Make Your Job a Calling

Make Your Job a Calling

*How the Psychology of Vocation
Can Change Your Life at Work*

Bryan Dik, PhD,
and Ryan Duffy, PhD

TEMPLETON PRESS

Templeton Press
300 Conshohocken State Road, Suite 500
West Conshohocken, PA 19428
www.templetonpress.org

Designed and typeset by Gopa & Ted2, Inc.

Library of Congress Cataloging-in-Publication Data
Dik, Bryan J.
  Make your job a calling : how the psychology of vocation
can change your life at work / Bryan J. Dik, Ryan D. Duffy.
      p. cm.
  Includes bibliographical references and index.
  ISBN 978-1-59947-380-2 (hardback)
  1. Job satisfaction. 2. Job satisfaction—Religious aspects.
  3. Work—Religious aspects. 4. Career development.
  5. Job enrichment. I. Duffy, Ryan D. II. Title.
  HF5549.5.J63D55 2012
  650.101'9—dc23
                                        2012014122

Printed in the United States of America

12 13 14 15 16 17   10 9 8 7 6 5 4 3 2 1

To Amy, and to our boys:
Eli, Silas, Abram, and Jasper
—B. D.

To my parents,
Michael and Dorothy Duffy
—R. D.

Contents

Acknowledgments

EASILY THE BEST PART of writing a book, for us anyway, happens before the real writing even starts. The excitement that comes from dreaming up a project, mapping it out, and creating the skeleton that will support the rest of the body is palpable. Once all that is done, the hard work begins. To be sure, bursts of vigor and excitement happen along the way, but for sometimes very long stretches at the writing desk, motivation and effort must be anchored by other factors. Our belief in the ideas we are promoting and our desire to share them are two such factors. But nothing is more powerful and valuable than the support, generosity, encouragement, and expertise of the people we are blessed to have around us. Yeah, it's cliché, but the truth is that, without them, the book you are reading right now quite literally would not exist.

Bryan would like to thank his colleagues and students (present and former) at Colorado State University who provided support and helped sharpen his thinking about this topic, especially Ernie Chavez, Kurt Kraiger, Michael Steger, and Brandy Eldridge. Thanks also are due to Jo-Ida Hansen and Wayne Joosse for their ongoing mentorship and support; to Terry Gray, Andy Tix, and Amy Van Guilder Dik for their extremely helpful feedback on earlier drafts of this manuscript, to Matthew Schaap for his expert advice early on, and to the team at Career Analytics Network for their encouragement. Bryan's extended family was extremely supportive and encouraging, especially his parents and siblings. But his biggest debt of gratitude is owed to his wife, Amy, and their four young sons, whose personal sacrifices were both significant and absolutely critical in allowing deadlines to be met. Their steadying influence, understanding, and encouragement made all the difference (and still does).

Ryan would like to thank his academic mentors—David Blustein, Bob Lent, and Bill Sedlacek—for helping him develop and refine his work on calling. Thanks to all the colleagues who have supported his work on this topic, especially Nicole Borges, and his colleagues at the University of Florida. Thanks to Ryan's five doctoral students—Alex Jadidian, Carrie Torrey, Liza Bott, Blake Allan, and Kelsey Autin—who have worked with him on several calling projects and provided support in various ways for the writing of this book. Finally, and most importantly, thanks to Ryan's parents, whose hard work and dedication to his education gave him the opportunity to pursue his own calling.

Together, we would like to thank the outstanding team at Templeton Press, who provided invaluable guidance, expert advice, and support. In particular, we wish to acknowledge Susan Arellano, Sharon Kelly, Natalie Silver, and Matt Smiley. We also recognize and appreciate the support that Dr. Jack Templeton provided for this project. Thanks also to David Myers for connecting us and for his ongoing support and encouragement. There are others who warrant mention and who we wish not to overlook—you know who you are.

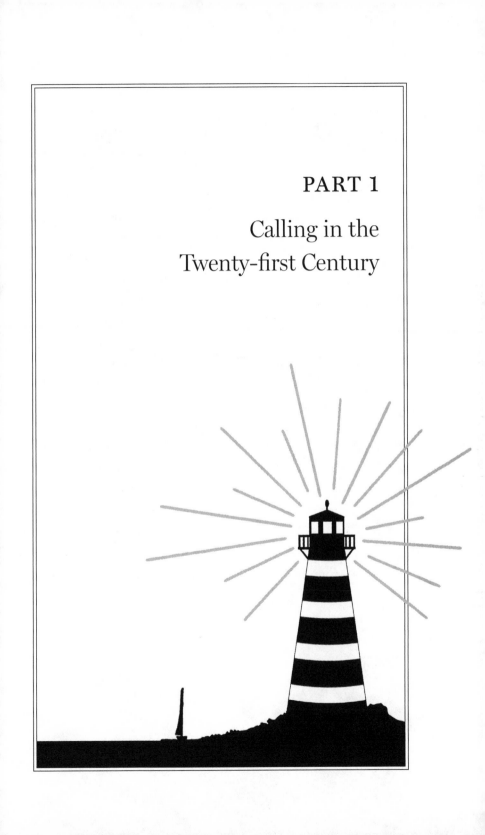

PART 1

Calling in the Twenty-first Century

1 Recovering Calling

ON A WARM August afternoon on U.S. Highway 50, at Monarch Pass in the Rocky Mountains of Colorado, Bryce Eldridge lightly tapped the accelerator in his car and inched forward. His eyes bounced from the clock to the speedometer to the long line of traffic ahead of him, and he sighed heavily. His dad waited for him in Gunnison for a long-overdue backpacking trip in the West Elk wilderness, and he was itching to get there. He didn't expect this kind of delay, and he could only speculate as to its cause. An accident? A fallen boulder? The countless procession of curves in the highway, which hugged the mountainside, made it impossible to see far enough ahead to identify the source of the slowdown. Finally, after fifteen more minutes and a slow crawl around a couple more hairpin turns, he looked ahead and saw the problem: A repair crew had closed down half of the two-lane thoroughfare, leaving just one lane for the Friday afternoon, get-me-to-my-cabin traffic to bleed through.

Ahead of the rest of the crew, marking the entrance to the coned-off single lane, stood a silhouetted figure leaning against the unmistakable octagon of a stop sign, affixed to a pole in his right hand. Bryce squinted into the sun, and the figure revealed himself as an orange-vested flagger. Bryce pondered the man's plight. Wearing jeans, a plaid shirt, hard hat, and work boots astride the newly patched pavement, his job consisted of barking directives back and forth across a two-way radio with the other flagger, at the other end of the construction zone. To direct the flow of traffic, every few minutes he rotated his sign from "stop" on the one side to "slow" on the other. Then, after a time, back to "stop." Then back to "slow." And so on, and so on.

Bryce braced himself as he approached the repair site. Always the victim of Murphy's Law scenarios, he watched the flagger turn the sign to "stop" immediately after the third car ahead of him steered around the cones and into the one open lane. He rolled his eyes and applied the brakes, submitting to his role near the front of what would soon become a long line of cars. Bryce turned back the keys in his ignition, and the hum of his car's engine went quiet. He knew he'd be waiting a while. He rolled down his window and breathed in the warm mountain air, which at this spot was accompanied by an unpleasant asphalt aroma. Noticing that he was within earshot of the flagger, he turned off his car radio and tried to hear what he could. The flagger began to strike up a conversation with the driver of the moss-green Subaru ahead of Bryce. With a tone of genuine, almost compassionate honesty, the driver said, "I'm sorry, but that has got to be the most boring job I can imagine. How can you stand it?" Bryce leaned toward the flagger, his head half out of the window, anticipating a response to the question.

The answer surprised him.

It surprised us, too, when we heard the story. The flagger perked with enthusiasm and proudly exclaimed, without hesitation and apparently without irony, "I love this job! Love it. You know why? Because it matters. I keep people safe. I care about these guys behind me, and I keep them safe. I also keep you safe, and everyone else in all those cars behind you. I get to make a real, tangible difference every day." After a drawn-out pause, as if the flagger was trying to decide whether to say this or not, he added, "I'm grateful that I was led here."

To most people, the flagger story might seem hard to believe. The driver who asked "How can you stand it?" is far from alone in imagining the work to be unchallenging and dull, only slightly more engaging than watching paint dry, and likely with more potent fumes. Even so, the flagger obviously was an enthusiastic believer in the purpose and importance of his work. We heard this story and wondered, how can a job that on the face of it seems torturously mind-numbing provide such a strong sense of meaningfulness? This guy was not a teacher, pastor, social worker, or doctor. He definitely was not Gandhi, Mother Teresa, or Martin Luther King Jr. He was a road construction flagger! Yet his work bears all the hallmarks of a calling. He mentioned that he had been led to his current job, implying the presence of a "caller," and hinted that he had listened to, and followed, this call. His work felt unmistakably meaningful to him and seemed to align with a broader sense of purpose ("I keep people safe"). And his work had an altruistic undercurrent. The way he saw it, he helps people—lots of people—by keeping them safe.

Of course, not all flaggers believe their work is a calling, just like not all teachers, artists, nurses, or attorneys approach their work as a calling. What is it, then, that separates this flagger from other flaggers who see work as a daily grind, little more than the means to a paycheck, for whom the phrase "Thank God it's Friday" is a life theme? What separates people within any profession—farmers, metal workers, janitors, administrative assistants, professors—who think of their work as a calling from those within their same profession who very clearly do not? Even more to the heart of the matter: What is a calling? What difference does having a calling make? What can people do to discern, experience, and live out their callings?

These questions drive us, the authors. Finding answers to them has become a primary focus of our careers. As psychological scientists, we are part of a community of scholars who have conducted dozens of research studies to help better understand this concept and the role it plays in people's lives. As career counseling specialists, we have worked with countless clients who yearn, sometimes desperately, for a calling—that is, work they feel compelled to do, that draws deeply from their sense of purpose, and that gives them a way to make a positive difference in their communities and world. A key part of our own callings consists of using carefully conducted, cutting-edge research to better understand and apply the kinds of lessons learned from the flagger Bryce encountered on the road—and from many other women and men, from all walks of life, who approach their work as a calling. Obviously, this matters to us.

It should matter to you, too.

Why?

Because understanding what it means to have a calling can help each of us examine our own lives and identify how we can transform our careers and jobs in deeply meaningful, satisfying, and life-giving ways—ways that, directly or indirectly, make the world a better place. The purpose of this book is to help you, the reader, put this understanding to use in the context of your own job, your own career, your own life.

To orient you, we begin by discussing why calling is the cause of some confusion, with diverse and sometimes competing ways of defining the term. Next, we present our approach to resolving the confusion by proposing a definition of calling in the context of work. Then we lay out our approach to the concept—one that stands on the shoulders of centuries of wisdom on calling from theologians and philosophers, but that is built on contemporary theory, a rapidly growing body of scientific research, and our own experiences as vocational psychologists. We close this chapter with a roadmap of sorts, outlining the rest of the book.

The Meaning of Calling

What does the word "calling" mean? The answer depends on whom you ask. Yale management professor Amy Wrzesniewski likens the word to a Rorschach test. The Rorschach, the projective test famous for its inkblots, provides psychotherapy clients with an ambiguous stimulus and asks them what they see, pulling for responses that are thought to reveal clues to the inner workings of their unconscious minds. Similarly, "calling" elicits a variety of definitions from people that reveal different assumptions and beliefs about the role and function of a calling in their careers and lives. In the first study to investigate directly the question of how people understand calling, we invited college students to answer a few open-ended questions about how they thought of the term.[1] Here are the questions; go ahead, answer them yourself before reading on:

1. As it applies to your career, how do you define the word "calling"?

_____

_____

2. What, specifically, does it mean for you to approach your career as a calling?

_____

_____

3. Does the word "calling" apply to areas of your life other than work? Please explain.

_____

_____

Of the 435 students with whom we started, a full 68 percent (!) indicated that calling was a relevant concern when they thought about their careers. Responses from this subset of students to the three questions above were analyzed to identify common themes. The results revealed that the idea of a guiding force was central to students' understanding of calling. Many identified external forces such as God, God's gifts, or destiny (one described it as "a path God has laid out for my life"); others pointed to internal sources such as an inner drive or passion (e.g., "a natural instinct or pull toward a certain field or career"). Students also stressed the importance of a strong fit between their gifts, passions, and sense of purpose with a particular job, often resulting in growth, clarity, and happiness (e.g., "It is a feeling that I can't explain, a feeling to be a part of something to better myself and others"). Finally, students pointed to making a positive impact on others as a defining feature of a call-ing (e.g., "being led to something because it helps others, not only myself"). Some noted that having a calling places responsibility on them to approach work with special effort and dedication. Most students expressed that calling was important not only for work, but for other aspects of life, too—relationships, education, leisure pursuits, spirituality. For some, *all* aspects of life were influenced by a sense of calling (one wrote, "anything you feel drawn to do for some reason, explainable or not").

Granted, these are young, idealistic college students, and we all know the real world does not run on college sophomore norms. So we followed up this study by asking these same questions to 370 university employees, representing a fairly diverse group of occupations, with faculty and administrators outnumbered by accountants, administrative assistants, information technology specialists, janitorial staff, librarians, and foresters, among others.[2] Sixty-two percent of them indicated that the concept of calling was relevant in their careers, just 6 percent fewer than in the college student sample. Analyses of their responses to the first two ques-tions revealed themes similar to those expressed by the students—a guiding force (with both external and internal sources identified), a sense of "fit," and altruistic motives, although a fourth primary theme also emerged that emphasized various aspects of well-being (e.g., passion, satisfaction, meaningfulness; one defined the term as "meaningful work based on my interests and values"). Also similar to the college students, the employees viewed the concept as far more expansive in scope than just one's career, with a few exceptions (one wrote, "One calling is plenty—it's pretty consuming").

Together, these two studies reinforce the reality that common themes cut across how people think of callings: the notion of a guiding force, a sense of personal "fit" with a job, and altruistic attitudes that align with a broader sense of meaning and purpose are typical for students and working adults alike, the latter of whom also think about calling in terms of the benefits it provides to well-being. Despite the overlap in how people conceptualize calling, though, some differences also emerge. For example, it is possible to sort the various ways of conceptualizing calling into two broad categories. First, *neoclassical* callings originate from an external source and emphasize a social duty (e.g., I am compelled or drawn to do this type of work by something or someone outside myself, and I will use it to help others). In contrast, *modern* callings arise from within and emphasize individual happiness (e.g., I have an inner drive toward a certain career that will make me the happiest).

This neoclassical vs. modern distinction is analogous to a sacred vs. secular distinction that scholars often make when trying to define calling. Roy Baumeister, one of the most influential research psychologists of the past half-century, was among the first social scientists to explore the contrast between externally originating callings, which he tied neatly to a religious perspective, and internal, secularized callings. The religious roots of calling in one's work, which we explore further in the next chapter, are simple enough. The *classical* view of calling was arguably developed by the Protestant Reformers, who taught that God calls people to serve him and to serve others, through whatever work they find themselves doing, and equips them with the gifts they need to do so well. The neoclassical view retains the themes embedded in this tradition, but expands the definition to make it more inclusive. In contrast, the modern view of calling revolves around the notion of self-actualization, and links to the Romantic and Victorian perspective of artists as inwardly called to their profession by yet-to-be-created masterpieces incubating within them. "Duty to the self,"

Baumeister wrote of the modern view, "seems to have replaced duty to God as the source of obligation to follow a calling."[3] Wrzesniewski concluded that the modern view is now the norm: "Callings have largely lost this religious connotation and tend to be defined in the secular sense as consisting of enjoyable or pleasurable work that the individual believes is making the world a better place."[4]

The assumption that a modern, secularized version of calling has replaced or supplanted the neoclassical usage of the term, as is often implied, is not based on research evidence, as far as we can tell. This doesn't mean it isn't true, of course; time and data will tell. Nevertheless, these two approaches clearly are dominant today. What are the options, then, for choosing a definition? We address this question in more detail in Q&A 1 (p. 221), but for us, the literal meaning of a word, and how that word has been used historically, is very important. We are reminded of another debate over the meaning of a word, in this case, "god." Stephen Hawking, in his classic book *A Brief History of Time*, argued that when modern physics arrives at its holy grail—a "theory of everything"—humans will finally see into "the mind of God."[5] Similarly, astronomer George Smoot reacted to the discovery of ripples in radiation still emanating from the big bang by declaring it "like seeing the face of God."[6] More recently, international news media trumpeted the historic discovery of the Higgs boson, the subatamic particle so critical to understanding space, time and matter that it is now more widely known by its alias: "the God particle." Such language recasts "god" as a metaphor for awe-evoking mysteries of science, not as an eternal being who cares for people on earth. This way of using the word "god" is not sanctioned by Nobel laureate physicist Steven Weinberg. "If language is to be of any use to us," said Weinberg in an interview, "we ought to try to preserve the meanings of words, and 'god' historically has not meant the laws of nature, it has meant an 'interested personality.' I rather grieve that they use the word 'god' because I do think that one should have loyalty to the way words are used historically."[7] On this point, we are in Weinberg's camp, and therefore our definition of calling reflects an attempt to preserve—indeed, reclaim—the literal and historic meaning of the word.

What We Mean When We Say "Calling"

Calling, when used as a noun, refers to a command, request, or invitation to go somewhere or do something. This implies a "caller"—that is, an issuer of the call, a source of the summons. Throughout history the term also has implied a responsibility to work in a way that is useful and helpful to others. Stuart Bunderson and Jeffrey Thompson highlight the importance of duty and destiny—"notions that figure centrally in the classical and neoclassical views but that play little if any role in modern conceptualizations."[8] The literal meaning of the term supports the idea that a calling comes from an external source, and its historic use emphasizes embracing and pursuing a calling as a duty to society and the common good.

Formally, we define "calling" as *a transcendent summons, experienced as originating beyond the self, to approach a particular life role in a manner oriented toward demonstrating or deriving a sense of purpose or meaningfulness and that holds other-oriented values and goals as primary sources of motivation.*[9] Admittedly, this is both wordy and academic-speak, so let's break it down into its component parts. (A quick disclaimer first: Callings can apply to potentially any "particular life role," a point we explore later. The focus of this book is on one's work and career, however, so that is our context for this discussion.)

A Transcendent Summons

The first dimension of the definition reflects our belief that a calling implies a caller—a source external to the person from which a call is heard, perceived, experienced. Historically, the caller has usually been understood to be God,[10] which still is very often the case, perhaps more so than is commonly assumed—especially in the United States, where 92 percent of adults say they believe in God or a universal spirit.[11] However, some people identify callings that they believe come from other sources, such as a need they see in society, destiny or fate, or a family legacy. One of the students in our study with college students described a calling as "something in your career field that makes you believe that you were destined to do [the work]." Often, when highly publicized disasters strike (like the September 11, 2001, terrorist attacks; Hurricane Katrina; or the 2011 tornadoes near Tuscaloosa, Alabama, or Joplin, Missouri), reports abound of people so moved by news footage of human suffering that they drop what they are doing and move to the site of the disaster, sometimes indefinitely, to help those in need. A forklift operator named Rohit,[12] whose story we tell in chapter 3, is a poignant example. Some people also describe experiencing a calling from more than one source, such as an Iowa farmer planting corn in response to a calling from God, ancestry, a hungry world, and a new generation of ethanol-burning engines.

Purpose and Meaning in Work

The second dimension of the definition focuses on a sense of purpose and meaning—in work, and also in life.[13] A calling may involve *deriving* a sense of purpose, as when a person's work actually contributes to the sense of meaning experienced in life. Imagine a pastry chef, for example, who is continually surprised by how much pleasure she feels from watching patrons' moods visibly improve when they are served her éclairs. Part of what makes life, well, delicious for her is the sheer joy that comes from using her artistic and culinary talents to create desserts that help people put their problems on hold and, for a brief moment, experience life more vividly. A calling may also involve *demonstrating* a sense of purpose, as when someone with a clear sense of purpose and meaning in life finds work to be an outlet for expressing that purpose and meaning. For example, an auto mechanic with a servant's heart may find his job at the body shop meaningful because fixing cars after an accident provides a clear and tangible way to help angry, inconvenienced drivers get on with their lives. When people have a calling, their sense of purpose and meaning in work aligns with their broader sense of purpose and meaning in life as a whole. As you might imagine, this kind of alignment gives a person a sense of stability and coherence in life.[14]

Other-Oriented Motives

The third dimension also highlights a key component of calling historically: the idea that work should support the well-being of others, and the common good in general. On a basic level and at least in theory, our economy is set up to support this idea. None of us do all the things we need to survive from scratch; instead, we rely on the work of others when we shop for groceries, turn up the heat on a frigid winter night, and change the oil in our cars. We need others, and others need the work that we do—again, at least in theory. Some people help others directly and tangibly—teachers, social workers, and physicians, for example. Others do so indirectly, but not insignificantly; every product we use has to be made by someone, every service we use is provided by someone, and every machine that runs has to be maintained or repaired by someone. Those with a calling understand how their work contributes; they can put into words the difference they make, whatever its magnitude. Not only that, but those with a calling do what they do *because* of the difference it makes. Enhancing the common good is probably not the only motivation behind their work, but it is a central one.

The Contours of Calling

Before we move on, let's clarify a few things.

First, a calling is not a thing to be discovered once and for all, as in one grand flash of insight. Indeed, among all the people we have interviewed concerning the development of their calling, informally and in our research studies, only a handful have cited an aha moment. People sometimes talk of needing to find a calling like it is a set of keys that might be buried under their seat cushions—something they are waiting to discover, and they expect that once they find it, they will stop searching and instead just revel in the enjoyment of doing the perfect job. If only it were so easy! In contrast, we view a calling as an ongoing process. Sure, approaching work as a calling includes choosing a career path, but it doesn't stop there. In fact, it *starts* there. Choosing a career is just the beginning, an entry point to a lifestyle of ongoing reflection and active shaping of one's job in ways that make it more likely for a sense of purpose in life to align with one's activities in work, with the goal of making a difference for others. Among other things, a calling is not only a career path that a person chooses to pursue, but that a person creates and cultivates. Even people who may not have landed in their ideal career can nevertheless craft or reframe their work, transforming it into a calling—or more accurately, transforming it into a vehicle for living out their calling.

Second, every person potentially has a calling. This may seem difficult to defend in an economy in which far too many are struggling with basic survival needs. Granted, pursuing a calling may well be the last thing in mind for most people wondering how their mortgage bill is going to be paid this month. However, hardship can actually catalyze pursuit of a calling. For example, interviewing a diverse sample of unemployed adults, researchers found "consensus that having resources can in some cases be a barrier to discovering a calling, as that removes a source of motivation to self-explore and try out different kinds of work."[15] Some may even consider it prejudicial to suggest that a certain level of privilege is needed before a person can experience work as meaningful.

Finally, any honest and legitimate area of work can potentially be a calling, even jobs that may not appear to enhance the common good in any obvious way, and jobs that people may have entered without having much of a choice. A calling has little to do, in fact, with a person's actual job, and everything to do with how that person approaches that job. Research evidence supports this claim; groups of administrative assistants, hospital janitorial staff, hairdressers, and restaurant kitchen employees are among those in low-prestige jobs who nevertheless indicate that they experience their work as meaningful, and as one way to improve the well-being of others.[16] Meaningful work indicative of callings also has been found among individuals with highly repetitive jobs[17] and those in "dirty" (i.e., extremely undesirable or stigmatized) jobs, who often derive meaning by reframing, recalibrating, or refocusing the function of their work tasks to emphasize the impact their work has on others.[18]

The Psychology of Vocation

A rich tradition of scholarship within disciplines such as theology, philosophy, and history holds that work can be approached as a calling. We value this work deeply, and our own scholarship has benefited tremendously from the foundation it provides. Wisdom gleaned from these fields of study pervades this book, naturally, as would be the case for any book on calling or meaningful work worth the paper on which it's printed. However, as scientist-practitioners in the field of vocational psychology, we are especially interested in two things: data and practical application. We like data—the results of scientific studies of calling and related topics—because data provide a close-to-objective means of examining the truth of claims people often make about what makes work meaningful and how people can find and create meaning on the job. All kinds of data are potentially useful, but we especially like data that translate into practical application. We read research studies and conduct research ourselves, not just because there is inherent value in contributing to the storehouse of human knowledge (although we absolutely believe there is), but because as vocational psychologists who work closely with people who have significant concerns about their work, we covet information that aids us in better helping others make good decisions about their careers. The data and applications that we find most valuable target two levels of knowledge that fall under our umbrella phrase "the psychology of vocation": research on calling and meaningful work specifically, and research on career choice and development generally.

Research on Calling and Meaningful Work

Research that specifically investigates the concept of calling is very new. Only within the last two decades have social scientists attempted to study the impact of a sense of calling on people's lives using scientific methods. Although we have tried to carefully differentiate the neoclassical view of calling from the modern view, up to this point researchers have hardly ever made this (or any) distinction, which presents a problem. Results can be murky and difficult to interpret, because researchers' and research participants' own unique definitions of the term end up ignored, masked by the (flawed) assumption that everyone thinks of calling in basically the same way. Funny thing is, despite this limitation, research to date paints a remarkably consistent picture. Across multiple samples of students and working women and men, and across multiple ways of conceptualizing calling, a sense of calling is surprisingly prevalent, and links repeatedly to positive outcomes.

When we say "surprisingly prevalent," we mean that far more people say the concept matters to them than most people would probably guess. Think about it. What percentage of people do you estimate report that calling is relevant to how they think about their careers? In one of the earliest empirical studies of calling (published in 1994), sociologists James Davidson and David Caddell[19] reported that 15 percent of their sample of working adults described their work as a calling. Given that their sample was drawn from affluent Christian church congregations in the U.S. heartland (South Bend and Lafayette, Indiana), one might expect even 15 percent to be an overestimate of the population as a whole. In the studies of calling since then, however, anywhere from one-third to the 68 percent we cited earlier indicate that the concept of calling is relevant to how they view their work. Whatever the actual percentage, calling evidently matters to a lot of people.

Researchers are interested in far more than merely estimating the prevalence of calling, of course. They want to know what difference it makes to have a calling. Are people with callings better off than people with other approaches to work? With remarkable consistency, the answer is yes, in terms of what people experience at work and also within their lives as a whole. People with callings are more confident that they can make good decisions about their careers, more committed to their jobs and organizations, more intrinsically motivated and engaged, and more satisfied with their jobs. They also are happier, more satisfied with life, cope more effectively with challenges, are less likely to suffer from stress and depression, and express a stronger sense of meaning and purpose in their lives.[20] Recently, researchers have begun to uncover *how* calling makes a difference. Some evidence suggests, for example, that people with callings are more satisfied with their work because they are more committed to it.[21] Other evidence suggests that those with callings experience a greater sense of well-being and psychological adjustment because they have a positive view of themselves and feel that life is meaningful.[22] Still other evidence indicates that simply having a sense of calling isn't enough; a person has to be living out the calling in order to experience its benefits.[23] So many positives have been associated with callings, but there can be drawbacks; people willingly make tough sacrifices to pursue their callings and often trade some types of satisfaction and well-being (e.g., material wealth and comfort) for others (e.g., the sense that they are making a meaningful difference in the world).[24] As we note in chapter 9, a sense of calling also can make people vulnerable to problems like workaholism or exploitation by unscrupulous employers. As Bunderson and Thompson put it, a calling can be a double-edged sword. Nevertheless, most people with callings say that if they were financially secure, they'd continue working in their jobs even without getting paid.[25]

The research on calling per se fits within a broader context of research on meaningful work. When people experience work as meaningful, and as a means of benefiting others, they tend to experience a stronger sense of well-being in their careers and in life. Where this research yields those two things we really like—data and practical application—we explore it and its relevance to you throughout this book. Of course, as much as we value research, we are the first to acknowledge that research on calling, while very hot right now, is also still very young, with more empirical studies of calling published since 2007 (the tipping point) than in all of history prior to that year. For this reason, throughout the book, we contextualize our discussion of the important but still new scientific research on calling by sharing our personal experiences, along with rich stories of calling we've encountered as we have talked with people about their careers, and provided some with career counseling services.

Research on Career Choice and Development

Given its level of scholarly newness, calling is a relatively small fish in a large pond of research on career choice and development. More than a century of theory and research exists on how people make good career choices, dating to Frank Parsons's posthumously published book *Choosing a Vocation*, which hit the shelves in 1909. We tell the ironic story of Parsons's career path in chapter 6. The ending doesn't give much of the story away, though, so we'll start with that: after his death, Parsons became known as the "father of vocational psychology," and his deceptively simple formula for making good career choices continues to be a primary strategy that nearly all career counselors use with their clients. Parsons advocated gaining a clear sense of one's self and a clear sense of the opportunities that are available in the world of work, then using "true reasoning" to find a good match between person and job. This "Person-Environment Fit" model, as it turns out, forms the basis of a good strategy for discerning one's calling. We'll get into all of this in more detail later.

Career development theorists in the generations after Parsons developed the idea that career decisions do not happen in a vacuum, but always in a life—and lives are complicated. People have all kinds of commitments and responsibilities; some are central and some exist on the fringes, but all change and fluctuate over time. People also change; they ripen with age. Circumstances change, too, along with economies and occupational fields that are never static. All of this needs to be taken into account when one seeks to identify, develop, and live out a calling in work, possibly among other callings in other spheres of life. We explore this more fully later also.

Finally, vocational psychologists have come to recognize that building successful careers, however that is understood, requires more than simply having the requisite talent, motivation, and opportunity. A successful career also requires the consistent belief that one can do what is required well, and that doing what is required actually leads to outcomes that matter. Not only that, but when facing obstacles, people have the capacity (to the extent that external constraints allow) to mold and shape their work into something that encourages, facilitates, and provides a means of living out their callings. This concept also is a subject of scrutiny later in the book.

Where We're Headed

This book is about exploring, discovering, and creating a sense of calling at work. The book is divided into four parts. Part 1, "Calling in the Twenty-first Century," starts with this chapter, in which we introduced this idea of approaching work as a calling, defined it, and laid the groundwork for exploring calling through the lens of the psychology of vocation. The second chapter places calling in context by tracing its roots and contrasting how work has been understood across cultures throughout Western history. History repeats itself, and the ways work has been viewed over time are clearly evident in how people view work today. In part 2, "Dimensions of Calling," we'll dig into calling's three dimensions: a transcendent summons, meaning and purpose at work, and other-oriented goals and motives. Part 3, "Discovering and Living a Calling," provides practical guidelines for discerning a calling when it comes to making a career choice and transforming an existing career path. We also explore the implications of having a calling at work for other roles and responsibilities in life. Finally, in part 4, "Boundary Conditions and Challenges of a Calling," we explore the perils, pitfalls, challenges, and opportunities of pursuing a calling, including the role that calling might play in the new world of work, as the norms of the workplace continue to morph into something that our grandparents would hardly recognize.

We frequently receive questions about calling from people trying to better understand the concept or exploring how it fits in their lives, and we welcome the chance to answer those questions directly and plainly. We do so after chapter 10, in a special section that contains some of the most commonly asked questions about calling, along with our answers to them. This "Questions and Answers" section is the beginning of what we hope becomes a dialogue between you, the readers, and us. To encourage this, if you have a question that is not addressed in the Q&As, please visit the book's companion website, www.makeyourjobacalling.com. Among many other things, the site provides an opportunity to submit your question to us. We will respond to user submitted questions on the site, contributing to a more exhaustive set of Q&As.

Throughout the rest of this book, our hope is that you engage this topic on a deeply personal level, reflecting on your own work and life and how the concept of calling might transform your path. Along the way, we'll try to help this reflection along by pausing to ask questions to ponder. The road to a calling may be a surprising one that is more accessible than you might have imagined possible. For some of you, pursuing a calling may require identifying and living out a new career path; for others, it may be possible to approach your current path—even your current job—in a new and different way that crafts it into a calling. Either way, we are hopeful that the pages that follow help illuminate your way.

2 What Work Means, and the Difference It Makes

IT'S NEARLY 1 P.M., finally time to pause for a lunch break. Today is your first day on the job with the local office of an upstart travel agency, and it's been a long morning. You're a brand-new travel agent. The learning curve feels pretty steep, although you're confident you're picking up what you need to do well. You're fielding phone calls. You're building rapport with prospective customers. You're gathering flight, cruise, and accommodations information and finding the right deals. You're preparing itineraries, getting your customers excited about them, and closing the sale. But you're still trying to get a feel for the company, and you're eager to get to know your coworkers.

You walk into the break room in the back of the office, open the refrigerator, and grab your container full of last night's chicken parmesan. As you wait your turn for the microwave, you take the last available seat at the small table in the corner and strike up a conversation with the three fellow agents whom you met for the first time that morning. "You three have been here awhile. Fill me in. What should I expect from this job?"

The first to respond is Shawna, whose dark rings around her eyes make her look tired and about ten years older than her age. "Honestly? You'll figure out ways to tolerate it. I mean, it's a job. It pays the bills, and on good months gives you a little to put away. That's not much to sneeze at these days. Some days are slow, some are really busy. I like the busy days because time passes more quickly.

You don't have time to realize you're trapped at your desk, instead of where you'd rather be—out having fun, at home relaxing, basically anywhere else. I've been here about six months, and it's been fine, but I don't know. I've got a friend with a bank job, and she's been talking to me about joining her there. If it pays more than this, I just might do it. A job is a job to me; I'm not looking to shake things up like Monique."

Monique chuckles from across the table. She has been furiously responding to e-mails on her smartphone, but sets it down upon hearing her name. She oozes professionalism, wearing a neatly pressed power suit, almost-but-not-quite-too-thick makeup, and a high-maintenance hairdo so obsessively coiffed it makes you wonder how early she has to get up in the morning to get ready. "Shawna just means that I have a lot of goals. I am going after the sales records here. If I keep pushing in the next couple of weeks, I think I can get agent of the month again. But I hope I'm not an agent too much longer. Don't tell our boss, but I know I can run this place better than she does. That's my plan—get manager here, then move up the chain with corporate. I'll go wherever they want me if I can keep moving up."

Nan smiles, taking it all in. She's been with the company the longest of the three and was identified earlier that morning as the go-to person when any questions or concerns about anything arise. Nan seems poised, content, comfortable in her own skin. "Here's what I love most about this job," she says. "Everyone out there has become way too busy. People don't have time for each other anymore. Members of the same family barely see each other, even when they live in the same house. We manage the details of people's travel, sure. But when we plan a vacation, we help people take a breather, relax a little, connect with each other again. Couples get away and have time to talk again. Families create memories they can share together for years to come. Think about your most cherished times with your family growing up. A lot of those happened on family vacations, right? That's what we get to help create. We are in the business of bringing people joy, helping them stay sane, and helping them stay together."

Shawna, Monique, and Nan represent three contrasting approaches to work in the United States: job, career, and calling. These three orientations were identified by Berkeley sociologist Robert Bellah and a group of his colleagues in 1985 in their ground-breaking book *Habits of the Heart*.[1] People work for a lot of different reasons, but according to this typology, most people resonate primarily with one of these three approaches.

What do the three work orientations represent? For Shawna and others who think of work as a job, what matters is making a living. What the work provides—a paycheck, benefits, and whatever stability it offers—is critical, and far more important than the nature of work itself, assuming it is tolerable. For these folks, work is a necessary evil. They tend not to like what they do, or are at best indifferent to it. They wish time would pass more quickly when they are at work, spend all week looking forward to the weekend, and can't wait to retire. They are biding their time in their current job, but if another job came along that offered better pay and benefits, they'd take it in a heartbeat. They complain about their job, turn up the volume on Todd Rundgren's "Bang the Drum All Day" ("I don't want to work/I just want to bang on the drum all day"), and if they could do it all over again, they probably wouldn't pursue the same career. Studs Terkel introduces his classic book *Working*, a fascinating collection of interviews with people discussing life in their jobs, as "by its very nature, about violence—to the spirit as well as to the body."[2] This is because many of the interviews that fill the book are with workers who have a job orientation, like the autoworker who would tease a coworker "just to break the monotony. You want quittin' time so bad," or the truck driver who "fantasizes something tremendous" to make it through the day.[3]

Monique and others with a career orientation derive the sense of self-worth they get from what they achieve and accomplish on the job. Work provides a clear set of rules for achievement they can follow and a tangible ladder they can climb. They may like their job, but whatever enjoyment they obtain from the work itself pales in comparison to the rush they get from climbing another rung on the success ladder. "Success" in this case is defined by promotion, advancement, and increasing power and prestige. Being seen as successful is extremely important to them; they are the types who might rent a BMW to drive to a high-school reunion.

Bellah and colleagues illustrate the career approach by describing Brian Palmer, a business manager who spent his twenties and thirties with his nose to the grindstone, chasing promotions. His career required moving from one city to another every few years, each time making new friends and then leaving for another city in another state, wherever the next promotion took him. Brian admits, "I got totally swept up in my own progress, in promotions and financial successes,"[4] yet his goals for the future remained focused on the next rung on the corporate ladder. We have found this to be a perhaps surprisingly common orientation in the academic world. Both of us work at research universities, where success is often quantified in terms of the number of articles one publishes, the quality of the journal in which they are published (as judged by a numerical "impact factor"), and the amount of money one brings to the university by landing large research grants. Such an environment seems to attract a disproportionate number of faculty with career orientations, for whom teaching becomes a nuisance (because it takes time away from research) and the workweek routinely sees the wrong side of sixty hours. On more than one occasion as graduate students, we had the experience of returning to the psychology building very late at night, only to find more than one professor holed up in their offices, plugging away at a paper.

Those with a calling orientation, like Nan, think of their work in the way we described in chapter 1—a way to make meaning from nine to five, and to somehow make the world a better place for people. Bellah and colleagues don't address whether a calling has an internal or external source. Instead, they focus on calling as an orientation that promotes discipline and wise judgment, and that views the work itself as meaningful, of intrinsic value, and as "morally inseparable from [one's] life." A calling also "links a person to the larger community, a whole in which the calling of each is a contribution to the good of all."[5] A calling links an individual to the public world; there is no such thing as a private calling that exists only for the self. The teacher who spends his own money to more fully equip his classroom so that students learn better has a calling orientation. So does the social worker who persists in a chronically underfunded position because the work she does matters so much to the people she serves. So does the hospital janitor who views her work as integral to the hospital's mission of helping sick patients get well.

The job/career/calling distinction is, to be sure, unrealistically simplistic. People are complex, with myriad motivations for why and how they approach work the way they do. Are there really just three types? Some scholars have suggested more. For example, Boston College management professor Mike Pratt and his colleagues believe callings may represent a blend of more basic orientations, such as craftsmanship, serving, and kinship.[6] Even Bellah and colleagues were quick to point out that it probably is typical for people to blend the types in how they approach work, a conclusion that research evidence supports.[7] With all their imprecision, however, the three types have provided a very useful way of thinking about different work attitudes since they were introduced in the mid-1980s. Three decades later, the types are every bit as relevant. They are not new, either, as we explore next.

A Very Brief History of What Work Means to People

In his marvelous book *The Fabric of This World*, philosopher Lee Hardy traces the story of how people have thought about work throughout Western history. We take a brief stroll through that history here, obviously only hitting selected highlights. The pendulum swings back and forth from work as a curse and a necessary evil on the one hand, to work as a way to become divine on the other. Both of these extremes are evident in how many people view their work today, a validation of Faulkner's most quoted line, "The past is never dead. It's not even past."[8] As you read what follows, pay attention to how your view of work syncs with the perspectives popular in the cultural contexts that precede you. Reflecting on this can give you a richer understanding of the foundation on which your personal view of work is built. Also, pay attention to where you see the job, career, and calling orientations. In one form or another, these have been with us for a very long time.

The Burden of the Beast

The Ancient Greek perspective on work was pretty clear: work was a terrible curse. To a Greek intellectual, the thought of work occupying more of our waking hours than anything else—true of most adults who are employed full-time in today's world—was totally depressing. Greeks associated work with the endless cycle of activity forced on us by our embodied existence. Spending our lives working means we sweat and toil and stay up late to meet deadlines, for what? We eventually die like animals, passing into oblivion without ever leaving a mark or making any real difference in the world. Sure, our work gives us the basic things we need to stay alive for a while, but in the end, what difference does it make?

All this fit into the very core of the Greek mind-set, which was built on the foundation of dualism, a parsing out of the mind from the body, of that which is sacred, higher, and honorable from that which is secular, lower, and banal. As a corollary of this worldview, popularized by Plato around twenty-three hundred years ago, a high value was placed on the realm of ideas, which was where resided the true reality, eternal and good. The life of the mind could connect with this realm, transcending our day-to-day physical reality and participating in the true reality. Of course, this meant that anything that keeps us from the realm of ideas—our physical bodies, our earthly responsibilities, certainly our work—functions like chains that imprison us in a cave, unable to see the world as it really is. Any kind of physical work therefore keeps us stuck in a hopeless, animal-like existence. Work was the burden of the beast.

The response to this, for the Greeks, was to escape work at all costs. The goal was to live in a way that takes part in the immortality of the gods, without obligation to do the kind of work necessary for survival, and pursue "worthwhile" activities. Working in politics or mustering courageous acts in the military were kind of worthwhile; they allowed a certain amount of immortality because future generations would remember these kinds of efforts. Most desirable, though, was pursuing the life of the mind, the contemplative life. Thinking deep thoughts is what really allows us to come closest to the true reality and therefore experience the highest possible degree of human happiness. This idea became so powerful, it formed the basis of a social hierarchy; the backbreaking labor of the slaves made possible the work of the professionals of the day, who freed up the philosophers to indulge the life of the mind. "The whole of human society is to be organized," wrote Hardy, "so that a few men can actualize the highest of human potentials,"[9] on the backs of everyone else.

All this was great for the toga-wearing philosophers, but as you might imagine, it was a real drag for the common Greeks of the day. For one thing, Aristotle and others used this way of understanding work to justify slavery. Some people were simply born to be slaves; it was viewed as the natural order of things. Without slaves, the philosophers' lifestyle of contemplation would be constantly interrupted by work, and maybe impossible altogether. For another thing, any kind of physical work was deemed completely void of dignity. Imagine toiling as a skilled stoneworker in ancient Greece, carefully and joyfully using your talents to craft the delicate scroll- and leaf-work on the Corinthian columns of some soon-to-be iconic building, maybe the Pantheon. You're creating nothing short of an inspirational (and functional!) masterpiece. But you'd have to deal with the likes of Plutarch. Plutarch may have liked the product of your work, but he didn't like you. He found it important to argue that "it does not necessarily follow, that, if a piece of work please for its gracefulness, therefore he that wrought it deserves our admiration." To drive the point home he picked on dyers and perfumers: "In perfumes and purple dyes, we are taken with the things themselves well enough, but do not think dyers and perfumers otherwise than low and sordid people."[10] Your work may well be breathtakingly beautiful and downright awe-inspiring, but since you're working with your hands and not dealing directly in the realm of ideas, you're still a shmuck.

The dualistic way of seeing the world didn't fall with the Greek Empire. In the early centuries of the first millennium, the fledgling Christian church established the monastic way of life. The earliest monks were hermits, radically rejecting everything worldly (including other people) and living in the wilderness or desert to pursue the things of God without distraction. Soon enough, though, monks toned down their asceticism a bit and joined forces, forming monastic communities to pursue the goal of a mystical union with God through meditative prayer. In this context the bishop Eusebius wrote about two types of work. One is "above nature, and beyond common human living. . . . It devotes itself to the service of God alone. . . . Such then is the perfect form of the Christian life." The other is "the more humble, more human, [that] permits men to . . . have minds for farming, for trade, and the other more secular interests as well as for religion." Then the clincher: "And a kind of secondary grade of piety is attributed to them."[11] Eusebius was only slightly more generous than Plutarch; if you had a mind for farming in the fourth century, you could aspire to a secondary grade of Christian! Two tiers of spirituality are present in this view; the second tier isn't all bad, but the first tier is clearly much better. Fundamentally, little had changed; an elite group was doing worthwhile work that was a worthy calling, and then there was everyone else, whose hard work was inherently inferior, spiritually speaking. This dualistic view and its two-tiered spirituality were more or less preserved over the next thousand years, with adherents spanning from Augustine in the fifth century to Thomas Aquinas in the thirteenth century.

The Pendulum Swings: Work Makes Us Divine

The low view of work in the West was turned on its head during the fifteenth century, thanks to a handful of Renaissance philosophers.[12] The basis for this was a different understanding of God's essence. Instead of thinking of God as a passive, eternally pure but distant mind, God was recast as a cosmic craftsman and creator, referred to with titles like "Supreme Maker" or "Mightiest Architect."[13] The view became as follows: Human beings don't become like God by just thinking, but by doing—that is, engaging in productive, creative activity. In the Renaissance, "The ideal human being is not the thinker who merely contemplates the idea of beauty," writes Hardy, "but the artist, who both contemplates that idea and shapes the world accordingly."[14] In his famous book, *The Lives of the Most Famous Painters, Sculptors, and Artists*, published in 1550, Georgio Vasari described Michelangelo's works as "divine" more than twenty times and increased that number to forty in the 1568 second edition. Even more poignant, Vasari describes Michelangelo himself as "divino."[15] The stoneworker in Athens was dismissed as undeserving of admiration, but the Renaissance artisan was lifted up as a demigod.

So by engaging in creative work, people can become like God. Not only that, but whereas for the Greeks, having to work is what made us *like* animals, the Renaissance philosophers argued that work actually *distinguishes us* from animals. Animals have no choice but to conform to their instincts, but people have no such constraints; we can correct and improve on nature with our nearly limitless resources. In this kind of creative activity, "We 'imitate God the artisan of nature,'" summarizes Hardy, "achieving a god-like rule over the animals, the elements, even matter itself."[16] By the end of the Renaissance, work was considered humankind's "essential activity,"[17] in which human potentialities are not hindered but developed and perfected. Greeks considered work to be undignified; for Renaissance philosophers, work is what gives people dignity.

Another philosopher from another era, one well-known for extending Renaissance themes on work, was Karl Marx, everyone's favorite philosopher of labor.[18] Marx argued that unlike animals, people can stand back, take in the fruit of our labor, and "see our own reflection in a world which we have constructed." In his view, the ability to do this is precisely what allows people true fulfillment. Remember the context for Marx: It was the heyday of industrial capitalism. Thousands of workers crammed into cities, living in postage stamp–sized apartments and working fourteen-hour days in blaringly loud, saunalike, mind-numbing factories. No education, no medical services, and few community resources were available—in cities full of crime, corruption, disrepair, and despair. Disgusted, Marx pinned the problem on private ownership. Private interests created a wedge between the haves and the have-nots, he thought, with the power brokers exploiting the hardworking laborers, stripping their work of its purpose as a means of self-expression. Famously, he predicted that the workers would eventually rise up and revolt against wealthy private interests, making the means of production public property and leveling the playing field so that exploitation would cease and people would once again be able to find themselves through their work. In doing so, they would control nature and master culture, essentially achieving a godlike status. Of course, at risk of oversimplifying things, we know how this vision played out. Instead of increased social polarization, a huge middle class developed, and labor laws and unions improved working conditions and slowed the exploitive tendencies of big business. Capitalism's collapse wasn't inevitable after all; instead of imploding, the system self-corrected, tweaking itself in ways that benefited workers. Although far from perfect, it seems a far less flawed system than Marx's vision, which paved the way for oppressive communist states that strip people of freedom rather than guaranteeing it.

The Middle Path: Work as Calling

So far, we've talked about work as it has been viewed at the extremes. On the one hand, work is at best a necessary evil and at worst a curse; it makes us like animals. On the other hand, work is where we find true fulfillment, a means to rule over the cultural world; it makes us like God. What is the middle path?

We can trace current thinking about what it means to have a calling to Martin Luther. Luther's story is a fascinating tale of transformation. He began his career as a monk so burdened by doubt about his spiritual adequacy that he would spend literally six hours at a time in confession, exasperating his spiritual mentor with excruciatingly detailed scrutiny of each and every daily sin he could conjure up in his memory. Luther operated within a "works righteousness" perspective, the prevailing view at the time, which held that eternal salvation is earned through hard spiritual work— confession, prayer, meditation, fasting. In striving to live up to this standard, monks clearly had an advantage over anyone distracted by running the farm, parenting children, tending the home, or any other kind of "nonspiritual" work. So there is spiritual work, which is good, and all other work, which is not so good. This was the same dualistic view of things we reviewed earlier, and it defined Luther's experience; knowing this makes Luther's next steps all the more revolutionary.

Engaged in scholarship as a University of Wittenberg professor, Luther found inescapable the conclusion that so many in the church had misinterpreted the path to salvation laid out in scripture: humans *cannot* earn their own salvation, but rather it has been earned for them by God's grace through Jesus Christ's sacrifice; people need only to believe this and own it personally. Good works are important, but as an expression of gratitude, not as a means of earning salvation points. This thinking turned Luther's entire worldview on its head, and at a time when some Roman Catholic leaders exploited desperate parishioners by teaching that donating cash to the church (by buying "indulgences") was a key way to gain the benefits of good works, his perspective was not particularly welcomed. When Luther famously made his disapproval of indulgence sales (among other things) public by nailing his "Ninety-five Theses" document to the church door at Wittenberg, it sparked the Protestant Reformation.[19] The Reformation changed everything—for Luther himself, for the church, for the history of the world, and certainly for how work came to be understood.

Darrow Miller describes Luther's view of work this way: "If righteousness is by faith, Luther reasoned, then the contemplative life of the monks and priests is neither higher nor lower than the active life of the faithful farmer, cabinetmaker, or homemaker. . . . Suddenly all work, so far as it is morally legitimate (not evil), is sacred. Priest and farmer, nun and homemaker, theologian and laborer, all stand, in faith, before God."[20] This perspective changed the view of work "decisively and irreversibly" in sixteenth-century Europe, according to theologian Alister McGrath, who noted that even the word for "work" in all European languages affected by the Reformation changed to reflect this perspective.[21] Luther also saw work as a call to love one's neighbor in whatever roles we occupy in our station in life—as workers, spouses, parents, citizens, and so on.

What is your calling? The answer prior to Luther was to leave your worldly occupation and join a monastery, but Luther insisted that rather than retreat to the cloister, you are called to serve your neighbor in whatever stations God has placed you. In other words, if you want to know your calling, look around you, and serve faithfully there.

This view of work started to take hold in the West, although one key modification was soon added. Luther lived in a very modest economy; to him the division of labor seemed a natural part of God's design. In the centuries following Luther, though, a convergence of technological advances, rapid urbanization, political reorganization, and an expanding market economy created an environment in which greed and power ruled the roost. In response, John Calvin, the famous Reformer in Geneva who largely echoed Luther's view, laid the groundwork for the perspective that some "stations" seemed out of whack with the created order. Calvin attacked the medieval institution of the bondservant in particular, and subsequent generations of Calvinists (most notably the Puritans) pushed things further: Individuals are subject to sin and are personally broken, but social institutions such as the order of stations in life also are subject to sin, and also vulnerable to brokenness. This shift in thinking was powerful. For one thing, instead of looking at our stations to find our callings, people should look at their gifts and talents to understand how they might best honor God and serve the common good. (As we explore in chapters 3 and 6, career counselors even today frequently practice versions of this strategy.) Also, part of living out one's calling means evaluating stations for signs of brokenness and working to improve them where problems are found.

We mentioned this classical view of calling in chapter 1, and it has stuck in the Christian church. The Roman Catholic position, articulated in Pope John Paul II's *Laborum Exercens* (On Human

Work), is now extremely similar, resulting in what Hardy describes as "a remarkable ecumenical convergence in the practical theology of work."[22] This view also represents the origin of the current neoclassical understanding of calling, which essentially takes the classical view and expands it, casting a wider net to include people who are not particularly religious, but who nevertheless feel compelled to do their work in a way that fits with their broader sense of purpose in life, with a goal of improving society in large or small ways. For people with a calling, work is far more meaningful than a way to survive and pass the time, or an achievement ladder to climb; it provides an arena for using one's gifts with purpose, to the benefit of the common good.

Distortions of Work, Then and Now

Not until the Protestant Reformation was the spiritual hierarchy leveled, but the dualistic worldview that originated with the Greeks has hung on stubbornly and remains to this day. Christian authors have noted that two-tiered spirituality is still widespread in the church,[23] and on a broader cultural level, this hierarchical way of viewing the world seems entrenched. Some people have exciting, respectable, high-profile jobs perhaps worthy of a calling; these people are held in high esteem, whereas others are stuck in more mundane jobs that surely warrant less respect. We see both sides of this when we meet people who almost sheepishly say, "I'm just a mechanic" or "I'm just a janitor," and others who say, "I'm a surgeon" or "I run a tech company" without quite fully masking their pride. Perhaps it is understandable given the cultural values in the United States; rags-to-riches stories are alluring because, well, the people in rags don't stay in rags, they move up to riches. This pecking-order view of the world reinforces job and career orientations. Blue-collar work, working with your hands, fixing things, cleaning things, serving things—all this is a grind, the burden of the beast, low on the totem pole, something to avoid. It's much better to move up the ladder, elevate yourself out of such jobs, and live the dream by working hard and making it big (which, of course, implies that people who don't make it big didn't work hard enough). With more money, more power, and more prestige come more respect and higher status. Of all the roles we occupy in life, work, probably more than any other, gives us clear rules for success and often enticing rewards for being successful.

The unbridled drive for more—more pay, more prestige, more power, more recognition, more respect—may be rooted in a dualist view, but in some ways it also reflects the Renaissance and Marxist emphasis on work providing a path toward self-realization. Some people strive to create because doing so is divine, but examples of unquenchable careerism seem the more contemporary path toward personal fulfillment. What drives the stereotypical young, top-of-her-class law associate mercilessly burning the candle at both ends in a quest to make partner in an up-or-out New York law firm? What gives the serial entrepreneur such a rush from working himself to the bone to translate another good idea into a lucrative revenue generator? Perhaps on some level, the career orientation is motivated by a subconscious desire to achieve a godlike status, with control over a world of our making. If that last sentence is controversial, this next one isn't: Self-fulfillment reigns supreme in the current milieu. Baumeister put it this way: "The assumption is that your work will elevate you to a position of eminence that will elicit respect, admiration, and acclaim from others, as well as allowing you to feel self-respect and self-esteem. Many people hold some mythical view of career success that promises personal fulfillment. They imagine that reaching certain goals will be automatically accompanied by living happily ever after."[24] But does it, particularly when getting ahead requires sacrificing time and energy from family, leisure, and other roles in life? Ultimately this is an empirical question—that is, one that can be addressed with research. Which work orientation—job, career, or calling—leads to the healthiest outcomes? We present initial answers to this question below.

The Difference It Makes

Why do you work?

Take a few minutes and answer this question. (If you are not currently working, answer whichever of these questions is more relevant: Why do you *want* to work? Why are you training for work? Why are you looking for work? Why are you avoiding work? Why *did* you work?) This question is one for which you probably think you'd have a quick answer, like why you went to school where you did, or why you are driving the car you have now. If you're like many people, though, you have never really articulated an answer to the work question. You may not have done so even now, despite being prompted a minute ago. So we'll ask again: Why do you work?

Your answer tells you something about what your work means to you. You may have answered with your current job in mind, or perhaps with a more abstract sense of your career as a whole. Regardless, if you took the time to reflect and formulate an answer, you may be surprised to see the variety of motivations behind why you work. Most of us work because we have to—to make a living, to provide for our families, to pay the rent or the mortgage, and to put food on the table. Some of us work because we feel obligated to work, because not working feels like we're not making something of ourselves, or because we are not sure what else we would do. Some of us work because we like to achieve, to do well, to feel competent, to develop a mastery of something. Some of us work because we have gifts and talents that we want to express and cultivate. Some of us work because working gives us a way to contribute, to make other people's lives better somehow. Some of us work because we feel compelled, drawn, called to our work. This list is far from exhaustive, but it offers a sampling of reasons that give you a good idea of how diverse people's motives for working might be.

You probably work, or want to work, for multiple reasons. Yet as we reviewed in this chapter, some discernable trends describe how certain ways of thinking about work dominate—across periods in history, across generations, and across individuals. Different people view their work differently. So what? What difference does it make?

As we noted above, one good way to answer the question is to turn to psychological science. In an instant-classic research study, Amy Wrzesniewski and colleagues devised a straightforward way to assess the extent to which people approached their work as a job, career, or calling.[25] They asked nonfaculty university employees representing a broad range of occupations, from doctors and nurses to computer programmers and administrative assistants, to read three paragraphs. Then they rated each paragraph according to how well it reflected their own way of thinking about work. Go ahead and try this. Read the following three paragraphs, and rate each one on a scale of 1–4, where 1 = *not at all like me*, 2 = *a little like me*, 3 = *somewhat like me*, and 4 = *very much like me*.

A works primarily to earn enough money to support life outside of the job. If A was financially secure, A would no longer continue in A's current line of work, but would really rather do something else instead. A's job is basically a necessity of life, a lot like breathing or sleeping. A often wishes the time would pass more quickly at work. A greatly anticipates weekends and vacations. If A lived life over again, A probably would not go into the same line of work. A would not encourage A's friends or children to enter A's line of work. A is very eager to retire.

To what degree are you like A? _____

B basically enjoys work, but does not expect to be in B's current job five years from now. Instead, B plans to move on to a better, higher-level job. B has several goals for the future pertaining to positions that B would eventually like to hold. Sometimes B's work seems like a waste of time, but B knows that B must do sufficiently well in B's current position in order to move on. B can't wait to get a promotion. For B, a promotion means recognition of good work and is a sign of success in competition with coworkers.

To what degree are you like B? _____

C's work is one of the most important parts of C's life. C is very pleased to be in this line of work. Because what C does for a living is a vital part of who C is, it is one of the first things C tells people about C. C tends to take work home and on vacations, too. The majority of C's friends are from C's place of employment, and C belongs to several organizations and clubs relating to C's work. C feels good about work because C loves it, and because C thinks it makes the world a better place. C would encourage C's friends and children to enter the same line of work. C would be pretty upset if C was forced to stop working, and C is not particularly looking forward to retirement.

To what degree are you like C? _____[26]

The researchers then assigned each participant to the category associated with the paragraph that she or he rated highest. You guessed right if you thought the first is the "job" paragraph, the second the "career" paragraph, and the third is the "calling" paragraph. Which category best represents you?

The researchers then compared people across each of the three categories. Clear differences emerged. Those in the calling group were more satisfied with their jobs, and more satisfied with life overall, than those in the job or career groups. They also were more likely to say "True" to questions like "I find my work rewarding," "My work makes the world a better place," and "If I was financially secure, I would continue with my current line of work even if I was no longer being paid," and "False" to questions like "I am very conscious of what day of the workweek it is and I greatly anticipate weekends." Compared to those in the job and career groups, those in the calling group also said they missed work less often. Recently, University of Michigan social psychologist Chris Peterson and colleagues[27] used the same three paragraphs to study more than seventy-five hundred workers from all over the world. Across all occupations, those with a calling orientation were more satisfied with their work and with life in general and scored highest on a measure of zest—defined as "the habitual approach to life with anticipation, energy, and excitement."[28]

Do you wake up eager to approach your day with "anticipation, energy, and excitement"? Do you feel highly satisfied with your job, and your life as a whole? Let's be clear up front: Approaching work as a calling is not a panacea that cures all that ails. But just imagine working a job where you consistently lose track of time because you are so delightfully absorbed in what you are doing. Imagine feeling like your job aligns with what you think is most important in life and allows you to live out a sense of purpose. Imagine feeling like your gifts and talents are being used well, that other people are benefiting from your effort, that your 9-to-5 is actually making the world a better place. Imagine having a job you'd want to do for free, one that makes you cringe at the thought of retirement.

Do you want this kind of experience at work? If you do, keep reading.

PART 2

Dimensions of Calling

3 Listening

EVER SINCE he was a kid, Roger Visker wanted to be a cop. He liked everything about it—the uniform, the car, the lingo, the sense of pride they must get from preserving the peace. He never seriously considered the possibility of doing anything else. In fact, in the program from his eighth-grade graduation ceremony, next to his name, it read, "Career goal: I want to be a Policeman." With a singular passion, Roger progressed through high school, graduated from college with a law enforcement degree, and landed a job with the Kalamazoo Township Police Department. It was a dream job that fit like a glove, and Roger thrived in it. He was well-respected and widely regarded as an exceptional cop: sharp, quick-thinking, decisive, cool under pressure, and equal parts firm and fair. He possessed an uncanny ability to de-escalate a tense situation by understanding, and speaking directly to, the anger and pain of desperate people doing desperate things. He quickly moved up the ranks and eventually was promoted to patrol lieutenant, second in command in the department and well on his way to becoming chief. He loved his job and cared rather deeply for his coworkers. He was making a difference. Life was good. Then one day something happened that changed everything forever.

He remembers the date: September 18, 1990. A Tuesday. Fourteen years into his career as a cop. That particular morning, he woke up early to spend time on a Bible study he was working through. Partway into it, he felt a strong urge to pray. "So I started to pray,"

Roger recalls. "And at that moment, God spoke to me. I am not sure if it was an audible voice; I looked across the table, and no one was there. I heard it, though, as if it were spoken into my ears. It was just a normal voice, not a booming voice from heaven, not particularly deep; remarkably neutral in a lot of ways. The message was very clear. He said, 'Roger, I want you to leave police work and go into the ministry. These are people I want you to talk to . . .'—and then he listed the names of seven people—'and this is the name of the person who will replace you as patrol lieutenant.' And he gave me the name. I sat there totally shocked, and in awe. I said 'Okay.' Then the only thing I could think to do was write down what he said."

It was time to go to work, so Roger walked outside to his car and started driving. The commute was all of four miles, and at about the two-mile mark, as he replayed the event repeatedly in his mind, tears began to flow. "These were not tears of emotion," he recalls. "They were just tears, like my tear ducts were operating. I felt like I was in God's presence. And I said 'Okay, I will do this, but you're going to have to help me.' God said, 'Okay,' and immediately the tears stopped." Roger spent that morning in a daze, walking around the station, trying to avoid everyone, unable to concentrate or think much about anything other than what had happened earlier that morning. "By the time lunch rolled around, I just needed to talk to my wife. I drove home, and she was still a little upset that I didn't kiss her good-bye when I left for work that morning. She could tell I wasn't my usual self, though, and I told her what happened. I was hoping she would tell me I was crazy, or stressed, or that it didn't really happen." Roger chuckled. "But to my dismay, she said, 'If this is what God wants us to do, let's figure it out.'"

The following weekend, Roger and his wife, Sue, were scheduled to lead a weekend Marriage Encounter retreat in Chicago, something they had done a few times before. It was a great weekend, until Sunday, when Roger started to feel ill. By the time they were ready to leave for home, a two-hour drive, he could barely sit up.

Sue helped Roger as he stumbled to the car, then laid down in the backseat with a vomit bag. Not long after starting the drive, Roger felt another urge to pray. He started praying, and asked Sue to do the same. Soon he noticed an unmistakable physical sensation, a sort of tingling; it started at his fingertips, then enveloped his hands, moved up his arms to his shoulders, then up to his head before heading down the rest of his body until it finally reached his feet. His whole body was shaking. Roger kept praying. "I recognized that this was a kind of spiritual battle. I had to either leave the job I loved for the ministry, or not, and at stake was my spiritual well-being. As I prayed, my focus was to release all my stuff to God—our kids, my career, our house, the dog, everything I could think of. I surrendered it over to God and told him all this is yours anyway, take it; more than anything, I need you. And strange though it sounds, I felt a sense of evil, and I rebuked it. I said, 'I don't want you around here.' When I finally had released everything to God, it was over. The tingling left in exactly the reverse order in which it came—it started at my toes, worked its way up to my head, then down my arms, hands and fingers, and then it was gone. Immediately at that moment, I threw up." At that point, Roger says, he knew that whatever he had been putting off, he had to stop. So he went to the list of seven people with whom he was supposed to talk—one couple he knew through Marriage Encounter, three coworkers, and two friends from church. "I didn't know what to ask them," recalls Roger. "I just told them what happened and asked, 'What do you think?'"

One told Roger to read the classic career self-help book, Richard Bolles's *What Color Is Your Parachute?* One recommended a local career counselor, who offered some assessments. One said to talk it through with a pastor. The others offered encouragement, support, and affirmation; they pointed out how they had recognized strengths in Roger that made them think he would be effective in ministry. Strangely, they could also relate to his situation. "The common thread was that all of them had themselves gone through, or were currently going through, a career change," said Roger. "Over the next several months, I did all the things they suggested. I read the book. I talked with my pastor. I scheduled time with the counselor and took some career assessments. Those were interesting; police officer came up as one of the top fits for me, but so did minister." He avoided telling his extended family until December that year. They were naturally surprised, but largely supportive. His mother-in-law asked, "How do you know this is from God and not from the devil?" Recalling this, Roger smiles, and says, "It was a fair question."

As dramatic as were the events of that week in September, the deliberate steps of exploration that Roger took those intervening months were important. They helped provide the assurance that, indeed, he had the interests, personality, abilities, and values to serve well as a pastor. The assessment results confirmed this, and the words of honest feedback from trusted friends confirmed it, too. "I had to wrestle with it for a while," recalls Roger. "It was too difficult not to, what with uprooting our four kids, moving to a new city for seminary, living on almost no income." Finally Roger met with the registrar at Calvin Seminary, which was about an hour's drive away. He told his story and had his transcripts ready. The registrar listened intently, then pointed out that because of the extra psychology and sociology courses he had taken as an undergraduate, along with an independent study in literature he took on a lark because of a good relationship he had with a professor, the only prerequisites he needed were introductory philosophy and Classical Greek. ("It was remarkable," recalled Roger, "how many of those courses I just happened to have taken when I was in college, never foreseeing this.") After pausing to let Roger take it all in, the registrar asked, "When do you want to start?"

From there, Roger followed through on his career 180. He finished his master's of divinity degree after four years and has since pastored three churches in three states, eventually landing in his current post on the staff at New Life Church, a large congregation in New Lenox, Illinois. Doesn't he grieve no longer being a cop, his lifelong dream job at which he so clearly excelled? "No, I don't," he said. "I said to God at that time, 'If this is what you want me to do, take my love of police work away from me.' He did. I left in 1992, and I have been back there only once. Those were great years. I loved them. But that was then, and this is now. And I have a deep love of what I'm doing now."

Roger's story is, hands down, the most dramatic contemporary example of a calling we have ever heard. It is simply astounding on many levels. When we share this story, we receive a fascinating mix of reactions. For some, it's just too incredible to be true; the knee-jerk reaction is one of skepticism. Maybe Roger accidently sampled the evidence from a recent LSD raid that September morning? For many others, the reaction is one of astonishment. Some, perhaps surprisingly, express envy. For those with a strong desire to have a sense of calling in their careers, who know what it means to struggle with indecision and uncertainty, the absolute clarity and specificity in Roger's calling would be, well, a godsend. This call was a burning bush–type sign, with Roger as a modern-day Moses, passively confronted with very clear instructions from what was experienced as an audible voice. This was a transcendent summons, if there ever was one.

The reference to Moses illustrates one reason that, of the three dimensions of calling, the transcendent summons dimension is most controversial. Some critics cringe at the close connection of the "summons" to the Christian tradition—too exclusive, too limiting. (See Q&A 2 for more on this issue.) Others object to the notion of a calling coming from an external source. Callings emerge from within, they say. Still others express concern that the idea of an external source encourages a passive approach to making decisions, essentially spending time waiting and hoping, rather than actively engaging in a thoughtful, intentional decision-making process.

We understand and appreciate the criticisms, yet we view the transcendent summons dimension as critically important to understanding what it means to have a calling. For one thing, the historic and literal meaning of "calling" implies an issuer of the call, an external source of the summons. The neoclassical understanding of calling broadens its applicability beyond any one religious tradition but retains the concept's fundamental meaning. For another, the notion of a transcendent summons matters for a substantial and diverse segment of people, at least in the samples we've collected. For example, one item we often include in our survey research is "I was drawn by something beyond myself to pursue my current line of work." In the sample of university employees we mentioned in chapter 1, 60 percent said that this statement is at least somewhat true for them, and 17 percent indicated that it was totally true of them. Obviously a transcendent summons in one's work is not a universal experience, but if these numbers are any indication of the proportion of the population who find it relevant, we are talking about a lot of people.

Finally, beyond its embeddedness in the definition of calling and relevance for people in today's world, a transcendent summons carries with it considerable power. Experiencing a summons from an external source fosters a connection of one's work activities to a broader sense of meaning and purpose in life, a linking of work tasks and broader purpose we explore further in the next chapter, but that clearly enhances the sense that one's work matters. Responding to a calling from God means honoring God and doing his will. Responding to a calling from a social need means orienting one's work activities in ways that address that social need. Responding to a calling from a family legacy means working to honor and extend that legacy. All of these make one's work tasks, however large or small, much more important and meaningful than they would be in the absence of a summons, because they connect to a deeper, beyond-the-self sense of purpose and responsibility.

Back to Roger's Moses-like experience and the jealousy some people express when they hear the story. Making career decisions is very difficult for many, many people. Without a doubt, choosing or changing a career is a major life decision, and feeling like there is a lot riding on it is very normal. There *is* a lot riding on it—a career choice or career change often determines the trajectory of the next several years of one's life, and often much longer. If part of having a calling means experiencing a transcendent summons, how does a person go about discerning that summons?

Make Room for Listening

As we explored in chapter 2, there is a diverse clutter of work attitudes and motives throughout history and today, most of which probably aim to distract from, rather than enhance, a process of honest discernment of a calling. Approaches to work that focus on pay and comfort, such as the job orientation described in chapter 2, provide one source of pressure. Have you ever been told you should pursue a certain career simply because it pays well and is in demand? Every generation has a hot job sector. As we were entering college, the message was "Go into computers" and Internet commerce; this was before the dot-com crash in 2000–2002. For Dustin Hoffman's character in *The Graduate*, it was plastics. Today it's green jobs. Such messages reflect a job orientation to the extent that these sectors provide the quickest paths to highpaying jobs, rather than pathways for using one's skills to address important social needs. When people evaluate options based primarily (or solely) on how easy they are to obtain and how well they pay, they are approaching the task in ways that run counter to discerning a calling. Let's be clear—we are not suggesting that in tough times, when it is not clear where the rent check will come from, one shouldn't look for a job that will put food on the table. We know, in no small part from personal experience, that this scenario is extremely stressful, and in such circumstances any thought of discerning a calling is appropriately placed on hold until basic needs are met, à la Maslow's need hierarchy.[1] However, taking the long view, the question is this: when survival needs are met and a range of possible career options does become potentially available, on what basis do you evaluate those options?

Similarly, the need to achieve, or to gain approval or power—characteristics of the career orientation—also are frequent obstacles in the process of discerning a calling. Here, too, clarification is needed: pursuing jobs that reward high achievement, that result in social approval, or that are equated with power (e.g., politics, administration, management) are by no means inherently anticalling. Such career paths can serve as very effective conduits for using one's gifts in service of the greater good. The problem is when a job is pursued solely or primarily for the sake of increasing one's power, gaining approval, or satisfying high-achievement needs. A number of our counseling clients over the years have fit this profile. They charged out of the gates as young adults in fields like law or business, orienting their lives around hoped-for promotions and awards. Many found success, objectively speaking, but eventually realized that such success not only came at a cost, it eventually started to ring hollow. In midcareer, they found themselves wedded to jobs they ultimately hated, but were at the same time reluctant to leave because they had become well established and well compensated. "Golden handcuffs" had kept them chained to jobs they did not experience as a calling.

Social and financial obligations are real, as are requirements for success within particular types of jobs. Such things cannot be ignored—but neither should they squeeze out deep reflection on how you might use your gifts in service of the greater good. The key to discerning a transcendent summons is removing the clutter and focusing instead on listening to the source of the call. Most of us never encounter an audible voice, like Roger did, in this life-time. You shouldn't expect such an event. For most of us, the voice of calling is, at least metaphorically, a whisper; while it provides clarity, it usually requires careful listening to discern it. Listening requires more than passive waiting; listening is an active process, as we explore next.

The Best Listening Is Active Listening

As amazing and spiritually profound as was his encounter that September morning, Roger would be the first to tell you that it is *not* how you should expect to discern your calling. "What happened to me is what God needed to do to get through to me," he said. "My hope for others is that God wouldn't need to do this for them." Of course, at the time, Roger was not searching for a sense of direction. He was happy with his career path. This situation is not the case for people who find themselves envious of Roger's experience, longing for a similarly clear sense of direction. We have on many occasions encountered what we describe as the "pray and wait" approach. Most often seen among highly religiously committed folks, but certainly not limited to this group, the pray-and-wait approach is just as it sounds: praying very hard for a clear sense of direction and waiting in anticipation for a clear response. If such a response doesn't come, the typical course of action is to pray harder, and to wait longer.

To be clear, praying is, in fact, helpful—plenty of research supports this claim.[2] Most people say they pray,[3] and for those who are people of faith, it is a prescribed behavior. By no means would we ever discourage someone from praying for guidance, wisdom, patience, or support. The problem is not with the prayer; it's with the waiting. Too often, the waiting is passive. When the hope or expectation is for some kind of audible voice, a burning bush–type sign, or an unmistakable sense of certainty, the frustration upon not receiving one can build quickly. The longer one waits, the more intense the uncertainty becomes. Research on people who are searching for a transcendent summons is sparse but it suggests that such passive waiting is indeed problematic: searching for a transcendent summons is negatively related to people's decision status, to how confident they are in their ability to successfully navigate the career decision process, and to their broader sense of meaning in life.[4] Furthermore, searching for a transcendent summons is unrelated to expectations of positive career outcomes.[5] In fact, every major theory of career choice and development assumes an active role on the part of the decision maker, every major career counseling strategy encourages active engagement, and research suggests that an active approach to career development tasks is very helpful.[6]

Roger's story involved hearing from an audible voice, true. However, it goes without saying that, just like in the Bible, this kind of dramatic encounter is not normative. It is remarkable because it is the exception, not the rule. Therefore, passively waiting for a compelling, existentially earth-rattling calling experience is very likely a misguided strategy for discovering one. Theologians recognize this. "Though there are exceptions," writes Douglas Schuurman, professor of religion at St. Olaf College, "generally God uses mediators to call individuals to particular places of service."[7]

What mediators? Schuurman attributes at least the following to the New Testament: gifts, needs, obligations, discussion, and prayer.[8] For Roger, the story didn't end with a voice imploring him to leave his law-enforcement career for the ministry. An active process of discernment was part of the instruction. The process involved talking with people, and those people recommended very practical steps toward engaging the decision-making and career-change process: reading a self-help book, meeting with a counselor, taking some assessments, talking it through with wise and trusted mentors. As it happens, these steps also align very closely with scientifically supported best-practice recommendations that have emerged within vocational psychology.[9] When we urge people to "pray and be active" rather than "pray and wait," or when we claim that the best kind of listening is active listening, this is the kind of "active" we mean. We explore these issues more deeply in chapters 6 and 7, but let's take a look at some of these steps now.

Gifts

In career development, "gifts" are best thought of very broadly. Your particular set of gifts consists of the attributes that make you uniquely "you"—for example, talents and abilities, such as perfect pitch, writing acumen, an affinity for numbers, or a penchant for understanding engines, organizing closets, or whipping up winning appetizers. Your gifts are broader than your skills, though. Gifts also include your particular pattern of interests, your temperament and interpersonal tendencies, your natural preferences for particular types of work environments. Your gifts make you different from other people—well-suited for some types of work and not as well suited for others. How can you gain a clearer sense of your unique pattern of gifts? We explore this later in the book, and we also recommend some strategies for assessment on this book's companion website, www.makeyourjobacalling.com.

Discussion

Think of at least three people who know you well, who have your best interests in mind, whom you consider to be wise, and whose opinions you trust. These people are important—they can serve as key resources for you. Here is what we have long instructed our career counseling clients to do: Arrange to meet with these people, one at a time, for coffee (or a beer, if that fits the nature of your relationship better). Seek their wise counsel. Ask each of them questions such as "What do you see as my most important strengths? Areas for growth? In which kinds of roles do you think I could thrive, and why? Which do you think I should avoid, and why? When you think about my areas of greatest potential, what comes to mind? What do you see as my blind spots right now? What important factors am I failing to consider?" Meet regularly with these mentors, draw from their encouragement, and seek their honest guidance. This process takes a lot of effort, but research evidence suggests that the process of building support for your career decision-making process can be a difference maker.[10] As we discuss later, research also indicates that trained career counselors can be an especially effective resource, providing a supportive and safe environment for exploration, while implementing some well-established frameworks for making wise, informed career decisions.

Obligations

Vocational psychologist Donald Super describes how at any given point in time, people find themselves navigating a complicated constellation of life roles.[11] Some roles are central; they dominate one's time, energy, and sense of responsibility. Other roles are peripheral, lurking on the back burner. These core and peripheral roles reorganize in importance over time. For example, most single adults have a web of close friendships and a heavy dose of leisure time to go with their work role; if they marry and have children, their friendships often leave the foreground and their leisure pursuits may go into virtual hibernation as their spouse and parent roles dominate. Similarly, the child and student roles are prominent early in life; as children come of age and eventually enter the workforce, both roles diminish in importance, until retraining is needed (in which case the student role becomes core again) and until aging parents require caregiving (at which point the child role becomes core once more). The point is that although things do change over time, right now, as you are reading this, you occupy certain roles that define your responsibilities in life.

Career decisions are never made in a vacuum, but in the context of a life—and discernment of a calling absolutely has to take into account one's other responsibilities in life. Baumeister tells the story from William Somerset Maugham's novel *The Moon and Sixpence* of a middle-class English stockbroker who abandons his family, job, and lifestyle of comfort, presumably to indulge in an illicit affair, until he is discovered holed up in a cheap apartment in Paris.[12] The "other woman" turned out to be an easel, a canvas, and some paint. Motivated by an inner passion to paint despite having no training or experience, the man's sacrifice of the responsibilities tied to his family and former career seemed perfectly justified to him—a perspective the novel eventually supports. This rather exaggerated example of the modern view of calling shows the call arising from within and driving the protagonist toward self-fulfillment. In contrast, the neoclassical perspective of calling, with its emphasis on duty and prosocial values, requires that a calling within the work role complement, not compete with, one's other callings in life. Therefore, part of discerning one's calling in work means ensuring that it fits in context with one's other roles and responsibilities.[13] Besides reflecting what for many are deeply held values, a large volume of research suggests that strategies promoting a balance of work and nonwork roles are associated with greater health and satisfaction with life and work.[14]

Needs

Obligations are relevant in another way, too. Recall Luther's notion that a person's "station" determines one's calling. Calvin and the

Puritans shifted the focus from one's station to one's gifts as the key mediators of one's calling, a view that persists today, even forming the basis of the core strategies used by most career counselors. This shift doesn't negate the relevance of duties, however; it just reframes things a bit. Our gifts don't equip us for successful pursuit of particular occupations purely for our own self-fulfillment. Instead, they prepare us uniquely for certain types of work in service of the common good. Within the values of this perspective, if you perceive a set of social needs that you are well equipped to address by virtue of your gifts and experiences, you bear some obligation to orient your work activity toward addressing those needs.[15] Part of discerning a transcendent summons, therefore, means evaluating the intersection of your gifts with needs you identify in your community and in the world around you.

How Big Is Your Calling?

We have undergraduate students whose approach to discerning a calling extends to what specific courses they should take next semester. Am I called to take Psychology of Personality as my elective, or should I take Psychology of Learning instead? Are callings that specific? Perhaps they can be. Certainly Roger's calling experience suggests very specific directives. But here again, for most of us, there is a fuzzy line between being called to *be* and being called to *do*. Religious traditions often differentiate between a general call—to discipleship, holiness, and righteous living, for example—and a particular call to serve in a particular role. But even with the particular call, perhaps the question isn't what specific job title you should pursue, but instead what constitutes your mission in the world and what types of occupations would allow you to use your gifts in pursuit of that mission. The authors of this book, for example, have distinct combinations of artistic, social, and investigative interests; we enjoy doing research, teaching, and writing;

we value understanding people and helping them; and we share a moderate degree of entrepreneurial interests. Each of us has ended up in jobs as psychology professors. Does this mean we discerned callings to serve as psych profs? Or are we called to use our abilities in writing, teaching, counseling, and conducting research to help people understand themselves and others better, and to use their gifts in satisfying, meaningful, life-giving ways that enhance the common good? This example admittedly oversimplifies things a bit, but we think the latter is closer to the truth and assume that callings are usually at least this general for most people.

This point has some pretty significant implications. For one, it means we didn't have to pursue jobs as psych profs to honor our callings. For example, Bryan considered other possibilities early on, including sociology, social work, business, and ministry roles. Ryan at one time aspired to work in architecture and (still in some small way) stand-up comedy. Could we have pursued one of these other options and still have "found" our callings? Absolutely, as long as we had been able to use our respective gifts in ways that aligned with our deeper sense of purpose in life, in service of others. How big is your particular calling? For most of you, your calling is not limited to a job title.

We hasten to add that the notion of callings being relatively general in nature—more general than a particular job title, usually—is more than just an assumption. If callings are mediated primarily by one's gifts, the research on individual differences in work-related personal attributes is highly relevant. What level of specificity can be achieved in research that predicts successful career choice on the basis of people's interests, abilities, needs, values, and personality? This area of research has layers of complexity as well as some holes, but the short answer is that people's unique profiles of such attributes seem to equip them for success within particular occupational domains or clusters of occupations, more so than within single specializations. For example, imagine a person who has strong interests in practical and intellectual activities, as well as high numerical and spatial abilities, and who values achievement and autonomy. This person, on the basis of her gifts, would likely do well and experience work as very meaningful within career paths related to applied math or engineering. However, without taking her experiences and training into account, do her gifts make her clearly a better fit for, say, an electrical engineer who focuses on improving computer chips that monitor fuel consumption in cars versus a chemical engineer who focuses on making cell phone batteries last longer? Research has not been very successful at predicting success with this level of specificity on the basis of such attributes, in part, we suspect, because most people are simply equipped with gifts that make them equally likely to succeed across multiple possible jobs within a more general cluster of similar occupations. We seem to have a fair amount of built-in flexibility.

If you are looking for clear and specific answers, this level of abstraction may be frustrating. However, you should also find it extremely freeing, because for most of us, there is no single right answer to the question, "To which job am I called?" Instead, that question has multiple right answers: you can pursue any one of several possible career paths while still honoring your calling. You don't have to make a choice and then second-guess yourself, wondering if you somehow should have chosen option B, C, or D instead, and are now doomed to work outside your calling. As we explore later,[16] even if you have a dissatisfying job, you could potentially, if external constraints allow, craft that same job into something that allows you to pursue your calling.

During the spring of 1997, the water in the Red River rose more than five feet beyond what the National Weather Service had forecast. The sister cities of Grand Forks, North Dakota, and East

Grand Forks, Minnesota, had no time to prepare for what followed. The icy water poured over the dikes, overtook the sandbag walls, and rushed into the cities, forcing what at the time was the largest evacuation in the United States since the Civil War. Thousands of homes were flooded, and the damage was estimated at $3.5 billion. On his sofa in his home in Minneapolis, Rohit watched the events unfold on his television with rapt attention. He saw the water rise over a period of days, and once it broke over the dikes he knew what he had to do. He got up, drove to one of the seven warehouses he managed, and pleaded with his boss for leave time, to no avail. "Either you give me some time off or I'm quitting" was his ultimatum, to which his boss replied, "See ya." Rohit drove straight up to East Grand Forks to help the flood relief efforts. When Bryan met Rohit in June of that year, he was operating a forklift in a makeshift Salvation Army food distribution center. He lived in a hotel room at the time, but for his first four weeks he slept each night in the back of his Honda Accord. He figured he could stay another month until his remaining four hundred dollars ran out, at which point he'd head back to Minneapolis or St. Paul to find another job.

Rohit's story is another dramatic example of a transcendent summons. Unlike Roger, Rohit didn't hear an audible voice commanding him to leave and serve in East Grand Forks. Yet he was called; the images on TV of houses under water and the thought of tens of thousands of people left homeless summoned him. Something beyond Rohit—a very intense, pressing, immediate social need— reached into his heart and dragged him, quite willingly, out of his job and home in Minneapolis and into the food warehouse in East Grand Forks. For the record, we invariably advise a more deliberate, planful, less impulsive process than the approach that Rohit took—yet at least at the time, Rohit had no regrets.

Also like Roger's story, Rohit's is quite unique. We shouldn't expect an audible voice like what Roger experienced, and few of us have the freedom, given our other responsibilities, to respond to a summons by quitting, relocating, and working until our money runs out like Rohit did. These dramatic and powerful stories nonetheless teach us some things about discerning a transcendent summons. Even after an audible voice clearly told him what path to pursue, Roger engaged in a period of exploration and discernment. For most of us, this kind of careful exploration and discernment allows us to listen to the quiet voice of calling as it is mediated through our gifts, our discussions with trusted mentors or a counselor, our obligations, and the needs we see in the world. Rohit's story shows powerfully how careful attention to needs in the world can stir something deep within us and serve as another source of a calling. For most of us, even despite having more constraints than Rohit experienced, Frederick Buechner's description of calling as "the place where your deep gladness and the world's deep hunger meet"[17] may ring true.

If Roger's and Rohit's experiences are dramatic and rare examples of discerning a transcendent summons, what does a more typical example look like? Consider the case of a former client, Maria, who had worked in the restaurant industry for several years, most recently as a cake decorator in a bakery.[18] She had grown deeply dissatisfied and longed for a change, but her wheels had been spinning while she waited for a clear sense of what such a change might entail. "I want to find my calling," Maria explained, "and working in food isn't what I thought it would be. I need to do something different." Maria's need to be creative was a core value for her, paired with producing art (broadly defined) that inspired people, art that was useful. In the process of working with Maria, we saw that discerning a calling would require attending to those factors through which the summons may be perceived particularly assessing Maria's gifts and helping her attend to needs she saw in the world around her. An avid hiker and camper, Maria loved the outdoors, and she expressed a hypothesis that being around beauty in nature gives people a needed boost. "It's good for the soul," she often said.

Maria's assessment results suggested that she resonated with artistic and pragmatic, outdoor-oriented interests, valued autonomy and achievement, and was skilled at spatial reasoning and math. A major pet peeve for Maria? "People have crappy landscaping out here. I can't stand it. It must be so depressing to live in houses surrounded by that stuff," referring to woody, overgrown shrubs and weedy grass. When she disclosed that she had recently attended a weekend workshop on xeriscaping (a form of landscaping and gardening, popular in the arid western United States, focused on reducing the need for water and irrigation) hosted by a local nursery, it wasn't a leap to ask whether she had considered exploring landscape architecture as a possible career path. After doing some investigating, Maria became convinced that it could be an excellent fit. "It's perfect. It would get me outside more, and I'd be able to express my need to create, but in a way that is really functional, that would make people happy, and would even be good for the environment. This could be one path for doing the kinds of things I was put on this earth to do." No audible voice or dramatic tugging on heartstrings, but Maria sensed that, based on her gifts and what she viewed as a need, landscape architecture provided a means for responding to her calling to create functional art that enhances well-being—both for the earth and for suburban homeowners.

How about you? What are your unique interests, abilities, personality traits, and work-related values? What needs from the world's "deep hunger" strike a chord with you, and how do they intersect with your "deep gladness"? What possibilities—now or down the road—would provide you with a path for living out your calling through your work? Actively engaging questions like these opens up channels for you to hear the quiet voice of calling, summoning you.

4 Making Meaning

MOST PEOPLE AGREE that experiencing a positive sense of meaning—defined as "the sense made of, and significance felt regarding, the nature of one's being and existence"[1]—is fundamental to living "the good life." Yet how many take serious steps toward living meaningfully at work? Before we dig into this, we are going to begin with a slew of questions to get you thinking. For starters, think about your life as a whole. What, ultimately, is most important to you? How would you describe your life's *purpose*? With answers to these questions in mind, list at least five *life goals* you are currently pursuing. (We recommend you write these down, either here on the page, in a journal, or on a separate sheet.)

1. _____

_____

2. _____

_____

3. _____

_____

4. _____

_____

5. _____

_____

Next, think carefully about your career for a moment—your current job situation, the kind of work you most want to do, and the steps you need to take to bridge the gap between these, if there is one. How close or far away are you from where you want to be? What role do you want your career to play within the broader context of your life? With your answers to these questions in mind, list at least five *career goals* you are currently pursuing:

1. _____

_____

2. _____

_____

3. _____

_____

4. _____

_____

5. _____

_____

Now look closely at the goals you listed above for your life and your career. To what extent are your career goals in line with your life goals?

Are you happy with your answer to this question? If not, what needs to change?

We'll do more than bombard you with questions in this chapter. The second dimension of calling is present when a person derives a sense of meaning from work, or when a person's job activity aligns with a broader sense of purpose or meaning in life as a whole. This chapter explores the pathways that research has identified for cultivating a positive sense of meaning at work. Along the way, we suggest practical strategies to help you nurture a sense of meaning and purpose in your own life at work.

Taking Stock

Part of what we've tried to do so far in this book is stimulate your thinking—about what it means to have a calling, about what your work means to you right now, and about where you might be summoned based on how your unique set of gifts has equipped you well for some types of work more than others. Above, we asked you to consider what matters most to you in life, your purpose, the goals you are striving to reach, and how your work and your career goals fit into that bigger picture. Regularly taking a step back like this and evaluating where things stand in your life right now, and where things are headed is very important—hence our suggestion that you make your life goals and career goals explicit by writing them out and taking a good look at them. The more closely your life goals and career goals align, the more likely you are to experience your work as meaningful, in support of your broader sense of purpose in life. We've found this exercise to be diagnostic. If your life goals and career goals support each other, you are experiencing the kind of congruence that fosters meaning. If you lack this kind of congruence, chances are you are unhappy, or at minimum feel somewhat disjointed and segmented rather than integrated and whole. If that's the case, changes are needed, and you probably already know it.

Questions like this also are helpful when you can use them as a starting point for assessing how you experience the two main components of meaning at work: comprehension and purpose.[2] *Comprehension* refers to your ability to make sense of your experience, to understand how you fit into the world around you. When it comes to work, people high in comprehension see how their day-to-day job tasks connect to something much bigger than themselves. If they work within an organization, for example, they understand how their tasks advance the goals of their organization, and what their organization is trying to accomplish in their community and world by pursuing those goals. If you work in the finance department for a health food company with products designed to help people live healthier lifestyles, and you can see how your hours of compiling expense reports and poring over spreadsheets really do meet a tangible need that helps the company better accomplish its mission, you have a high degree of comprehension for your work. Think about your current job, or if you are out of work, your most recent job. In what ways do (or did) your job tasks connect to a broader goal—one you value, one that makes a difference?

Purpose, according to Stanford professor Bill Damon and colleagues, is "a stable and generalized intention to accomplish something that is at once meaningful to the self and of consequence to the world beyond the self."[3] Whereas comprehension focuses on understanding, purpose focuses on action. One common purpose, for example, is to have a consistently positive impact on others. Someone pursuing this purpose might have life goals that include being a loving and supportive spouse and parent, a person who provides a listening ear and encouraging words and deeds, and who uses her gifts to give back to her community out of a sense of gratitude. If this person is pursuing this purpose in her work as, say, a marketing manager, she might have career goals that include using her training and skills to promote useful products that make people's lives better, and to share ideas and information in ways that help her employees develop their strengths. Purposes drive pursuit of more specific, shorter-term goals, and provide thematic structure and a sense of coherence for activities in which a person engages. Take a look again at your life goals and career goals. What purpose do they reflect?

How Can You Make Work Meaningful?

As useful as it is to think about things like comprehension and purpose in the abstract, ultimately you have to actually do something to help you gain a sense of meaning in your work, and, by extension, in your life. Here we get practical. What specific steps can you take to enhance the meaningfulness of your work? Research from the fields of psychology and management suggests several strategies. One obvious strategy is to find a meaningful job—that is, an especially meaning-inducing work environment. Of course, even if you have an unusually ideal set of circumstances, finding such a job is much easier said than done. Fortunately, you can take other steps within most any job that can make your work more meaningful: integrating your spirituality, using your strengths, linking your day-to-day activities to down-the-road outcomes that you find personally meaningful, and infusing your work with a focus on benefiting the greater good. We address each of these in turn.

Find a Meaningful Job

Bonnie Wurzbacher, senior executive and almost thirty-year veteran at Coca-Cola, claims, "There is no such thing as meaningful work. You must learn to bring meaning to it."[4] This probably sounds familiar, because earlier we wrote that a sense of calling has little to do with a person's actual job, and everything to do with how a person approaches that job. Even so, not all jobs provide a level playing field for experiencing the work as meaningful. One recent review of research on meaningful work identified particular aspects of the work context—such as the nature of one's job tasks, the organizational mission, and the quality of one's workplace relationships—that make some jobs simply easier to experience as meaningful than others.[5]

Different jobs come with different demands and provide different kinds of opportunities for employees. Jobs that allow considerable autonomy—in other words, that give employees a lot of latitude and control over how they get the job done—are associated with a greater sense of meaning than other jobs. So are jobs that provide opportunities to use a variety of skills. Similarly, jobs that give workers a clear sense of how their efforts contribute to the completion of a piece of work they can identify—a visible, tangible outcome—are easier to experience as meaningful, especially when that outcome clearly has a positive impact on others.[6]

To get a sense of how important such factors can be in experiencing work as meaningful, imagine working in a job that *lacks* these things—one that gives you no autonomy, no opportunity to use your range of skills, no sense of how your efforts contribute to a tangible outcome, and no sense of the work's impact. For example, think of a factory job that consists of standing on a line with pieces of machinery moving by you. Your task is to pick up one large piece of metal with two gloved hands, turn it, lay it down on a press, and push a button. You are told that there is only one way to do this task right, so don't freestyle it. What exactly are you making? Parts for a large piece of construction equipment, you're told, but who knows? Does this sound meaningful to you? Let's not pretend this kind of low-autonomy monotony is limited to blue-collar manufacturing, either. In the same vein as *Dilbert* and *The Office*, the cult classic film *Office Space* poignantly (and very humorously) depicts life for software engineers in a barren wasteland of cubicles—with a soul-crushing boss incessantly demanding TPS reports (whatever those are) and with a constantly failing printer—where employees have little control over their work and are almost wholly detached from the fruits of their labor. Actor Ron Livingston's character, Peter Gibbons, reflects on his experience and comes to this conclusion: "Ever since I started working, every single day of my life has been worse than the day before it. So that means that every single day that you see me, that's on the worst day of my life." Peter's hypnotherapist, Dr. Swanson, asked, "What about today? Is today the worst day of your life?" Peter blurted, "Yeah," and it's hard to disagree with Dr. Swanson's professional opinion: "Wow, that's messed up!"

In contrast, philosopher and motorcycle mechanic Matthew Crawford affirms the importance of autonomy, skill variety, significance, and impact in his book *Shop Class as Soulcraft*. For Crawford, meaningful work took a serious hit when the Industrial Revolution and its technological advances separated thinking from doing. He lifts up manual trades—like his own job operating a motorcycle repair shop—as examples of work that weaves thinking and doing back together, requires legitimate skill, produces a genuinely useful outcome, and ties workers to those who benefit from their efforts. Crawford writes,

> Seeing a motorcycle about to leave my shop under its own power several days after arriving in the back of a pickup truck, I suddenly don't feel tired, even though I've been standing on a concrete floor all day. Through the portal of his helmet, I think I can make out the edges of a grin on the face of a guy who hasn't ridden his bike in a while. I give him a wave. With one of his hands on the throttle and the other on the clutch, I know he can't wave back. But I can hear his salute in the exuberant "BwaaAAAAP! blum-blum" of a crisp throttle, gratuitously revved. That sound pleases me, as I know it does him. It's a ventriloquist conversation in one mechanical voice, and the gist of it is "Yeah!"[7]

Work like this promotes comprehension and purpose, leveraging skills to accomplish a tangible outcome that makes customers very happy. Crawford certainly finds it meaningful.

The nature of a person's tasks on the job is important, but those job tasks usually occur in the context of an organization, and the mission of that organization also makes a difference. New Belgium Brewing Company, the third-largest craft brewery in the United States, is as mission driven an organization as it comes. New Belgium is very clear about the importance of "remembering that we are incredibly lucky to create something fine that enhances people's lives while surpassing our customers' expectations." Their mission centers on producing innovative, top-quality craft beers, modeling environmental stewardship, developing their employees' potential and promoting their wellness, and having fun.[8] These phrases are more than mere platitudes at this company: their beers consistently win awards; 100 percent of their electricity comes from renewable sources; their employees benefit from gym memberships, yoga classes, a climbing wall, a limited-edition bike after one year of employment, and career development training; and they employ a director of fun who, among many other things, installed a twisty-slide in the brewery. We have interviewed several New Belgium employees and talked with many more informally. A common theme is their intense passion for their work, and the unmistakable sense of comprehension and purpose their work provides. Nearly every New Belgium employee with whom we've talked assures us that this job will be her or his last, and their annual employee retention rate hovers around 97 percent. At least in part, these results come from a strong alignment of personal values with those that their company promotes—an observation consistent with research showing that such ideological congruence provides positive meaning for employees.[9] If you work in an organization right now, do you know its mission? If you don't, this is a pretty significant problem.

If you do know the mission, how well does it fit with your own personal values?

Relationships on the job are important, too. Part of how we make sense of the world is by looking to others for cues on how to think and behave, using these cues to inform our own ways of understanding things,[10] especially when it comes to the meaning and value of work.[11] Have you ever worked alongside fellow employees who seemed to truly enjoy their work—who were engaged, energized, and excited about what they were trying to accomplish? Such attitudes are infectious. Unfortunately, so are attitudes that communicate disengagement, disinterest, and dread.

We've personally experienced both ends of the continuum of social environments. On one end of the spectrum was the part-time job at a discount sporting goods store where a manager was arrested for embezzlement the same month that two cashiers were embroiled in competing affairs with the ex-Marine in the hunting and fishing department. It was a soap opera that, while certainly never dull, hardly inspired a sense of purpose in the work. On the other end of the spectrum was the college counseling center where staff members were so driven by a deep and profound value for the importance of their work, it was hard not to feel like a valuable part of what they were trying to accomplish. Undeniably, people differ in the extent to which they value their relationships with coworkers,[12] but for most of us, given the sheer amount of time we spend with these folks, their collective attitudes set the tone.

Leaders also set the tone. At their best, leaders help employees understand the organization's mission and their role in accomplishing that mission. Some leadership styles are especially effective at helping employees derive meaning from their work. For example, transformational leadership involves effectively communicating a clear vision (and walking the talk by behaving in ways consistent with that vision), expressing genuine personal concern about employees, and encouraging workers to take calculated risks and solve problems creatively. Transformational leaders have a knack for broadening the goals and aspirations of employees, and instilling the confidence they need to perform beyond expectations.[13] Scholars have cited everyone from Gandhi to Steve Jobs as examples of such leaders. What do you think? Would following a leader like this make your work seem more meaningful? In one pair of research studies with health-care workers and service workers in Canada, employees who had transformational leaders also tended to view their work as meaningful—and as that sense of meaning increased, so did their psychological health.[14]

Let's wrap this section up with a summary: You can increase the odds of experiencing your work as meaningful if you land a job that gives you the following:

- ► Autonomy—that is, the freedom to try out your own ideas
- ► A chance to use your skills—not just one, but a variety of them
- ► A sense of how your work contributes to a tangible product or service you can identify
- ► A sense of how that tangible product or service matters to society
- ► Coworkers who enjoy and value their work, and with whom you get along well
- ► A leader who can communicate a clear vision that you value, who lives out that vision in her or his own life, who expresses genuine concern about you, who encourages you to take risks and solve problems creatively, who gives you confidence, and who broadens your goals and aspirations
- ► An organizational mission that aligns well with your values and broader sense of purpose

In looking over this list, we can't help but have a reaction we expect many readers share: This stuff is great, but it might be hard to find all of it in one place. To be sure, some jobs out there actually provide all these things, but nevertheless we have described an ideal-world scenario. For readers trying to choose a career or find a job in the real world, getting hired into a position that resembles anything in the ballpark of this is much easier said than done. Of course, a job that provides even a subset of the bullets in this list makes a big difference. Still, what if you are currently suffering through a job you hate, but are reluctant to leave because of the risks involved? Job changes tend to be high-risk, high-reward, but without a doubt, the high risk cannot be easily ignored or dismissed. Fortunately, as important as these features of the work context and workplace relationships can be, people are not passive recipients of their environments; they can and do proactively influence the tasks and relationships in their work to help shape its meaning.[15] In short, to the extent that constraints allow, you can make your current job more meaningful. How? Research points to four strategies, to which we now turn.

Bring Your Faith to Work

Calling has been described as inherently spiritual, a concept "that challenges us to see our work in relation to our deepest beliefs."[16] The link of calling to spirituality should be unsurprising by now. As we reviewed in chapter 2, calling was very closely linked to religious worldviews throughout history, and in chapter 3 we explored how the notion of a transcendent summons can be viewed through a spiritual lens. In the context of research on the workplace, spirituality has been described as "one of the fastest-growing areas of new research and inquiry by scholars and practitioners alike,"[17] as sure an indicator as any that many workers view their work in spiritual terms. This research has shown that workers with spiritual commitments tend to think of their work as contributing to a higher purpose beyond themselves, particularly in terms of caring, service, and transcendence, which in turn provides a sense of meaningfulness.[18] This point is clearly evident for Roger Visker, the cop-turned-clergy in chapter 3. Similarly, Peggy, a participant in sociologist Susan Crawford Sullivan's study of work and faith in low-income mothers,[19] described wanting "to have a pure heart before God . . . pleasing him" by how she approached her work cleaning houses. "A lot of times in these homes that I cleaned, it was in my mind a way that I could give a gift back to somebody . . . to go in there and . . . clean everything with a touch of love."

University of Connecticut social psychologist Crystal Park proposes that people make meaning by integrating their big-picture beliefs, goals, and sense of meaningfulness, then translating those global meaning frameworks into a day-to-day experience of meaningfulness.[20] People with strong religious or spiritual worldviews may be especially inclined to approach their daily experiences in a way that connects to their broader framework of meaning, and a sense of calling provides a path for doing this in the work domain.[21] For example, imagine a forester who believes that God created and sustains the natural world and calls people to take care of it as responsible stewards. For this person, coordinating an effort to cut down swathes of lodgepole pine that have been decimated by beetle kill might be conceptualized not just as merely getting the job done, but as serving as a caretaker of God's creation. Or consider Bonnie Wurzbacher, the Coca-Cola executive, who has described work as "the way we participate with divine intention in this world." From her perspective, her work at Coca-Cola is less about satisfying shareholders' unquenchable thirst for profits and more about advancing the economic well-being of communities around the world. Driven by this calling, she leads Coca-Cola's North American global customer management teams, as well as the company's 5 BY 20 initiative, a global program designed to inspire and empower 5 million women entrepreneurs by 2020.[22] "When women are lifted up economically, socially, intellectually, and spiritually," she said recently, "so are their communities."

We should note that integrating one's faith at work may seem within mainstream American culture to be a highly personal, individualized quest, yet some religious traditions have been very active in providing resources designed to help people live out their callings in a context of support, guidance, and mentoring. Enough books on faith-work integration have been published to warrant at least one published annotated bibliography of works on the topic,[23] and the Cardus organization in Canada[24] and the Center for Faith and Work[25] in New York City are examples of networks that provide support for people who strive to integrate their faith with their work. Even Princeton has gotten into the act, establishing the Princeton Faith & Work Initiative to "investigate the ways in which the resources of various religious traditions and spiritual identities shape and inform engagement with such workplace issues as ethics, values, vocation, meaning, purpose, and how people live out their faith in an increasingly diverse and pluralistic world."[26]

If spirituality and faith are important to you, don't check these things at the door when you go to work. To do so would deny a core part of who you are. It would lead to fragmentation rather than wholeness. Work is more meaningful when you seek paths of integration.

Use Your Strengths

Above we discussed how one of the features of meaningful workplaces is the opportunity to use a variety of skills. Using multiple skills staves off boredom and makes work more dynamic and engaging, but when it comes to the link between skills and meaning, variety is only part of the picture. A good strategy for deriving meaning is to find or create ways to use your strengths. Much has been written on the benefits of identifying and using strengths,[27] and we provide a more detailed summary on this book's companion website, www.makeyourjobacalling.com, about abilities, character strengths, and the benefits and drawbacks of formal approaches to assessing strengths. Using one's strengths without knowing what they are is difficult, and although formal assessments are useful, informal strategies for identifying strengths provide another good place to start.

One informal strategy for assessing your strengths is to think carefully about a recent situation when you were at your best. Give it a shot. Start by identifying the situation, a specific event within the last few weeks in which you felt you were clearly at your best. Got it? Now, replay it in your mind a few times, focusing carefully on the details of the moment. In a journal or on another sheet (because you will need space for this), write out answers to these questions:

- Using a step-by-step account, how did the events of this situation unfold?
- What did you do well?
- What was the outcome?
- Thinking back on it, what specific personal strengths did you show in this situation? List as many as you can.
- Circle or highlight the top five. In which other situations have you observed these strengths?

Once you have those top five strengths, try this experiment: Make a conscious, deliberate effort to use these strengths more often, and in new ways, in your job (or in other areas of your life, if you are not currently employed) every day for the next week. Over the course of that week, as you do this, what do you notice or experience? In what ways has using these strengths changed the way you feel about your work?

Martin Seligman and colleagues have shown that people instructed to write about a "you at your best" experience, reflect on their personal strengths illustrated in the story, and then review the story once a day for a week to further reflect on their strengths were significantly happier and less depressed compared to people in a control group at the end of that week.[28] However, these effects didn't last into the weeks and months that followed. Why not? One explanation is that merely reflecting on your strengths is not enough; you have to *use* them. Another finding from the same study supported that interpretation: Individuals who were given feedback on their top strengths, and who were then instructed to use one of their top strengths in a new and different way each day for a week, were significantly happier and less depressed not just at the end of that week but even six months later! Of course, these participants were instructed to use their strengths generally, not only at work, and happiness and depression are not the same thing as meaning. However, another recent study demonstrated that when people use their strengths at work, they are in fact more likely to experience their work as meaningful.[29]

You might recall from chapter 2 that a key element of calling has historically been using one's gifts in service of the common good. As it turns out, some scholars have suggested that this very strategy— using one's gifts to promote the well-being of others—is a primary path to meaning in life.[30] Other research suggests that people who act consistently with their strengths experience positive emotions and well-being as a result,[31] and some scholars have referred to the use of one's top strengths as one way of living out a sense of one's true or authentic self,[32] which in turn has been described as a source of meaning in life.[33] To summarize the obvious conclusion: identify your strengths and use them!

Link Your Work to Outcomes That Matter

A classic story about different perspectives on work[34] goes like this: Three workers were assigned the miserable job of breaking big rocks into smaller chunks. Each worker was asked to describe what he was doing. The first paused and said, "Making little ones out of big ones." The second followed with "Making a living." The third: "Building a cathedral." All three of these responses were technically correct, but you can imagine that the way each worker felt about his job would have differed. The difference in focus for each of the three workers in this anecdote—a surface-level objective (making little ones out of big ones), an extrinsic reward (making a living), or a broader vision of accomplishment (building a cathedral)—harkens back to the work orientations we described in chapter 2. The same job can be approached in different ways, and perspective matters a great deal.

As you've likely guessed, we'd predict that the "building a cathedral" worker derives the most meaning from his work. Why? Because he understands how the daily grind of his job, insignificant though it seems, contributes to something bigger, something that matters to him, something from which others benefit. This strategy is very fruitful for making work meaningful. Think about your current job or a job you've held in the past. Do you know what "cathedral" your effort is or was helping to build? If you need some examples of how a job might connect to something of broader importance, here are some from our own work histories, dating back to adolescence:

- *Corn detasseler* (for the uninitiated, the job happens in the cornfields and consists of pulling the tassel off one type of corn plant so that they can be properly fertilized by pollen from another type of corn plant, which is essential for cultivating high-yield hybrid seed corn): Helping a team of workers create the conditions needed to make farming corn more efficient, which in turn helps the families that own the farms and those who consume the corn.
- *Salesperson at locally owned, independent toy store*: Helping customers find unique gifts to spread joy to (mostly) children, and working with coworkers to create a store atmosphere designed to make shopping fun. Dressed as the Easter bunny at one point (fortunately no pictures exist).
- *Salesperson at Firestone tire store*: Helping customers identify the most effective fixes for their car problems and identifying

the most cost-effective solution for these problems. Worked here during a period in which a certain tire model was blowing up unexpectedly on the road, and thus also worked with customers to obtain new tires so that they could travel safely as soon as possible.

▶ *Salesperson at sporting goods retail*: Helping equip people with clothing and equipment that they need to live healthy, active lifestyles; to feel confident about their appearance; and to help maximize their ability to perform in athletic competition.

▶ *Dining hall dishwasher*: Working with a team to maintain the standards for cleanliness and sanitation necessary to fulfill the larger purpose of providing college students with nutrition they need to optimally engage their education.

▶ *House painter*: Working with a crew to enhance the well-being of families by helping maintain and improve the appearance of the homes in which they live.

▶ *Personal care attendant*: Providing assistance with various activities of daily living for a friend confined to a wheelchair after a diving accident, helping him pursue his goals of completing his education, obtaining employment, and living an active life.

▶ *Landscape and lawn maintenance worker*: Working with a crew to improve the well-being of families and performance of companies by installing, improving, and maintaining the aesthetics and functionality of the grounds surrounding their homes and places of work.

▶ *University instructor*: Designing and implementing learning experiences to deepen students' knowledge about psychology, to establish a base for additional learning, and to help them develop useful strategies for engaging in critical analysis, creative thinking, effective oral and written communication, and other intellectual skills.

▶ *Staff psychotherapist*: Facilitating one-on-one and group-based psychological interventions designed to help struggling clients identify and better understand the nature of the problems, build skills for coping with hardship and implementing more satisfying approaches to living, and navigate their relationships and responsibilities in healthier, more life-giving ways.

Theoretically, the tasks of *any* legitimate job can connect to a broader purpose, if it is true that society is interdependent, with each job supported by common needs met by mutual service. Our premise is that focusing on that broader purpose imbues the work with meaning.

Of course, we don't want to oversimplify things. In looking back on that list, a few things become apparent to us. First, although the sample tie-ins of each job to broader, more meaningful, down-the-road outcomes provide the jobs with a level of dignity and meaning in retrospect, we certainly were not always thinking about such things at the time. Staff psychotherapist, university instructor, and personal care attendant are easy to frame as meaningful, but corn detasseler? In Bryan's mind at the time, working that job felt a little like occupying one of Dante's circles of hell. In his better moments he thought of the work as a way to make a buck and spend some time with friends, but most often, with the oppressive sun beating down on him through the muggy Michigan summer air, the focus was on little more than how much time was left before the crew finally quit for the day. Admittedly, it is hard to identify—much less consciously focus on—such distal outcomes while drenched with sweat, when the muddy earth has soaked through your socks and new blisters are forming between your fingers. Second, the process of reframing a job's broader purpose can sometimes raise questions about whether the job connects to something ultimately of value after all. Making corn production more efficient is great when it helps a family farm, or when ears of sweet corn end up on a hungry family's table, but what about when you know the work ends up lining the wallets of corporate farm executives, or facilitating the production of the high-fructose corn syrup that is making Americans obese?

These kinds of challenges are real—and to be sure, in some circumstances, trying to identify the broader purpose of your job results in a realization that your efforts simply don't align with a broader purpose that you value. If that's the case, and a better-fitting job is accessible to you, you should probably begin planning for a transition. Still, within most jobs, tying work activities to broader purposes in life can make work more meaningful.[35] Dirty jobs like corn detasseling may be more difficult to connect to an overarching purpose than other jobs, but the question is, if Bryan had been able to make such a connection and focus on it with any consistency, would his attitude toward the job have improved, and would he have felt that the job mattered more? Undoubtedly yes and yes. As we noted in chapter 1 and explore further later on, even those in low-status jobs (e.g., hospital janitorial staff, hairdressers, racetrack backstretch workers) seem to find benefit from reframing, recalibrating, and refocusing their work responsibilities in ways that connect them to a broader purpose.

Focus on the Greater Good

As you've no doubt noticed by now, when we discuss ways to make work more meaningful, we usually connect meaning to things like the well-being of others, societal impact, and prosocial motives. The notion of meaningful work as tied to the greater good harkens back to some of the oldest ideas about what makes work meaningful. The emphasis on the greater good seems woven into the fabric of meaningful work, a part of its very nature. This point is true conceptually, but also empirically; statistical analyses of meaningful work items have identified the greater good as a core theme of what makes work matter to people.[36] The roots of this theme seem to dig deep; evolutionary theorists even postulate that early human groups were more likely to survive if they acted in ways that enhanced the survival of other members of the group, which means they also passed along to subsequent generations a willingness to help others.[37] This possibility suggests that helping is part of our biology—in short, that we have been made to help. Psychologists have postulated that helping others is stimulated by a wide range of factors, such as our ability to understand and identify with others' emotions,[38] a tendency to incorporate others into how we view ourselves,[39] and a sense of gratitude for what others have done for us.[40] Serving the greater good through work seems to be a useful way to connect our immediate concerns to a broader sense of purpose. This focus on the greater good and other-oriented sources of motivation also is a defining characteristic of calling, and the focus of the next chapter.

What Good Is Meaningful Work?

In one of our recent research studies,[41] we sought an answer to the question: if you want to experience meaning in life, does it help to find meaning in work? We started by asking a group of students to fill out a survey assessing their career attitudes and general well-being. Sure enough, those seeking meaning in life were more likely to experience it if they reported that they approached their careers as a calling. We followed up the survey by randomly assigning another group of students to either a brief, two-session career decision-making workshop intervention or to a control group with no workshop. We assessed each group before and after the intervention period. Here, too, results suggested that people seeking meaning in life and who were able to build career-related meaning by participating in the workshop were more likely to experience global meaning—and were slightly less depressed, to boot—compared to those in the control group.[42] The answer to the initial question, therefore, appears to be yes: approaching work as a calling seems a good strategy for cultivating a broader, global sense of meaning in life.

The accumulating research suggests that a sense of meaning in life as a whole is just one highly desirable characteristic to show up alongside meaningful work, among many others.[43] Meaningful work has been closely associated with authenticity; a sense of self-efficacy or confidence; a sense of personal control, responsibility, and initiative; successful navigation of obstacles; and self-esteem. It has been linked to a sense of interconnectedness, belongingness, community, and identification with others. Employees who describe their work as meaningful also report greater overall well-being, satisfaction with their work, and a sense of their work as important. All of these patterns of results are, of course, consistent with research on individuals who experience their work as a calling. Whether cultivated by finding a meaningful job, integrating one's spirituality with work, using one's strengths, linking work to down-the-road outcomes they value, connecting work to the greater good, or some combination of these strategies, people who demonstrate or derive a sense of their work as meaningful will tell you: meaningful work matters.

5 Serving Others

IMAGINE FOR A MOMENT you are living in a hunter-gatherer society several thousand years ago. Life is, to say the least, hard. On any given day, you may not be sure when you will eat next, what you will eat, or (gulp) what will try to eat you. Such harsh conditions make it a necessity to band together with other humans who, like you, want to increase their chances of survival as much as possible. So you form a community of sorts, and a pragmatic (if primitive) social system emerges, governed by a "you scratch my back, I scratch yours" philosophy. For example, while you are out hunting prehistoric bison, other members of your community are taking care of your children, gathering firewood, and protecting against hairy intruders of all kinds. When one of your four-day forays into the wilderness in search of some much-needed protein finally reaches its apex with a kill, you are exhausted, parched, starving, sunbaked, filthy, and in a positively foul mood that even a successful hunt can't undo. This attitude is understandable given the strain you now face in hauling a two-thousand-pound carcass back home.

When you arrive at home base, however, something glorious happens. Someone hands you a salty hunk of pemmican to eat and a round gourd brimming with fresh water to drink. Members of your tribe take the weighty creature and begin the lengthy process of procuring the meat. A trip to the local river to bathe in its frigid but refreshing current follows, and a straw bed is prepared for you to rest after the long journey. You've done your job, and now others are doing theirs. These shared tasks combine to make a big difference for you and the community as a whole and are typical of the highly practical, prosocial mentality that sustains your people. Everyone has figured out that working together and helping each other leads to the community's survival and, as a result, to your individual survival. Anthropologists studying these early communities consistently find this theme; ancient communities that maximized their ability to help one another tended to survive and prosper, and those that didn't inevitably failed.[1]

Fast-forward a few millennia to the present day. A relatively new area of psychology has emerged with the goal of better understanding how the behavior of our ancestors influences our current behavior. The basic contention of scholars within this field, usually called *evolutionary psychology*, is that the way we behave today is tied to behavior that led to successful survival and reproduction in the past. (This view is not without its skeptics, who raise some important points, but we won't have that debate here.) Those of us with ancestors who survived over the generations are naturally—indeed, biologically—more likely to enact modern versions of those behaviors that helped ensure our current existence.[2] For example, even though men today no longer have to tangle with saber-toothed tigers or fight hell-bent rivals from neighboring tribes with their bare hands, there is still an inherited desirability (obviously reinforced by the culture) for guys to be strong and in shape. Even though we live in a world where some might think they can focus solely on themselves and survive just fine (à la Ryan Bingham, George Clooney's character, in the first half of the film *Up in the Air*), we continue to act as a species motivated to help others. Stories about people acting in others' best interest often find time in news coverage (to counterbalance the gloom from the rest of the broadcast), are often a central theme in movies or television shows (think *Extreme Makeover: Home Edition*), and are usually what people talk about when describing what is "good" about another person. How many times have you heard someone say, in an admiring tone, "She always puts others above herself," or that the best trait of a person is that he is kind, caring, or a really nice guy? If people describe you in such a manner, they probably do so because they have experienced you performing acts of kindness, perhaps accompanied by some kind of personal sacrifice, to their benefit.

On average, people in the United States between twenty-five and fifty-four years old, with children, spend 8.7 hours per weekday working, more than any other activity, according to the 2009 American Time Use Survey conducted by the U.S. Bureau of Labor Statistics.[3] (In case you're curious, out of a 24-hour block, Americans averaged 7.7 hours sleeping, 1.3 hours caring for others, 1.1 hours eating, 1.1 hours doing household activities, 2.6 hours enjoying leisure or sports, and 1.5 hours classified as "other.") Given the sheer amount of time most people spend working, the workplace seems to be the most consistently available venue for doing something that has beyond-the-self benefit, or for displaying kind, caring, and compassionate behaviors—behaviors that are central to living out one's calling. In this chapter, we describe how jobs across the full occupational spectrum are tied to the common good. We also offer some ideas for considering how your work—whatever it is—makes a difference for others. We discuss the latest, most innovative research in psychology that has tied helping behavior, in and out of the workplace, to happiness and health, and offer a few simple strategies you can use to express your calling by serving the greater good through, and at, your work.

Your Work, Whatever It Is, Makes a Difference

Most societies today are, obviously, profoundly different from the hunter-gatherer community we described above. Yet even now, people are bound together by common needs and mutual service. Consider a typical morning in the life of a hypothetical suburban professional, Mikayla, starting the moment she walks out of her front door. Because it is Thursday, Mikayla leaves the trash and recycling containers by the curb before climbing into her sporty sedan, backing out of her driveway, and motoring to the corner gas station to fuel up for her morning commute. She picks up a bagel and a latte from the drive-through on her way into the office, and catches the first half of the news on the radio before fortuitously finding a parking space right in front of her office building. After feeding the meter, she heads up the elevator to her office suite on an upper floor, exchanging a smile with the receptionist as she strolls in. Once at the office, she settles into her ergonomic chair, powers up her computer, and turns on a little music to stimulate her creative thinking. It's barely 8:30, and already Mikayla has demonstrated a direct or indirect reliance on the services of people in the following occupations: trash and recycling collectors; car designers, engineers, manufacturers, distributors, dealers, salespeople, financing underwriters, and insurance agents; oil refinery workers, tanker truck drivers, gas station clerks, and gas pump engineers, manufacturers, and installers; wheat farmers, bagel makers, coffee farmers, coffee roasters, coffee distributors, espresso machine manufacturers and salespersons, and a barista; news reporters, anchors, producers, sound engineers, radio antennae maintenance workers, car stereo manufacturers; architects, construction crews, and subcontractors; elevator engineers, manufacturers, and installers; electricians and power plant workers; chair designers, ergonomic consultants, computer hardware and software engineers, computer manufacturers; recording artists, producers, sound mixers; and so on and so on.

The above list, as long as it is, leaves out many, many other jobs responsible for creating the products and services Mikayla used— in less than an hour of her life. If you actually tried to identify all the work that was required by other people to enable you to do the things you typically do en route to your 10:00 a.m. coffee break, you'd be overwhelmed in a hurry.

This example highlights the interconnected nature of the complex web of occupations and workers in which you operate. This point is important to understand, because occupying a place in that web means that your efforts also have some level of social impact, however small or far removed from its beneficiaries. For those who approach work as a calling, understanding that social impact is very important and has a motivating effect on their efforts. Of course, the broader societal impact of one's work activities is only one way of behaving prosocially on the job; relationships with coworkers, supervisors, or customers provide other opportunities, as might identifying and mitigating the impact of one's job on the natural environment or on the unequal distribution of resources across groups. Although our focus is on the psychological dimensions of work, there are undeniably moral dimensions, too. Approaching work as a calling, which urges consideration of how your gifts intersect with societal needs, requires not merely acknowledging this reality but taking active and intentional steps to work in a way that enhances the common good.

The focus on using work to enhance others' well-being is altruistic in nature. As we highlighted in the last chapter, such altruistic attitudes also increase a sense of meaning in one's work. Some workers may sacrifice personal pleasures (like higher salaries or comfort) to increase the extent to which their job has a social impact—like the teacher who spends personal resources on school supplies for students in need. But does prosocial behavior always, or even often, come at the expense of personal happiness? Over the last few years, CNN has highlighted "everyday heroes" who, through their work, have made a positive difference in the lives of others. Ten people who stood out from among those nominated in 2011 were engaged in the following activities:

- ► Providing support to teens who suffer spinal cord injuries playing football
- ► Supporting military widows
- ► Using a newspaper column and a nonprofit to help people who have fallen on hard times pay for food and rent
- ► Providing a safe refuge for children in the inner city who want to escape gang violence
- ► Helping low-income mothers have safe birthing experiences
- ► Starting a nonprofit youth soccer program for children in Haiti's poorest slums
- ► Using recycled hotel soap to improve the health of children in impoverished countries
- ► Serving free pasta dinners to impoverished children
- ► Providing wheelchairs to people with disabilities in rural Mexico
- ► Connecting South African teens with online mentors from all over the world[4]

We'd expect these types of activities to yield a tremendous sense of meaning, but go to CNN's website and watch the footage that tells their stories. Touching lives in these ways clearly does more than express a burdened sense of purpose for these heroes. It also produces profound happiness. As we explore next, psychological science confirms that genuine acts of service to others not only makes the beneficiaries of those acts happier but it tends to make the people doing those acts happier, too.

What's So Good about Doing Good?

Psychologists have long speculated that, despite the view that nice guys finish last, doing good has plenty of benefits. To be sure, a remarkably expansive range of pathways have been found that link altruistic or prosocial activities with a meaningful and satisfying experience of life. In one recent study, for example, psychologists

Michael Steger, Todd Kashdan, and Shigehiro Oishi followed a group of sixty-five college students over a three-week period while they completed daily diary reports of their activities, levels of happiness, and general mood.[5] The researchers wanted to know if engaging in different types of activities had different levels of impact on students feeling happier and in a more positive mood. Do certain types of activities make a person feel good, more so than other activities?

The researchers collected information about all kinds of activities that the students reported and split these activities into two groups. The first set of activities concerned actions that were tied to immediate feelings of pleasure, such as having sex purely for hedonic gratification, getting drunk, or getting high on drugs. The second group of activities concerned actions that were tied to a larger sense of purpose, meaning, and community, such as volunteering, giving money to a person in need, or listening carefully to another person. What the researchers found supported their hypothesis: students who engaged in more meaningful and other-oriented daily activities were more likely to be happy and in a good mood during that day. Intriguingly, engaging in these types of activities even had a positive impact on how happy they felt the *next* day.

Let's be clear: if your primary motivation for serving others is to benefit yourself, you are badly missing the point. Nevertheless, if engaging in acts of kindness does benefit the people who do those acts, understanding how would be helpful. In her book *The How of Happiness*, social psychologist Sonja Lyubomirsky synthesizes years of research on the effects of serving others and highlights a variety of reasons that doing good results in feeling good. First, acts of kindness can have a host of positive consequences for social relationships. They can help you feel more enmeshed in your community, leading you to feel part of something greater than yourself. Think back to the hunter-gatherer society. Perhaps because of the importance of social bonds for survival that have become ingrained over millennia, something naturally feels good about being connected with others, and helping another person is an easy way to forge that connection. Serving others also can lead others to appreciate and like you more, and in turn, to treat you better and potentially help you in times of need. Research has shown that people who behave in the most prosocial ways over time reap the most social rewards.[6]

Second, helping others can impact your emotional state. On the one hand, it can help relieve your personal feelings of guilt or discomfort over the suffering of another person. Consider the feelings you may have had when you first saw footage of the attacks on 9/11, images of the thousands left homeless by the 2004 South Asian tsunami, the grisly aftermath of a school shooting, or news reports of child abuse or abductions. Many people describe feeling literally sick to their stomachs when they reflect deeply on such raw human distress and agony. Plenty of research in psychology has shown that when we do something good, these negative feelings often decrease, perhaps because we come to view ourselves, in some small way, as part of the solution. On the other hand, even small acts of kindness can also make us aware of how good we have it. When we spend an evening serving in a soup kitchen, light a candle in prayer at a vigil, mail in a donation to the Red Cross or even put a few coins in the red Salvation Army kettle, it often forces us to reflect a little on our own good fortune. Most of us probably don't think about this enough, but when we do, we tend to feel better about our lives and grateful about how good we have it.

Third, acts of service that benefit others cause us to change the way we think about ourselves. Something about helping other people is refreshing, and when we do this we tend to think of ourselves as helpful, caring, compassionate people. For example, in a recent study, psychologists Neeta Weinstein and Richard Ryan followed a group of undergraduate students over a two-week period, tracking their daily helping behaviors and well-being. When participants' motivation to help others was autonomous—that is, when their altruistic attitudes aligned with their view of themselves or what was important to them—the helping behavior that resulted related to increased happiness, vitality, and self-esteem. Imagine walking around every day knowing that you are a genuinely helpful, kind person, a catalyst for good whose presence makes others' lives better. Without delving into philosophical matters about whether people are inherently good, or whether any act can be truly altruistic,[7] it seems obvious that thinking of yourself this way would probably make you feel like a pretty valuable person, and rightfully so.

Seeing this combination of social connection, positive feelings, and positive thoughts enriches our understanding of why when we do good, we feel good. And for the 65 percent of us in the United States over the age of sixteen who are in the labor force, opportunities to do good at work abound. The workplace provides a venue where most American adults spend a ton of time and interact closely and regularly with fellow employees, customers, or both. If they know where to look, people can find near-limitless opportunities to help others at work. Bottom line: if doing good is a good thing to do, good for others, and good for you, and if work is a good place to do good, why not do good at work?

Doing Good at Work

Some of the most enlightening studies we have conducted over the last few years have been those in which we interviewed people who view their career as a calling. In one of these studies, we interviewed eight psychologists—some therapists, some professors—who felt called to their careers, and we coded the interviews in search of common themes. A total of fifty-five themes emerged, five of which were endorsed by every single participant: feelings of satisfaction at work, calling as a key influence on how one approaches work, calling as a process (as opposed to an event, or something a person finds and then is set for life), having support from others for maintaining one's calling, and believing that a critical part of one's calling is to help and nurture others. We cannot emphasize this final point enough: for everyone in this group anyway, their callings were always in some way about serving others.

One of the participants in the study was Emily.[8] In her fifteen years of experience in the mental health profession, Emily had seen it all. She worked as a school guidance counselor, a therapist at a teen center, a psychologist at a college counseling center, and ultimately started her own private practice. Emily displayed a true passion and commitment to her work, noting that her purpose in life and her calling were essentially the same thing. Like anyone who devotes so much energy to work, Emily discussed the struggle of balancing her work with the rest of her life, meeting her clients' needs but also her own. Clearly, however, the impact Emily had on the lives she touched was a driving force that fueled her fire. Emily remarked, "I see my calling being sort of witnessing with people what their lives are—witnessing what their pain has been, what their pain currently is, what their successes have been, witnessing growth and supporting my clients in their life journey."

To be sure, Emily is in many ways a privileged case when it comes to pursuing other-oriented values at work. She is well educated and well paid, and she has a job that might be considered at the peak of the "helping others" pyramid. In fact, Emily's job exists for the sole purpose of serving others, and she has the opportunity to do so on an hour-to-hour basis. Most of us do not have anywhere near this level of direct contact with the people who ultimately benefit from our work. However, this does not mean that the privilege of providing benefit for others at and through work is only relegated to a select few, the people helpers in full-time social service roles like Emily. Our sense is that most scholars interested in calling and meaningful work agree that virtually any person, in any job, in any place can either use the products or services they help provide at work to serve others, or can serve others at the workplace itself.[9] Shortly, we provide some suggestions for how this proposition might play out, even for those in jobs without any immediately obvious social impact.

Before we get there, let's address another question: does doing good at work have the same benefits as doing good in general? That is, can we take the research conducted on prosocial behavior in general and use it to draw inferences about what people can expect from behaving prosocially at work? Consider for a moment what motivates someone to serve others in the workplace. Certainly personality factors play a role; some people are simply predisposed to be generally more social, more conscientious, and more agreeable than others, and these folks are more likely than others to behave in an altruistic manner. But important situational factors also can promote a motivation to serve. Adam Grant, a professor of management at the University of Pennsylvania, has devoted his career to studying helping behavior in the workplace and understanding employees' motivation for doing so, conducting innovative studies with workers representing a wide range of occupations.

In one study, Grant and his colleagues conducted a field experiment with a group of call-center fund-raisers who were seeking donations for a scholarship fund at a university.[10] Their work consisted of cold-calling people, giving them information about the scholarship fund, and then asking for a donation. He split the fund-raisers into two groups. One group spent five minutes interacting with an actual recipient of the scholarship, during which the recipient expressed gratitude and shared details about how the scholarship had made a big difference in helping him earn a degree and pursue his life goals. The other group had no contact with the scholarship recipients. Grant's research team tracked the work output of employees in both groups, and one month later, they compared the groups to each other. The results? Fund-raisers in the group who had contact with a scholarship recipient spent more than double the amount of time making calls and raised almost three times the amount of money. This evidence suggests that having face-to-face contact with the very people one is helping, and having conscious awareness of the impact one's work is having on others, can dramatically affect a person's motivation to help and performance in doing so.

This study by Grant and his colleagues is just one example. Across dozens of studies, the two critical workplace precursors to wanting to help others is having contact with the people you are potentially helping and feeling that your job has a real impact. The greater the frequency, duration, depth, and breadth of contact with beneficiaries a person has, and the greater the magnitude of the impact one perceives, the more that person feels committed and motivated to help—and in turn, the more frequently and effectively the person actually performs helping behavior.[11] As is the case for Emily, when people help others in the workplace, they reap the same types of emotional rewards as helping outside of work. Helping others makes you feel better about yourself and more satisfied in your job, but these aren't the only benefits of doing good at work. Consider another study conducted by Grant and his graduate student, Justin Berg, this one with a group of firefighters. Grant and Berg distributed a survey to this group, asking questions about the degree to which they viewed their job as a way to help others, and also how much they found the work intrinsically motivating— that is, enjoyable and engaging. The researchers then tracked the number of overtime hours the firefighters put in over a two-month period. Here again, the results were clear. Firefighters who found their work intrinsically motivating and had a strong motivation to help others put in three times as many overtime hours compared to those with low intrinsic and altruistic motivation. They simply wanted to work! This pattern of results is consistent across many studies: having the motivation to help others can lead people to perform better, to work more productively, and to commit more deeply to their jobs.[12]

Some evidence even suggests that helping others, or being motivated to do so, makes workers more creative. A recent field study with a group of water treatment employees[13] found that, as in the study with firefighters, those with a high level of intrinsic motivation and prosocial motivation were rated as much more creative by their supervisors, using criteria such as "comes up with new ideas," and "is a good source of creative ideas." The reason that these ratings were higher? Compared to other employees, those with higher prosocial motivation were better able to understand the perspective of others. People who venture outside of their own heads and think from other points of view have access to better, more creative ideas.

Happiness, job satisfaction, productivity, and creativity—all have been identified as by-products of having the motivation to help others at work, and actually engaging in other-oriented behavior.

How Can You Better Serve the Greater Good at Work?

Hopefully by now we have convinced you that, at the very least, it is a good idea to try to help others, at work or otherwise. Doing so provides tremendous benefit for the beneficiaries of that help and for the person doing the helping, too. But if you are not a psychologist like Emily or anywhere close to one of CNN's everyday heroes, how can you serve the greater good in your own career and life?

Choose a Prosocial Job

The surest way to put yourself in a position to help others through your work is to find a job in which helping others is a critical component. Employees in the social service professions, for example, can see easily how their work serves people. These workers usually have direct contact with their beneficiaries and can experience the impact of their efforts firsthand. More than likely, their motivation to serve others played a dominant role in their career choice, which is the case for many people. In a study we completed a few years ago, we analyzed data from more than thirty thousand college students who were asked what the most important factor was in making their long-term career choice.[14] The most frequently endorsed answer was selecting a job that matched their interests. The second most-endorsed answer was selecting a job at which they could make a lot of money. In third place, totaling 14.4 percent of the sample, came selecting a job that focused on making contributions to society.

What makes it tough for many people to choose a job based primarily on serving others, however, is that doing so very often comes with a cost. For example, it may lead people to take jobs that don't pay very well (like teacher or child-care provider) or that require an immense amount of work hours (like emergency room physician or public defender). Work that has the strongest combination of contact with beneficiaries and potential impact is not only often lower on the pay scale and higher in terms of workload, but it also can be extremely stressful (as many nurses, Peace Corps volunteers, and social workers can attest). For some people, though, the motivation to help others is so strong it can overcome any of the undesirable characteristics that might come with a highly other-oriented career. If you are one of these people, do yourself a favor and go after one of these jobs. Trust us when we say that in the long run you will be happy you did. The suggestions that follow are for the other 85.6 percent of you.

Whatever Your Job, Identify and Focus on Its Prosocial Impact

Perhaps you have a job that isn't directly and inherently about helping others. Maybe you are a software engineer. Maybe you work in accounting. Maybe you are a stockbroker. Maybe you own a restaurant. And maybe, like most Americans, you can't just pick up and leave the job you have right now to test the waters for a job in which helping others is a more primary focus. If helping others is indeed so important, then what are you supposed to do?

One place to start is to recognize that your job may actually benefit others more than you realize. "The Horseshoe Nail," one of the Grimms' fairy tales, describes what we refer to as the "for the want of a nail" principle: "For the want of a nail the shoe was lost, for the want of a shoe the horse was lost, for the want of a horse the man was lost, for the want of a man the battle was lost." When it comes to the social impact of our jobs, some of us are nails—doing work that occurs behind the scenes, that is seldom noticed, that appears insignificant, but that plays a critical role nevertheless. A sermon by the late Peter Marshall, chaplain of the U.S. Senate, illustrates this principle in a less abstract manner.[15] It tells the story of an old man working in obscurity in a quaint Austrian village along the eastern slopes of the Alps. His job was to clear debris out of the pools of water that fed the narrow river flowing through the heart of their town. He cleared out leaves and branches, dug out accumulating silt, and made sure the water kept flowing. In time, the village's immaculate views attracted tourists, farmers enjoyed the irrigation the narrow river provided, and mill wheels relied on the water for power. One night, the town board noticed the old man's salary buried in the payroll record. None of them even realized he was employed by the town, and they voted unanimously to cut his job in a cost-saving measure. Not much changed at first, but as weeks turned into months, silt, dead foliage, and debris accumulated in the narrow river. Eventually the water took on a yellowish tint, a film covered sections of the water near the banks, and it started to smell. The mill wheels slowed and then stopped, crops dried up, the waterfowl left for better options, and tourism all but ceased. Eventually some townsfolk became sick with disease. In an emergency meeting, the town board eventually put its finger on the cause and rehired the old man. Within weeks the water began to flow again, wheels started to turn, and life returned to the mountain village.

Seemingly small and insignificant work ignored by society or by the organization in which you work may well be both highly important and impactful. Focusing on the impact of such work provides a sense of meaning for hospital cleaning staff, noting that patients would get sicker without their work,[16] and for racetrack "backstretch" employees pointing to how their tasks, usually considered menial, are extremely important for making horses fit for racing.[17] What problems would occur if your work tasks were left undone for any length of time? Thinking about such things might help you recognize that your work does indeed matter.

Actively Seek and Create Opportunities to Help Others

Identifying and focusing on your work's impact is an important way to recognize how others are affected by your effort, but you can expand your reach by actively seeking new and more opportunities to use your work to benefit others—and to create such opportunities if they seem hard to find. To help spur this on, we offer three suggestions.

First, during your next workweek, go out of your way to spice it up by using your work to serve others. Typically, people get into a rhythm at work, and often that rhythm includes little to no engagement in helping activities. Imagine that you are a bank teller responding to the needs of a hundred customers a day, every day. Doling out the minimal amount of extra effort in helping make your customers' day better would be very easy. Maybe you feel that helping others means working harder, which may not be an appealing option given how exhausted you are at the end of the day already. The reality, however, is exactly the opposite. Helping others energizes and builds enjoyment, putting a spring in your step and making time seem to move faster. Try this: Before your next work week, spend just ten minutes mapping out your week's schedule. While you do so, identify three new ways that you could use what you are required to do that week to help others, without even having to adjust your week's schedule. To start, keep things simple. Sell your customer the car he really needs and can afford, rather than the one for which he's willing to break his budget and overpay. Donate the light fixtures you are tearing out in a kitchen remodel to a family who could use them, rather than just tossing them in the dumpster. Make the phone call to a patient's insurance company for her, rather than having her pay out of pocket and deal with the reimbursement on her own. Don't stop with merely identifying such things; during the week, make a concerted effort to actually try them out and evaluate at the end of the week how it went.

Second, consider using the skills you have developed at work to help people outside of work. If you are a cook, make a meal for a family you know who just had a baby or who has been dealing with health problems. If you are an accountant, reserve some time around tax season to do pro bono work for senior citizens living in an area nursing home. If you are a construction worker, donate an afternoon of your time and skill at a Habitat for Humanity project. If you are an administrator, volunteer on the board of a nonprofit in town. Will doing these activities cut into time you are enjoying away from work? Yes, but trust us, the personal and social rewards that come from using your skills and expertise in these kinds of voluntary activities will be more than worth the time. Try this, even just once, in the next couple of months. You'll see what we're talking about.

Finally, let's talk about the worst-case scenario for a moment. What if your job is so far removed from helping others that you cannot possibly conjure up anything you might do differently to have any kind of prosocial impact? Maybe you sit in a gray fabric-walled cubicle all day, staring at a flickering computer screen, double-checking numbers on an endless spreadsheet. Your job tasks are mind-numbing, and your job likely will be obsolete as soon as someone devises the inevitable software to automate it. You have to do mental gymnastics to convince yourself that anyone benefits from your work at all. Especially if this situation sounds like yours, try our third piece of advice: Go out of your way to do something good for the people with whom you work—your coworkers, boss, support staff, or anyone with whom you interact on the job.

As we mentioned earlier, for many people, the workplace is unique in the number of available opportunities to serve others. Many people interact with more people at work than in any other life role. Even if you are not fortunate enough to have close contact with the beneficiaries of your work tasks, almost all of us have contact with coworkers. Look at these relationships as opportunities for you to flex your altruistic muscles, because like all of us, these people could use some goodwill once in a while. Management scholars refer to these ways of serving others on the job as "prosocial organizational behaviors."[18] The easy examples of prosocial organizational behaviors are things like making the coffee in the morning or bringing in a batch of home-baked chocolate chip cookies for the break room. These actions are simple enough, but other options are available that may have a longer-term impact, too. For example, what's stopping you from actively mentoring a younger colleague, offering yourself to other employees as a supportive confidant if problems should arise, or organizing a weekly lunch forum where people from different parts of an organization come together informally, sharing in each other's lives, venting frustration, and brainstorming ideas about their current projects? Like other strategies we discussed in this chapter, prosocial organizational behaviors like this have been identified in research to be good for you (resulting in higher satisfaction, performance, and commitment) and the organization (resulting in higher sales, employee involvement, and retention).[19] Try out these behaviors. You may be surprised at how much more connected these types of activities make you feel to your coworkers, and how much office morale improves.

Prosocial Work and Calling

Throughout this chapter we explored how serving others at and through work is good for the people being served and good for you, too. We also suggested some strategies you can use to work more prosocially, applying some of these principles to your own work and life. Using your work to serve others and enhance the greater good is, along with a transcendent summons and a sense of purpose and meaningfulness, a core dimension of calling. Without other-oriented values and goals, people could conceivably pursue a calling solely for the purpose of their own personal gain.

Yet in all of our experiences interviewing and working with people who embody what it means to have a calling, the goal of personal gain almost never emerges. Living out a calling means focusing on others, which makes a sense of calling unique compared to other work motivations. People often think of discerning a calling as involving a sequence in which a person finds a job that helps her or him live out the goal of serving others through that job. For many people, identifying the calling comes first and helping others comes second. However, the reverse also can be true. Start helping others in and through your current job. Doing so may be the best and easiest way to start discovering and living a calling.

PART 3

Discovering and Living a Calling

6 Forging a Path

To RECAP, we've introduced what it means to have a calling. We explored where the idea of work as a calling comes from and how it stands in contrast to other ways of thinking about work. And we looked closely at the three dimensions of calling. The next two chapters focus even more directly on where the rubber hits the road—in practical terms, what kinds of things you should do to figure out your calling and to live it out in your work. We start with the question of career choice. At one time, choosing a career was considered a rite of passage for young adults, part of the gateway to productive adulthood. In an era in which the classic career narrative (finding a job, getting established in a stable organization, working one's way up the ladder, and then hanging on until retirement) is now the exception rather than the rule, however, career choice is relevant to those far along in their career journeys, too. When choosing a career is the issue, how can you discern your calling? Of the job options potentially available to you, which should you pursue? What practical steps can you take to make informed choices?

The Father of Vocational Guidance

On a Thursday night in the summer of 2008, we joined a few dozen colleagues for dinner in the second-floor meeting room of La Famiglia Giorgio's Ristorante, a quaint Italian eatery in Boston's

North End. It was a special night; the Society for Vocational Psychology was celebrating the one-hundred-year anniversary of the opening of the Vocation Bureau of Boston, the first agency in history devoted to vocational guidance and career counseling. The sense of history in the room was undeniable, because the Vocation Bureau had operated, a century before, in the very same redbrick row house where we met that night.

Frank Parsons, whom we introduced in chapter 1 as "the father of vocational guidance," was the first director and vocational counselor at the bureau. He had worked tirelessly to establish the agency, presiding at its opening in January 1908. Based on the few details that have survived history, Parsons's personal story is fascinating, in part because his own career path was extremely chaotic. How is this for a smooth and coherent path to the top?

- Parsons trained at Cornell University as a civil engineer. In 1873, as an eighteen-year-old, freshly minted college grad, he accepted a job on the engineering staff at a railroad company. The company went under. He lost his first job.

- Parsons looked hard for another engineering position, but because of an economic downturn, he settled for a job as a laborer in a steel mill. He worked sixty-hour weeks lifting and shearing iron and loading it on wagons. He hated it.

- Within the year, he left the steel mill for a public school teaching job near Boston.

- At the urging of a top attorney who admired Parsons's debating skills (which he put on display at local literary society meetings), he left teaching to study law. However, he worked himself so hard in preparation for the bar exam (which he passed) that he developed health problems that affected his vision and culminated in "some kind of general breakdown."[1]

- On medical advice, he "lived in the open" for three years in New Mexico.

- In 1885, at age thirty, he returned to Boston to practice law.

- After ten years as an attorney, moonlighting as a lecturer at Boston University, he decided to run for mayor of Boston. He finished with less than 1 percent of the vote.

- From there he moved to Manhattan, Kansas, to teach economics and social sciences at what is now Kansas State University. Three years later, he was fired.

After that firing in Kansas, Parsons landed back in Boston, where he persuaded a philanthropist to fund the Vocation Bureau. Parsons's tenure as director didn't last long, though. The summer after the bureau opened he became very ill, and before the end of that September, Parsons was dead, the victim of a kidney infection. That was it—an abrupt and tragic end. The irony, of course, is that the career of Frank Parsons, the man widely known as the father of vocational guidance, can only be described as a convoluted pattern of trials and errors—and his experience as a career counselor amounted to a grand total of about six months!

Parsons knew full well that his own career path was a lousy example of sound career decision making. "Late in life," wrote H. V. Davis, "Parsons did call himself 'a damn fool,' disparaging his own career as unplanned and wasteful."[2] Perhaps due to the wisdom he gleaned learning from his own mistakes, Parsons used his time at the Vocation Bureau (brief though it was) to devise a strategy for helping others do what obviously did not come easily to him: make good career decisions. He tried out the strategy with a very tough clientele—unemployed immigrants—and presumably found it effective. After his death, his friends published the decision-making model in a skinny 1909 book called *Choosing a Vocation*, and the model is foundational for career counselors even today. Of course, we don't have to take Parsons's word for it. Since his classic book hit the shelves, a century of research within vocational psychology has tested and refined his approach to making wise career choices, wisely.[3]

Finding a Fit

What wisdom does the father of vocational guidance have for us? Parsons's strategy is deceptively simple. "In the wise choice of a vocation," he wrote, "there are three broad factors: (1) a clear understanding of yourself, your aptitudes, abilities, interests, ambitions, limitations and their causes; (2) a knowledge of the requirements, conditions of success, advantages and disadvantages, compensation, opportunities, and prospects in different lines of work; and (3) true reasoning on the relations of these two groups of facts."[4] As we noted in chapter 2, many contemporary writers on the topic of calling advocate essentially this very process as a starting point for understanding one's calling. Discerning a calling is, after all, fundamentally about finding and establishing a fit. What is your place in the world? Where can you most effectively contribute in a way that is meaningful to you and that makes a positive difference for others?

From a scientific perspective, this person-environment (P-E) fit strategy builds on a very simple truism: people are different, and those differences matter. The critical questions are as follows: What are the most important ways that people differ, and how do those differences make them better suited for some types of jobs than others? Psychological scientists have identified the key work-related individual differences dimensions, and have come up with good ways to measure people on those dimensions. They also describe occupations on those same dimensions, establishing psychological profiles that are characteristic of people who are satisfied and successful within each type of work. This is one reason the P-E fit strategy has great appeal; it is not only intuitive, it is systematic and empirically tested. Sophisticated, heavily researched, scientifically supported inventories are available for helping you gain "a clear understanding of yourself" and "a knowledge of [the key features of] different lines of work." In fact, you can now go online, take a battery of psychological inventories, immediately see a feedback report, and then obtain a list of job titles selected for you based on how well they match your profile. Then you can click on each job title and find a wealth of information about what kinds of characteristics are typical of successful people in that job, what kind of training is required, what the economic outlook is like for that job, and so forth. Easy!

It *is* easy, and we usually urge people who face a career choice to start with this strategy. It is an excellent starting point—but usually only a starting point, because real life is not this easy. If the P-E fit model sounds simplistic, that's because it is; the P-E fit can only get you so far. We base this appraisal not just on our experience, but on decades of research suggesting that fit is an important predictor of outcomes like job satisfaction and job performance, but it is very far from a *perfect* predictor. Occasionally we are contacted by potential counseling clients who say something like, "I want to take that test that will tell me what career I should pursue." Unfortunately, no test can possibly tell a person what she or he *should* do for a career. Information culled from psychological tests is valuable and can help people make informed choices about possible good fits, but it cannot make those choices for them.

Career decision making thus remains at least as much art as science. Even the best tools currently available for assessing fit seldom take into account your current life circumstances, such as your responsibilities as a significant other or spouse, a parent, a child of aging parents, and a friend in a complex network of relationships. They rarely take into account the simple realities of the job market, where some types of jobs and training opportunities are more accessible than others—and where some jobs may not be available at all, at least not now, near where you want to live. And they almost never formally assess what is most central to your identity, what defines you, what you understand to be your central purpose in life, and where you see the most important needs in the world around you. P-E fit is important, but absolutely must be augmented by a broad appraisal of your personal context, your deepest values, the needs you see in the world that speak to your heart, the concerns you find most meaningful, and your personal life mission.

How, then, to proceed?

Actors, Agents, and Authors

Internationally renowned vocational psychologist Mark Savickas describes people in the throes of career development as actors, agents, and authors.[5] No, these aren't the first three occupations he found in an alphabetical list (as far as we know, anyway). Rather, people have to play these three roles when they navigate the process of discerning a calling in their career and living it out day to day. People are *actors* who represent a particular pattern of traits that, objectively speaking, fit some work environments better than others. People are *agents* who have to devise ways not just to find work that is a good fit but to fit work into their lives as they confront transitions, manage their different life roles, and meet the responsibilities, expectations, and challenges they face. Finally, people are *authors* who narrate the story of their purpose in life and how their work might provide a key way to pursue that purpose. If these concepts seem a bit abstract, don't worry. We aim to make them more concrete in the rest of this chapter.

Actors: Cast for a Role That Fits

The goal of an actor trying to make it in show business is to understand his unique strengths and attributes as an actor, figure out what types of roles are out there, work to audition for a role for which he is particularly well suited, land the role, and then successfully perform it. This scenario is simply a restatement of P-E fit. Indeed, people in jobs that capitalize on their strengths, satisfy their interests, and reinforce their values—in short, jobs that allow them to be who they are at work—usually feel as if they are swimming with the current rather than against it. Their work comes easy to them, relatively speaking.

So how do you find a fit? Follow Parsons's three steps:

Step 1: Understand how you are unique. Personality theorist Henry Murray once observed that every person is in some sense like all other people, like some other people, and like no other person.[6] It is hard to argue with this logic. Some aspects of being human are universal: we all have the same basic biological systems, the same basic needs (e.g., food, water, oxygen), and the same basic predicament in the universe. Some aspects of being human make us truly unique. Like fingerprints, we each have our own quirks and idiosyncrasies, our own peculiar patterns of thoughts, feelings, and behaviors, things that no one else shares with us. When it comes to understanding how people fit to jobs, however, what is critical is knowing what makes us similar to *some* other people—specifically, to people within a particular occupation who are good at what they do, and who love it. Psychologists point to four such characteristics that are especially relevant to work: interests, personality, abilities, and values.

When people talk about having a passion—something they find captivating, that draws them in and sustains their attention—they are talking about interests. When people talk about general, innate tendencies they have, dispositions that influence their patterns of thinking and feeling and doing, they are talking about personality. When people talk about their capabilities and talents, tasks that come naturally to them and at which they excel, they are talking about abilities. And when people talk about the things they absolutely need to have on the job in order to be satisfied, they are talking about work values. These four characteristics combine to create a psychological profile, your work personality, the unique gifts that we described in chapter 3.

You can assess your work personality in a few different ways, which range in terms of expense and quality. The first approach, informal and totally free, is to appeal to your own experience, intuition, and ability to self-assess. For starters, think about how you would answer the following questions:

- What kinds of activities, jobs, and school subjects have you enjoyed most?
- What are your strongest areas of ability? Alternatively, thinking back to chapter 4, what strengths do you display when you are at your best?
- If we were to ask your closest friends and family members to describe your personality, what would they tell us, and what would you add to that?
- If you had to create a list of the three to five most important things that you absolutely needed to have in a job in order to be satisfied—your nonnegotiables (maybe a chance to be creative, good relationships with coworkers, the opportunity to advance, etc.)—what would they be?

Reflecting on questions like these provides an initial window into your particular pattern of traits. You can find more in-depth self-help strategies on the website that accompanies this book, www.MakeYourJobaCalling.com, or in workbooks that are usually available at a reasonable cost. For example, Richard Bolles's classic self-help book *What Color Is Your Parachute?*—billed as "the best-selling job-hunting book in the world"—provides numerous do-it-yourself activities that we find highly engaging, practical, and useful as strategies for assessing fit. But do such self-assessment exercises really help, and are they enough?

The answer to the "do they really help?" question is, well, "it depends." Informal self-assessment exercises probably help most by asking the right kinds of questions and stimulating self-reflective thought. Such exercises are especially helpful if you are highly motivated, know yourself well, and are adept at integrating different types of information. However, when Indiana University professor Sue Whiston and colleagues compared different types of career development interventions in their analyses of research studies spanning more than four decades, they found that self-help strategies were significantly less effective than other options.[7] We've talked to enough people who have used these strategies to vouch for the fact that they certainly seem helpful for some people. These folks would say the answer to the "Are they enough?" question is a resounding yes. The limitations of self-help strategies are real, though. We are not always the best judge of our abilities—or other aspects of our work personalities. Sometimes an outside perspective is valuable.

A second approach to assessing your work personality, more formal in nature and increasingly popular, involves taking one or more online psychological tests. As we mentioned earlier, good tests are available that can provide an objective, reasonably accurate picture of your unique profile of work-related characteristics—your gifts. But here, too, we urge caution. We have talked with people who tell us they simply Googled "career test" and then took the first free assessment that popped up, which is a terrible idea. Why? Simply put, not all tests are created equal. Some are painstakingly developed with careful attention to ethical standards and with a concerted effort to demonstrate scientifically that the test meets the claims made for it—for example, that scores are consistent over time, that they seem to measure what they are supposed to measure (such as interests or values) instead of something else, and that they actually predict real-world outcomes like happy employment or career success. Developers of tests like this, usually research psychologists, also usually make technical information about reliability and validity publicly available, too, so that impartial analysts can properly evaluate the test. This approach to test development is highly technical, expensive, and labor-intensive, usually taking years of revision and refinement before a test is made available for people to use. How can you access the good tests? Here again, on the companion website for this book, www.MakeYourJobaCalling .com, we provide more information about quality-control criteria for career tests, a checklist you can use to evaluate online assessment systems, and information about a new assessment system called jobZology that Bryan is helping to develop.

The third strategy for assessing your gifts is to enlist the services of a skilled counselor. Career counseling (delivered individually or in small or large groups) is the most formal and the most expensive type of career help available. However, it also is the most effective form of career intervention, according to Whiston's research, which is no surprise considering the advantages of working with a good counselor. For one thing, counselors offer encouragement and emotional support, and indirectly they provide accountability. Research has shown that a strong working alliance between counselor and client plays a very important role in facilitating change— in career counseling just like in other types of counseling or therapy. Counselors are able to provide fine-tuned interpretations of test results, helping you identify themes that cut across multiple assessment instruments and your own life experience, a skill that online assessment tools do not simulate well. Counselors often see things that you don't see, filling in your blind spots and helping you think broadly and comprehensively about your career and its role in your life as a whole. What type of counseling strategy is most effective? Research by psychologists Steve Brown and Nancy Ryan Krane identified five "critical ingredients" that are found in particularly effective career interventions: written goal-setting exercises, individualized interpretation and feedback, provision of accurate occupational information, modeling of successful career exploration and decision-making behaviors, and attention to building support from family, friends, and mentors in a person's life.[8]

Step 2: Understand the opportunities in the working world. After developing a clearer sense of your unique work personality or gifts, the next step is to gain a good understanding of different areas of work that are potentially available to you. Here again, the quality of information about jobs varies from one source to the next. Some sources of occupational information present data from a panel of experts who use their best judgment to estimate the characteristic work personalities for people employed in particular jobs. A better strategy is to use what is called the "incumbent approach," which actually assesses a large, random sample of happily employed workers within each occupation, then derives the information about that occupation from the data they provide.[9] One very good source of information developed using strategies like these is the Occupational Information Network (O*NET, www .onetonline.org). This searchable database, updated and maintained by the U.S. Department of Labor, provides detailed information for each of more than a thousand occupations—information that includes the characteristics of happy, productive employees within each occupation, training requirements, salary data, and projected job growth in that field. The information in O*NET is not perfect, mind you—a certain amount of error is present in any approach to describing occupations—but it is at least as accurate as anything else currently available.

Step 3: "True reasoning." Parsons's third step involved using "true reasoning" to identify a match. With self-help strategies, this means tracking down career information yourself and using your best judgment to identify a fit. Some online assessment systems remove the guesswork by using mathematical "fit" algorithms to generate a list of potentially good-fitting occupations, sort of like an eHarmony or Match.com for job seekers and occupations. Of course, any list of jobs recommended for your profile still requires critical evaluation and scrutiny; remember, tests (or some combination of several tests) never tell you what you *should* do. Counselors can help you appraise both objectively and subjectively how well certain opportunities may fit for your profile of gifts. Good counselors respond to your questions in a way that makes you feel understood, tailor the process to meet your specific goals, help you identify the role that your emotional experience is playing in the process, and make all this happen in an environment of care and support.

To illustrate how all this works, we'll tell you Sheryl's story.[10] Sheryl, one of our counseling clients, was in the middle of a successful career as an electrical engineer. She was paid well, had been promoted twice, and was now beginning to manage projects—but she was miserable. For one thing, her recent move to project manager had not gone smoothly. She clashed with coworkers and felt little control or support when problems came up that needed solving. It was stressful. For another thing, the project manager role gave her a reason to take a step back and look at the big picture of what she was doing with her work. Her company specialized in developing innovative, high-end speaker systems, and the work rang hollow to her. "In the grand scheme of things, I just don't feel like what I'm doing is really making a difference. I want to wake up in the morning eager to go to work, spend the day excited about what I'm doing, and at the end of the day I want to look at myself in the mirror and feel like what I did that day mattered. I have never thought of my work as a calling, but that's exactly what I long for. How can I find it?"

Sheryl began with an informal assessment of her gifts and also took a battery of tests. Her interest profile suggested that she enjoyed mechanical and intellectual tasks, especially those that provided an outlet for creative self-expression. Her personality scores suggested that she was extremely conscientious, open to experience, and neurotic; she had an average level of agreeableness and was not very extroverted. Her profile of abilities suggested that she was adept at reasoning with numbers and accurately understanding and mentally manipulating spatial patterns. She mentioned that she could write well, which was consistent with a very high verbal-ability score. Her values suggested that it was most important for her to have a feeling of accomplishment on the job, to have a chance to try out her own ideas, to have support from her supervisors, and to feel like her work benefited others.

The mismatch between her gifts and what she was doing in her current job started to become clear for Sheryl as we talked through all this. Engineering fit well for her as a profession—indeed, she loved her current job when she first started—but the project manager role didn't feel right from the start. She had to give up some of the hands-on work she loved to focus on the tasks of managing people (which, she quickly found out, she didn't love); hence, her interests were not well satisfied. Her high neuroticism meant she was highly vulnerable to job-related stress (of which she had a lot), and her low extraversion did not make it any easier to manage people the way she felt she must. Her abilities were partially satisfied: she could map out well what needed to be done, and her written reports were outstanding, but when challenges arose or her coworkers' performance wasn't up to par, relationships quickly became strained and she felt overwhelmed and unable to handle it. Her values? In theory she should have felt like she was accomplishing things, but because her team members were doing the nuts and bolts of the projects, she felt a step removed from the work itself. Her ideas were sometimes challenged by know-it-all coworkers, and although she felt supported when she was a subordinate, as a project manager she felt more or less on her own.

Questions followed. What now? Should she ask her company to move her back into a staff engineer role, possibly closing herself off from future promotions? Should she try to obtain some training and support to make the manager role work? Or should she consider starting over at another company? Maybe her current misery was telling her that another occupation altogether might be a better fit—something in medical science, for example, or technical writing, two possibilities that her test results suggested, along with engineering. Here we run into the limits of processing the parameters of personal fit, of looking only at the role of actor as a level of analysis. Sheryl said she longed for a sense of calling. What is her work all about, in an ultimate sense? How does her work fit in the broader context of her life, and with her broader sense of purpose? How does it contribute to the world around her? What kinds of needs in the world matter to her and beckon for her attention? Such questions require a more expansive approach to looking at the problem.

Agents: Adapting to Change and Challenge

In the 1950s the aptly named vocational psychologist Donald Super described career development as unfolding in stages.[11] Early on, children start thinking about the future, imagine themselves in different types of jobs, learn work habits (hopefully good ones), and build confidence (the *growth* stage). Adolescents explore various options before deciding on a path to pursue and landing a job (the *exploration* stage). Young adults work hard to establish themselves in that position (*establishment*). As they enter middle age the focus shifts to sustaining what they have established, which means coping with constant changes in the workplace, learning updated skills, and innovating (*management* or *maintenance*). Eventually, people start to plan for and transition into retirement (*disengagement*).

Most Americans probably still use these stages—even unknowingly—as a kind of outline when they try to describe to people how their career paths have unfolded. The stages have long served as a template for the typical career, a cultural grand narrative that many people in industrialized nations share that guides the stories we tell about how we ended up in our current work situations. Career changes are not part of a natural progression in this model, but a departure from the norm, and people commonly talk about them that way. However, a linear progression through these stages within one organization is nowhere near the norm in today's world. A 2010 report published by the Bureau of Labor Statistics revealed that the younger half of the baby boom generation (born between 1957 and 1964) held an average of eleven jobs between the ages of eighteen and forty-four.[12] In another report published that year, the median number of years people had worked for their current employer was 4.4,[13] a statistic that prompted use of the phrase "the four-year career."[14] There is little agreement on how "career change" should be defined, but the actual number matters less than the obvious conclusion: For most people born after the classic stage theory was introduced, a whole lot of change has been going on.

Authors have been talking about the changing world of work for years.[15] The world has become more globally interconnected, the economy increasingly knowledge-based, and organizational structures are no longer safe havens. In today's world, fluidity is a fact of life; career changes are the rule, not the exception, and more and more professionals have become free-agent types who work for whichever company is paying at the moment. The notion of spending an entire career in one organization is viewed as a quaint relic of a bygone era. Now, you can barely get established in a position before you face a transition, requiring renewed growth, reexploration, and reestablishment. Super himself recognized this, and later in his career described these transitions as a "recycling" in which people have to redo the stages, often repeatedly, over the course of their careers.[16] Getting a pink slip, for example, requires a forced disengagement; searching for a new job and eventually reentering the workforce requires new growth, more exploration, and establishment in the new position. Moving from one job to another, retiring, and leaving the workforce to parent full-time all involve a similar process of recycling through the stages.

With all this transition and change as the new norm, the most useful skill a person can develop is the ability to adapt, to anticipate change, and to cope effectively when it arrives. In this way, people are agents in their careers. They actively take the reins and prepare themselves for the transitions they will encounter, then confront those transitions head-on with personal resources for navigating the change. Adaptable agents confidently respond to the developmental tasks they face, whatever their career stage, and they have strategies for fitting their work into the broader context of their lives in satisfying ways. What challenges are you facing? If it is indifference, what explains your pessimism and reluctance to plan? If it is indecision, what gives you the clarity and decisiveness you need? If it is a lack of initiative, what engages your motivation and gives you momentum? If it is low confidence, where can you find encouragement and boldness?

Agency requires activity—that is, effort. There is no passive agency; agency shows when someone is actively gathering information, evaluating options, and calculating risks. Agency is more than wise anticipation, though; it is built through determined striving, through tearing down emotional obstacles and assembling sources of support. How do you do this? One way is to recognize that managing transitions does not usually go well in a vacuum. You are a social being, and enlisting the support of trusted others is critical. Author Richard Leider has long encouraged people facing career decisions to put together a "personal board of directors," a group of mentors who know them well and whose counsel and advice they trust. Whom in your life have you relied on for wisdom and encouragement in times when these qualities are most needed? In chapter 3 we suggested the strategy of identifying at least three specific people whom you trust, who have your best interests in mind, and who are willing to provide ongoing support as you navigate this process. Take our word for it: their input and support will make a big difference. Good counselors also provide support and a more objective perspective and are well versed in helping people put into practice effective approaches to coping with transitions and challenges in careers and in helping to navigate those changes and issues within the broader context of life.

Think back to Sheryl, the electrical engineer. She was at a crossroads. Her job no longer fit well, and something had to give. Just knowing that, though, was not enough; in fact, knowing that something had to change without being sure how to change it was overwhelming and stressful. Part of Sheryl wanted to curl up in a ball and wait for all the stress to pass, but passivity would have the opposite effect, fanning the flames of her anxiety instead of dousing them. She knew the time had come to investigate her options, figure out the details, and attempt to predict what movement in each of the directions she was considering would mean. Throughout this process, Sheryl leaned on her husband for support. She called a professor from college with whom she had kept in touch to get her take. Sheryl talked things through with her aunt, with whom she grew close after her mother passed away. Counseling helped pull everything together. She knew that a change would be risky and hadn't yet ruled out another role in her current company, but she decided that she had hung on long enough to the hope of making the project manager role fit. As she sifted through her lists of pros and cons, it became clear that she wanted a role which made her feel more like herself again. Not only that, but she found herself continually coming back to the work value of making a difference. "I'm not saying the work my company does is not of value," she said. "I know firsthand how much more beautiful really good music sounds through our best speakers. It is otherworldly. But I feel like I'm past that now. I want to use my gifts to help people with more substantial needs."

You may be wondering whether these tactics are really unique to thinking about work as a calling. Isn't all this just plain good strategy for making career decisions and adapting to challenges, whether a sense of calling is at all relevant or not? You bet it is. As we touched on in chapter 3, we are concerned that some people who long for a sense of calling, or who are in the process of trying to live out a calling, start to believe that they are somehow immune to the often harsh realities of career decision making. Perhaps they hope their choices will be revealed to them via an audible voice or a burning bush–type sign. Perhaps they expect that because they are responding to a calling, the choppy waters will part and provide a callus-free path forward. The truth is that almost nothing of value comes without preparedness and hard work, whether you view work as a job, career, or calling. Indeed, the obstacles often are all the more salient for people who think of their work as a calling, because the broader mission that a calling beckons often requires an extra measure of persistence and perseverance to pursue and maintain, when other work orientations might encourage pursuit of whatever path provides the least resistance. Sound career decision making is essential in discerning and living out a calling. It is virtually always necessary, even if seldom sufficient.

Authors: Narrating Meaning into Work and Life

Actors address the *what* of a career by assessing their gifts and evaluating their fit with particular career options. Agents address the *how* of a career by anticipating and coping well with the career development tasks at hand, managing career transitions in the midst of changing life circumstances. For people seeking a sense of calling, an essential component of career decision making is the *why* of a career—as in, why are you doing this? What is it ultimately about? How does that fit with your sense of identity, the overall direction of your life, and the needs you see in the world? What is your purpose in life, and how does your career help you pursue that purpose?

In the author role, people narrate their life stories and identify the themes that emerge from them, exploring the meanings they convey. How did who you were in the past develop into the person you are today, and how will it influence who you become in the future? Savickas's counseling strategy, the Career Story Interview, elicits these stories by asking individuals to describe their childhood role models, their favorite magazines and movies, books, sayings, school subjects, leisure and hobbies, and their earliest life memories.[17] (What are yours?) The actual historical content revealed in the answers to such questions matters, but the narration of the stories matters more, because it reveals the meanings people already are making in their careers. All people interpret their past experiences in light of their present realities; they build coherence in the way they understand the events that unfold over the course of their lives, and they seek to maintain that coherence in the future. In this way, themes from stories like this clue us into a person's most desired goals, hopes for the future, and the sense of purpose that emerges as a result. For example, a person might identify Batman as a childhood role model, explaining that he was one of the very few superheroes who didn't have actual superpowers, relying instead on his athleticism, training, and a tool belt full of gadgets to help rid Gotham of its evils. A story like this reveals a theme of wanting to succeed and be helpful, but having to work hard to make up for having lower levels of ability than others seem to have. As it applies to career decisions, this theme is important; if such a person views himself as a scrapper who gets by on working hard, this quality is in itself a strength, one that usually is admired and that in many work environments is rewarded.

This strategy is insightful and artful, but we often start by simply and directly asking people to describe what they see as their purpose in life. We also ask them to identify the most important needs they see in the world around them. People usually can answer these questions forthrightly—not with how they feel they *should* respond, but with how they actually feel. Answers to these questions about purpose and important needs reveal possibilities for a person's "social fit." Earlier in this chapter we described the level of P-E fit we refer to as "personal fit," the match between a person's work personality and the requirements and rewards of particular jobs. Social fit refers to, quoting Frederick Buechner once again, "the place where your deep gladness and the world's deep hunger meet."[18] What is your purpose in life? What are the most important needs you see around you, needs that you are well equipped to address?

A core aspect of Sheryl's identity was her work as an engineer, an occupation in which men outnumber women by a ratio of about nine to one.[19] She was good at what she did and endured a tough path to get there. She wasn't ready to consider other occupations. As she talked about her mother, who had died four years prior from bone cancer, Sheryl became emotional and passionate. Years before her death, her mother had her hand and forearm amputated to prevent the spread of the cancer. Sheryl remembers being fascinated at the time by the prosthetic arm her mother wore, and the upgraded version she started using after a couple of years. She also remembered the expression of frustration on her mother's face when she tried to play golf with her new arm, a sport she had loved before the surgery but that she struggled with afterward and eventually gave up. "I remember wishing I could give her a better arm, so that she could do what she loved again without feeling so limited," Sheryl recalled. She started reading about prosthetic limb technology and innovations in brain-controlled limbs. The more she learned, the more she became convinced that she could use her gifts and her training in this way, to make the kind of direct and tangible difference she valued. The fact that this kind of work honored her mother's memory was the clincher. She had to do it. It became her calling.

Sheryl's story is a poignant example of someone using the resources and supports available to her to manage the process of discerning a calling. She quickly confronted challenges in trying to implement her choice; most notably, no companies working on prosthetic limb technologies were anywhere near where she lived. Her husband's family lived in town, and with the possibility of having a child on the horizon, they decided they couldn't think about moving. Life—it has a way of complicating things. After about six months and two interviews that didn't result in an offer, Sheryl accepted a position with a biomedical technology company in a neighboring town, about forty minutes away. "It's not what I was hoping for at first," she explained, "but I'm going to love it, and I really feel it still aligns with my calling. The projects I'll be working on will eventually result in new treatments for heart disease. My calling is not so narrow; it's about using technology to affirm life, help alleviate suffering, and keep families together longer. My mom would be proud."

7 Job Crafting

IN THE DAYS immediately following the birth of Bryan's third son, he and his wife, Amy, encountered one of their favorite people at Poudre Valley Hospital. She was a member of the custodial staff. Her name was Maggie; she was a middle-aged Latina whose job it was to empty the trash, clean and restock the sink area, wipe down surfaces, and mop the floor, among other such duties. They barely noticed that she was doing these things, although she was effective, leaving her area immaculate in her wake. Instead, it seemed to Bryan and Amy that her job was to dote on their new baby, to share openly in their joy, and to express genuine empathy when talking with Amy about her lingering pain from childbirth. Her cheer was infectious, and she had a way of making them feel like her visit to their room was the single most important event of her day. She obviously had a passion for her job, despite the fact that housekeeping is near the bottom of the prestige hierarchy at the hospital—as it is within most any organization. No matter to Maggie. "My coworkers are constantly giving me applications for translator positions at the hospital," she said, "because I speak English and Spanish equally well. But they don't realize how much I love the job I have now."

Born to migrant farm workers (her dad from Texas, her mom from Mexico) in a car (!) in Wyoming, Maggie Garza, now sixty-two, has lived most of her life in Fort Collins, Colorado. After dropping out of high school ("the worst decision of my life," she says), she worked for a laundry service and later as a day care provider. For the last fifteen years, however, she has worked as an environmental tech for the hospital. "They call it that to make it sound important," she said. "We just say we work in housekeeping."

Can a housekeeping job be a calling? "For me it is," said Maggie without hesitation. "I believe God put me here for a reason." Ask Maggie for her job description, she'll tell you: prepare her cart; clean the utility rooms; check which patient rooms are occupied and go to each one, knock on the door before entering, then clean the sinks, tables, restrooms, and floors; take out the trash and replace the trash liners; evaluate whether the walls need to be wiped down; if they do, wipe them down.

Ask Maggie to simply describe what she does, though, and you get a different answer. She cleans, sure—and does so well. But she also checks in with patients, assesses their needs, expresses concern and care, and assists them where she can. She talks with them, gets to know them, and helps them feel more at ease. Other hospital staff members notice this. Sometimes pediatric nurses call Maggie into a room to help soothe a frightened child or calm a patient who is acting out. Consider this story: "There was a kid who the nurses were having trouble with. They called me over and said, 'Maggie, maybe you can break the ice.' So I went in, and to get his attention I started crawling underneath the bed, from one side to the other. Another nurse came in and saw me down there, and thought I fell or something. 'Oh Maggie, are you alright?' she kind of yelled. She really kind of ruined it, because I was crawling to the other side to surprise the boy and make him laugh."

That story illustrates how Maggie approaches her job. She makes silly faces at children to coax a smile. Sometimes she dances around the room while she cleans and meows quietly like a kitten, invariably causing her child patients (indeed, she sees them as *her* patients) to roar with laughter. Their parents, often swimming in stress and concern, see this and laugh right along with their kids. It helps take the edge off. Maggie also provides words of encouragement, and she prays for patients in rooms where she cleans. As an environmental tech, Maggie could say her job is fundamentally about cleaning rooms. Technically, she would be correct. For her, though, the job is much more than that. It's ultimately about keeping hurting people comfortable, relaxed, cared for, satisfied. "I like to converse with people, see what they need, and see how I can help them," she said. "It makes them feel good. It makes me feel good, too."

One myth we attack whenever we can is that only specific types of people, within specific types of occupations, can experience their work as a calling. Although we readily acknowledge that far too many workers toil in job situations in which a sense of calling is thwarted, sabotaged, and otherwise blocked from nearly every angle, we contend that most people have more potential than they realize to transform their current work into a calling. The previous chapter focused on the question of how a person might discern a calling during the process of choosing or changing a career—both privileges that are not extended to some workers, who may have limited career options from the start, and who are inclined to cling to a job they may not like because an unpleasant job is better than no job. Others may dream of jobs other than the one they hold, but due to geographic constraints, family responsibilities, aversion to risk, or any number of other factors, do not see alternative career paths as viable. This chapter addresses the challenge of cultivating a calling in the context of one's current job, when a career change may be impossible, impractical, or for whatever other reason simply not on the table. People can take a range of approaches to cull a stronger sense of calling from their jobs. Perhaps the most promising approach—the one we focus on in this chapter—is engaging in a process known as job crafting.

Job Crafting and Calling

The concept of job crafting was formally introduced to workplace scholars in 2001 by management professors Amy Wrzesniewski and Jane Dutton, who argued the basic premise that "work tasks and interactions that compose the days, the jobs, and, ultimately, the lives of employees are the raw materials employees use to construct their jobs. . . . Job boundaries, the meaning of work, and work identities are not fully determined by formal job requirements. Individuals have latitude to define and enact the job, acting as 'job crafters.'"[1] Stated most simply, *job crafting* refers to those things that workers do to elicit a stronger sense of purpose, meaning, engagement, resilience, and thriving from their jobs. In crafting their work, employees might change their work tasks; branch out into alternative work activities; build stronger relationships with coworkers, supervisors, and customers; and reenvision the very purpose of what they do all day. Such strategies ultimately lead to changes in the design of a job, the social environment, or the job-crafter's perspective—and research so far seems to suggest that it works. Scholars have found that workers across a variety of occupations (e.g., managers, teachers, salespersons) who implement job crafting strategies become more engaged, satisfied, and productive at work.[2] Can job crafting transform one's work into a calling? The only study of which we are aware that begins to answer this question suggests that the answer is probably yes. Based on in-depth interviews of thirty-one employees who had "unanswered callings" (that is, one or more callings not satisfied by their current job), Justin Berg and colleagues found that workers were more likely to experience the satisfaction and meaning that is usually associated with "answered callings" in their current jobs when they used job crafting strategies.[3] In short, job crafting, even in jobs that are not ideal, can help evoke the same psychological outcomes that typically accompany living out a calling.

As in most other aspects of life, chronically dissatisfying circumstances at work are hard to just accept and live with; when we're deeply unhappy, we want to make changes. People are motivated to craft their jobs when they want more control over their work, when they feel isolated and want a closer connection with others, and when they want to experience a greater sense of purpose and meaning. When people are successful at job crafting, they feel more engaged, satisfied, and content—the results of effectively implementing one or more of three crafting strategies. The first, *task crafting*, focuses on redesigning the job itself, changing the array of tasks in which the worker engages while still tending to the responsibilities for which she or he is held accountable. The second, *relational crafting*, targets the social environment and seeks ways to expand and improve the worker's relationships at work. The third, *cognitive crafting*, centers on developing new, more enriching understandings of the very purpose of the work. We explore each of these strategies in turn.

Task Crafting

For most people, task crafting is probably the first thing that comes to mind when thinking about job-crafting activities. In almost any job, workers have formal responsibilities, a specific set of tasks laid out in their job description that they are required to complete. Sometimes the tasks for which a person is responsible feel like a mismatch with that person's gifts—one's interests, abilities, values, and personality. Task crafting refers to the process of altering those responsibilities to better align them with the unique features of one's work personality. This change usually occurs by adjusting how tasks are completed, attempting to add new tasks or remove others, and potentially allocating one's time or energy for tasks in a different way.[4] How one goes about task crafting, of course, depends on the amount of freedom or power a person has to change the tasks while still performing the essential requirements of the job well.

Berg, Wrzesniewski, and Dutton conducted a landmark study designed to provide a window into the motives, strategies, challenges, and outcomes of job crafting.[5] They interviewed thirty-three employees, twenty of whom were employed at a for-profit manufacturing firm and thirteen of whom worked for a nonprofit political agency. From employees' responses to their questions, two types of task crafting emerged: one that focused on altering the scope or nature of tasks and one that concentrated on adding new and different tasks. Employees who used the altering strategy adjusted their approach to carrying out their required tasks, approaching the same activity in a novel way or directing more attention to those components of an activity that they find most engaging. "I really enjoy online tools and Internet things," reported one of the study's participants. "So I've really tailored that aspect of the written job description, and really 'upped' it, because I enjoy it. I spend hours exploring what else we're paying for with this service. So it gives me an opportunity to play around and explore with tools and web applications, and I get to learn, which is one of my favorite things to do."[6] This employee identified a specific portion of her job that struck a chord with her, and she devised ways to spend more time and energy on those tasks. Doing so allowed her to use her strengths more effectively, to satisfy her interests and values more directly, and to simply be herself to a greater extent on the job—all of which are characteristic of people living out their callings. If she is able to maintain this focus while also fulfilling the other duties her job requires, her employer will be at least as happy with her as she is with her job.

Adding tasks quite literally involves supplementing the tasks a person is required to carry out with additional tasks that a person especially enjoys or values. For example, another employee from the nonprofit organization stated, "We have an annual luncheon, and I have become the person who runs the registration table. It would normally be something that a coordinator would do and was before I got here . . . but I've taken it on myself because I'm good at it and like the challenge and like being able to control it. I could have just as easily set it up, and removed myself, but instead, I stay much more actively involved."[7] This employee obviously doesn't *have* to do this task, but chooses to do it because of what the task offers her: a chance to use her strengths and satisfy her needs for challenge, control, and mastery. By running the registration table, she is actively improving the extent to which her job fits with her gifts.

Berg, Wrzesniewski, and Dutton's study highlights two key points. The first is that task crafting allows your job to be what you make of it. All of us have a set list of tasks we have to carry out to stay employed, at least some of which probably feel like they have little to do with our calling. Even those living out their callings can acknowledge that no job is perfect; virtually everyone has to put up with demands for completing tasks they really can't stand in order to support the parts of the job they love. Nevertheless, to the extent that external constraints allow, people in most any job can potentially accentuate certain tasks (like learning about new web tools and applications) or add in other tasks that are not required (like running a registration table) to help bring their jobs into closer alignment with their callings. The second point is that accentuating or adding tasks into your current job is almost always surprisingly easy. It is probably natural to assume that adapting one's work tasks means an entire overhaul of the job, and for most of us, such drastic and comprehensive change is impossible. In actual practice, though, effective task crafting targets the little things, like a restaurant server or cashier spending a bit more time talking to each customer, a teacher shifting more of his energy to individual instruction as opposed to class lecture, or a counselor deciding to run a grief therapy group once a week on top of her individual clients. Whereas task altering can turn one's job from a fruitcake to carrot cake, task adding can serve as the icing on the cake. Either way, the cake tastes better.

Relational Crafting

In their influential article "The Need to Belong: Desire for Interpersonal Attachments as a Fundamental Human Motivation," Roy Baumeister and Mark Leary discuss the ingrained desire that humans have to socialize with each other, likely due to the benefits people reap when they are in relationships.[8] As we explored in chapter 5, any person living in society by definition relies on the contributions of others to survive, and those who engage with others in consistently positive ways experience a wealth of psychological benefits. This statement is as true in the workplace as in any other sphere of life. Establishing stronger, more positive connections with others around you at work will generate a greater degree of meaning and on-the-job happiness. Positive relationships at work also create more opportunities to engage in prosocial behaviors, a critical component of calling. Like task crafting, relational crafting entails both altering the nature or quality of one's relationships and creating new ones.

As we settled into our roles as professors at large research universities, both of us were a little surprised by the level of isolation that can easily come with an academic lifestyle. Despite what may be a common perception, we don't enjoy buffet lunches in a faculty dining room, and friendly philosophical debate over drinks at happy hour is a rare occurrence. Given the importance our universities place on maintaining productive, independent programs of research, during some weeks our computer screens get more face time than all of our coworkers and students combined. For Ryan especially, the dynamics of his department reinforce a fairly solitary existence. After his first two years struggling with this reality, Ryan (who happens to be highly extroverted) had reached a tipping point: Should he just accept the system as it is and check out, or would it be worth the effort to craft a stronger relational experience? Fortuitously, at the same time Ryan hit this point, a colleague down the hall was reaching his own tipping point: after three decades in the department, he had informed the university that within the next five years he would retire.

Though he and Ryan had never talked that much, he openly shared with Ryan his feelings of sadness about putting an end date on his academic career and pondered how he would be remembered once he left, especially considering how little anyone talked to each other around the department. The two of them quickly formed a bond over their shared angst about the everyone-is-an-island departmental culture. Ryan decided to ask, "What would you say to grabbing lunch every couple of weeks or so?" Their biweekly lunch meeting continues today, providing both of them with a chance to share in the ups and downs of their respective professional careers, naturally often spilling into their personal lives, too. This kind of relational crafting is obviously very easy, and for Ryan, it has provided an enormous return on the very minimal investment of time and energy the lunches require.

Improving the interpersonal climate of the workplace is one important outcome of relational crafting, but not the only one. Another participant in the study by Berg and colleagues, a customer service representative, established relationships with coworkers who could teach her new skills and knowledge that enhanced her ability to do her job well. "I have taken initiative to form relationships with some of the folks who fulfill orders," she explained. "That's not my area, but I was really interested in how that worked and wanted to . . . learn. . . . I have learned a lot from them, and that's helped me in my job. I know more about how the ordering process goes so now I can explain it up front to customers."

Of course, effective relational crafting does not always require expanding one's social network or investing more in already-existing relationships. Sometimes *decreasing* relational involvement in strategic ways can have a positive effect. A senior manager in Berg and colleagues' study provided an example: "I've tried to limit some interaction with my supervisor because sometimes she wants a really high level of . . . kind of pre-work. For example, we've had meetings before where it was literally . . . like a two- or three-hour meeting for something that I think we could have discussed really in a half an hour. . . . I enjoy working with her overall and we can have fun together, but there are certain types of interactions that I try to limit. Like for instance, sometimes if it's a meeting that I know could be much shorter, and I know it will go longer, I may schedule another meeting like an hour after that meeting starts so that we have to finish it up."[9] People are able to more consistently sustain their callings when they can alter relationships in both directions where appropriate, increasing positive interactions and decreasing negative interactions. The goal, obviously, is to maximize the overall quantity and quality of positive interactions they have with others at work.

Cognitive Crafting

The third form of crafting is cognitive crafting. Cognitive crafting involves redefining one's perception of the kinds of tasks or relationships involved in one's job, or of the extent to which one's job is meaningful. At its core, this type of crafting involves a change in the way a person thinks about the job, regardless of whether any change takes place in the job itself. In its most basic form, cognitive crafting involves a simple attitude adjustment in which a worker adopts new and improved ways of thinking about the job's nature, purpose, and impact. This strategy has some key advantages, particularly for individuals in highly structured jobs (e.g., production worker, toll booth collector, truck driver) who may have little latitude for proactively changing their required tasks or their workplace relationships. Before we explore this further, consider a few examples of cognitive crafting from the participants in Berg, Wrzesniewski, and Dutton's job crafting study.

One brand manager talked about how she defines the tasks she is responsible for carrying out on the job: "I'm . . . passionate about beauty. I love it . . . because in marketing, you can try to influence the way people think about beauty. You can have people think about it differently, because there's more than one standard of beauty. For example, I might ask, 'Well, is that all that's beautiful or are there some other images that we can think of that are beautiful?' . . . I see it as a chance to change the way people think about beauty."[10] We are willing to bet that this brand manager's contract says nothing about changing the way people think about beauty. Yet for her, all the effort she devotes to creating logos and ads, and designing marketing campaigns, is fundamentally about influencing what people see as beautiful. Another customer service representative stated, "I'm passionate about . . . just doing a good job and doing my job well and going above and beyond what basic thing that I can do, not just giving an average phone call, going above and treating the customer well. . . . Technically, [my job is] putting in orders, entering orders, but really I see it as providing our customers with an enjoyable experience, a positive experience, which is a lot more meaningful to me than entering numbers."[11] Here again, the job description focuses on one set of responsibilities—handling phone calls with customers and entering orders—but she sees those tasks only as means to a more important and meaningful end: providing customers with a positive, even enjoyable experience.

Think for a moment about these two employees. Who do you think experiences work as more meaningful, the brand manager who thinks of her work responsibilities as a pathway for promoting beauty, or a brand manager who focuses solely on accomplishing what is spelled out in the job description? The customer care representative who thinks of her work as a way to give customers a pleasant experience, or the representative who focuses exclusively on filling her weekly quota of answered phone calls and completed orders? Now think about this from the perspective of an employer. Which employees from among these pairs would you prefer to have working for you?

Whether redefining a particular task or redefining what is meaningful about a job altogether, these strategies can help people alter the perception of what they do at work. Such alteration is probably most powerful when it helps workers view their jobs as more meaningful, more prosocially oriented, or both. Because these components tie directly into a calling, crafting one's job to have these components is critical.

Remember Maggie Garza? Maggie is a shining example of all three types of job crafting. While engaging in the essential duties of the job, which center around cleaning and sanitizing, Maggie adds other tasks, such as asking patients if they need anything and then finding a nurse, a meal menu, the TV remote, or whatever else they require. She expands the relational boundaries of her job description by interacting meaningfully with patients and their families— encouraging them, joking with them, making them feel welcome and cared for. She also thinks of her job as consisting of far more than the discrete tasks that technically define it; for her, the job is about providing high-quality care to sick and suffering children. Maggie's approach to her job also conforms to what Jane Dutton and colleagues found in their interview study of twenty-eight members of a hospital cleaning staff.[12] An analysis of the interview data revealed two groups of employees. One focused rigidly on the job requirements as described; they punched in, punched out, did the minimum number of tasks necessary in between, and limited their interactions with others as much as they could. This group disliked cleaning, described the skill level of the job as low, and were generally unwilling to do anything outside of what was articulated in the job description. The other group consisted of cleaners who adopted an approach like Maggie's. They took on additional work tasks; freely conversed with patients, visitors, and medical staff; and planned their days in ways that made the whole system work more smoothly (e.g., by timing their regular duties in ways that made the work flow maximally efficient). They considered their role as critical in advancing the broader goal of healing patients. Here again: Which group do you think derived more meaning from their jobs? Which group would you want working in your hospital?

How to Craft Your Job

Are you ready to give job crafting a try? You've seen the advantages of crafting the tasks, relationships, and cognitive appraisals of a job. Crafting may seem very appealing and (deceptively) simple. Still, we advise you to prepare yourself before you jump in. The most important component of job crafting is, without a doubt, your mind set.[13] Embarking on the job-crafting path with skepticism and half-hearted reluctance is likely to sabotage its effectiveness and leave you more discouraged than before you started. Believe that your job is not set in stone but is malleable enough to be changed through your own efforts. Be on the lookout for opportunities to engage in crafting, and be willing to experiment and make at least small changes to your normal work routine. Then prepare yourself to be persistent and patient, seeking small wins that will accumulate and result in bigger changes in due time.

The job crafting pioneers—Berg, Dutton, and Wrzesniewski—developed the Job Crafting Exercise, a tool designed to help workers identify and plan ways to put into practice some of the strategies they have uncovered through their research. Readers interested in completing Berg and colleagues' formal exercise, which we strongly recommend, can purchase the materials at www.jobcrafting.org.

Below, we summarize a more informal approach, a teaser of sorts that we've adapted to help you begin exploring opportunities for crafting your current job.

Outline Your Job Tasks

To begin, take inventory of the tasks for which you are responsible in your current job. In a journal or on a separate sheet of paper, write "Current Job" on the top of one page, and create three columns, labeled "Low," "Medium," and "High." Under each of these columns, create lists of the various tasks you are required to carry out in a typical workday, organized according to the level of time and energy they require. In the Low column, list five or six of those little things that don't take much effort; in the High column, list the major tasks that require a considerable amount of effort; and list the in-between tasks in the Medium column. As an example, if you are an elementary school teacher, you might list "arranging desks and chairs" in the Low column, "developing a lesson plan" in the High column, and "teaching that lesson" in the Medium column. Try to list five or six tasks under each column, although obviously the number of different tasks depends on the job. When you've finished, take a moment to evaluate the chart. Does this look like your typical workday?

Outline Your Gifts

On the top of a second sheet of paper, write "Gifts." We've used the term "gifts" broadly, to describe interests, abilities, personality, and work-related values. We broaden the term further here to include the three personal characteristics that are the focus for Berg, Dutton, and Wrzesniewski: motives, strengths, and passions. Under "Gifts," create three more columns, this time using "Motives," "Strengths," and "Passions" as the column headings. In the Motives column, create a list of five or so specific outcomes you hope to attain by working in your current job—things like financial security, happiness, meaningful relationships, or making a difference. In the Strengths column, write down lists of strengths that you can apply in some way to your job. [Refer back to the "you at your best" exercise in chapter 4 (pp. 78–79), if that helps.] Examples include making connections with people, computer programming, problem solving, mediation, and public speaking. Finally, in the Passions column, create a list of your strongest areas of passion—those things in which you are most interested or that you most value—that apply in some way to your current job. Examples might include helping people learn, mentoring, creating order out of chaos, persuading people, or being creative.

Integrate Tasks and Gifts

For the third step of the exercise, write "New and Improved" on the top of a third sheet of paper. Your goal now is to combine your job tasks with your gifts in a way that reflects how you most want to use your motives, strengths, and passions in your job. To accomplish this, begin by creating the same three columns you have on the Current Job sheet—"Low," "Medium," and "High." Then transfer the tasks from the Current Job sheet onto the New and Improved sheet, but this time put them in the column that reflects how much time and energy you *wish* you were devoting to each task. For instance, if talking with parents about their children was in your Low column before, but you would like it to be a bigger part of your job going forward, write it in the Medium or even High column this time. Strive to be both ambitious and realistic as you do this. If developing lesson plans simply takes an enormous amount of time for you right now, it won't make sense to write it in the Low column. However, by adjusting your strategy (e.g., adopting a higher-quality curriculum with excellent preplanned lessons, identifying and revising your favorite plans from among those you've used before), your planning efforts could become efficient enough to warrant its placement in the Medium column.

While reorganizing your job tasks to reflect your preferences, you will probably notice some themes emerging. Circle clusters of tasks that illustrate those themes, and give each theme a name. For example, classroom instruction and tutoring students one-on-one might be grouped under a "Directly Helping Students Learn" theme; creating lesson plans, meeting with parents, and consulting with other teachers might be grouped under the theme "Behind-the-Scenes Student Support." Try to identify at least three themes.

Once you have transferred your tasks onto your New and Improved sheet in a way that reflects your ideal job, start incorporating your gifts. Focus on the themes that emerged from your task list. Look back to your Gifts sheet (where you listed your motives, strengths, and passions), identify the gifts that support those themes, and write them near each other on the New and Improved sheet. For example, your motive of wanting meaningful relationships might map well onto the overall theme of Behind-the-Scenes Student Support, which includes the tasks requiring you to interact with parents and other teachers with whom you could foster mutually supportive working relationships. Similarly, your strength in problem solving and your passion of helping people learn would fit well with the theme of Directly Helping Students Learn. Keep in mind that the same motive, strength, or passion may support more than one theme; do not hesitate to use them more than once. When you complete this process, you have a visual representation of what your job could become. This visual representation, ideally, also converges well with what you understand to be your calling.

Take Action

The final stage of this process is to develop an action plan for making your hypothetical New and Improved job more of a reality. Task crafting, relational crafting, and cognitive crafting come into play at this point. You don't have to do this on your own. We suggest inviting a counselor, one or more members of the personal board of directors we invited you to name in chapter 4, a trusted colleague, or your supervisor (if you feel safe in doing so) to look over your New and Improved sheet and help you brainstorm some realistic approaches for crafting your job in ways that bring it into closer alignment with your calling.

After identifying specific job crafting opportunities, however small, make a commitment to engage in at least three of these behaviors per day for a trial period of at least a week. Write about these behaviors in a daily diary, evaluate your effectiveness in executing them, record their consequences, and check in with your counselor, friend, coworker, or supervisor about your progress. Challenge yourself to take some calculated risks, stir the pot, and change the status quo, because the very nature of job crafting *requires* you to do something different in your work tasks, your relationships at work, or the way you think about your job. This can be a scary proposition for anyone, even (and perhaps especially) people who are highly dissatisfied with their jobs. Developing the necessary level of commitment, attention to possible opportunities, and willingness to take the risk of trying out these strategies may be the most challenging step in the job-crafting process, especially for those who are naturally risk averse. If this applies to you, don't worry. Your initial experiments with job crafting do not, and probably should not, involve big changes or jumps. Rather, experts in job crafting suggest that small steps are the best way to start, because small steps result in small successes, which accumulate and become larger successes. As this process moves on, you'll feel encouraged to take slightly larger calculated risks later.

One last piece of advice for the potential job crafter. Properly choosing the types of job-crafting activities in which you might engage will almost certainly influence your level of success with these activities. For this reason, we urge you to remember your gifts, and choose crafting strategies that align closely with your motives, strengths, and passions. If you are a mechanic with a passion for German imports and strengths in creative problem solving, consider crafting opportunities that capitalize on those gifts, such as working with your shop's boss to design a marketing strategy intended to bring in more Volkswagens and BMWs. If you have strong interpersonal skills and value positive relationships, focus on strategies that strengthen your network of relationships at work, such as organizing a monthly happy hour, lobbying management for funds to celebrate birthdays with a cake at lunchtime, or garnering support for a workplace mentoring program. The bottom line is that aligning crafting activities with the unique features of your profile of gifts will, in time, turn the job you have into more of the job you want, one that resembles your New and Improved sheet, and ultimately, your calling.

A Job Is Like a Marriage

To better imagine how successful job crafting might unfold, think of a job as similar to a marriage. For more than fifty years, researchers have studied how happy people are in marriage and how their level of happiness changes over the course of the marriage. Results from these studies are not particularly encouraging: on average, the longer people are married, the more unhappy they tend to be with the marriage.[14] This conclusion seems like a real downer, but buried in this research is another finding to consider. Although on average, people who are married become less happy in their marriage over time, a subset of people stay consistently happy or grow even happier as the marriage endures. What do these people have in common? The common thread is that, one way or another, they have learned that being happy in marriage is not just about marrying the right person, it is about working really hard as the marriage goes on to build and maintain happiness. They focus on learning to communicate better, to spend quality time with each other regularly, to learn more and more about each other, and to stay enmeshed in each other's lives. They are active and vigilant about addressing and readdressing the strengths and weaknesses of their marriage over time.

Perhaps the most compelling evidence of how commitment, hard work, and persistence translates into happiness comes from research on couples in arranged marriages, still practiced in some cultures in South and East Asia, Africa, and the Middle East. According to a *Scientific American* article by Robert Epstein, couples in arranged marriages often report that their level of happiness has increased over time, the opposite of what is found for most couples in "love marriages."[15] Epstein speculates that couples in arranged marriages focus less on maintaining happiness and more on building it, and therefore work harder at investing in the relationship in ways that lead to long-term happiness. If you find yourself in a work environment that wouldn't have been your first choice, or that ends up seeming less perfect than you assumed it would be—as is inevitably the case in a marriage—you can choose to stick with it and be miserable, to give up on it and leave in the hope that the next job will be the right one, or to work hard at improving the fit, adapting to it, making it work. Job crafting helps you carry out this last option.

Viewing your job as a calling is likely influenced by a combination of factors that may include a transcendent summons perceived either directly or indirectly through that job's degree of fit with your gifts, as well as the extent to which that job provides a strong sense of purpose, meaningfulness, and a means of contributing to the greater good. This chapter has focused on the challenge of turning an existing job into a calling by improving its fit with what you perceive to be your calling. Task crafting, relational crafting, and cognitive crafting individually and together offer avenues for shaping your current job into closer alignment with your ideal job. Will job crafting turn any job into the perfect job? Of course not, but if crafting is done effectively, it moves things in the right direction, making your work a better fit for your gifts, providing you with a stronger sense of meaning, and establishing new pathways for serving the greater good. As we have maintained throughout this book, a calling is best approached not as a thing to be discovered once and for all, but an ongoing process of evaluating and reshaping work in ways that continue to use your gifts meaningfully, in service of others. Indeed, one of the most important lessons we have learned from interviewing workers with a calling is that actively striving to keep their passion alive is every bit as critical as discerning their calling in the first place. Job crafting provides a useful set of strategies for molding your work over time in ways that continue to support a sense of calling, even—indeed, especially—when work tasks or the work environment starts to shift in ways that threaten your opportunities to live it out.

8 Callings outside of Paid Work

PAUL PRIESTER began his career working a variety of jobs in the restaurant industry, and like too many in the kitchen before him,[1] he developed an addiction to alcohol and cocaine. After coming to grips with the impending self-destruction of that trajectory, Paul entered treatment and sobered up. ("Literally my first real calling [was] to get sober or die," he remembers.) In anticipating the changes he would make in his life, he began to think seriously about his career path. Many substance abusers who respond successfully to counseling find it a transformative experience, and some even end treatment with a strong sense of calling to help others overcome the same demons that nearly undid them. Paul's experience with his counselor was not exactly transformative ("I had such a horrible substance abuse counselor. . . . She was so ineffective, and I thought, 'Oh, I can do that. I can make more of a difference in that . . .'"), but it had the same result: he sought some paraprofessional training and started working as a substance abuse counselor himself.

Paul's journey from substance-abusing waiter to substance abuse counselor was far from a straight road. It was full of twists and turns and littered with obstacles. Yet inexplicably, a series of seemingly serendipitous events helped him overcome each barrier. For example, upon taking a new job at a clinic in Iowa City, Paul was in desperate need of a place to live—until one block away from the clinic, he ran into an old friend who was about to move out of a really nice, cheap apartment and needed a renter to take his place. As he was about to move, his beat-up, rusted-out car finally died—and out of the blue, without knowing about his clunker's smoking engine, his aunt called and offered him a car she no longer needed. "You see what I mean?" said Paul. "An obstacle would be there, and it would just dissolve. It would melt away when it seemed like I was going in the right path. The energy felt good; I felt invigorated by it. I was actively praying for what God's will was for me, and the answer would come, and the barrier would just dissolve."

Paul loved the work, whether he was delivering services at a homeless shelter or a community-based treatment center. He was living out his calling, but also looking for ways to extend his reach further. One day he asked one of his professors for advice. "I remember him saying, 'If I were you, I would get a PhD in psychology,' and at that point, it blew me away," he noted, "because it seemed like such a far-off, impossible thing to achieve." In time, though, a PhD in psychology became Paul's goal. He kept a picture of the campus that was his top choice on the wall to motivate him as he worked his way through a master's degree and prepared for the GRE (Graduate Record Exam). He applied to a handful of PhD programs and waited for his acceptance letter. Unfortunately, the letter never came. As the rejections rolled in, Paul was crushed. "I just really felt like this one time the barriers were appearing and not disappearing," he explained. "I was really torn on what I was going to do." Around this same time, Paul became a father, and having an infant daughter in his life caused his priorities to shift. After a period of intense prayer and some serious soul-searching, he ultimately concluded that he could not escape his sense of calling to a career in psychology. Paul swallowed his pride, summoned his inner fortitude, and spent a year beefing up his credentials by volunteering in a research lab at a nearby hospital and studying with reckless abandon for his second go-round with the GRE. The effort paid off. A year later Paul landed in a PhD program that fit his gifts perfectly.

After taking jobs at two other universities, Dr. Priester is now a professor at North Park University in Chicago, and he loves his work. He teaches courses, conducts research, chairs two departments, and manages an active consulting practice that often takes him overseas. All of this work serves what Paul views as his calling, a perspective reinforced by his conviction that God opened up the doors that led him there and removed the barriers that threatened his path. When he steps back and takes it all in, Paul expresses a profound sense of gratitude, recognizing how fortunate he is that he can do what he loves and use his gifts meaningfully in service of others. Paul's tale is a dramatic success story: from an alcoholic, cocaine-addicted restaurant server to a passionate teacher, productive researcher, effective administrator, and international consultant, Paul not only earned a living but also made a global difference. If his story was a fairy tale, we would be at the happily-ever-after moment. Right?

Here is where Paul's story gets even more interesting. After such a long and remarkable journey to his current job—one he loves—you might think that Paul had come to a place of ultimate contentment. Not quite. Paul feels called to serve as a professor, sure, but after attending to another nagging summons, he found himself with a second calling: to operate, of all things, an organic farm. "Now I'm being called in a totally different direction," he told us. "I have this fifteen-acre organic farm. . . . [There is] a complete sense of calling there that's totally away from academics, and now, even though I really enjoyed academics [and] I'm really sort of satisfied with it, it has become really sort of secondary . . . The primary thing is this small, organic farm. And once again, it's a pure sense of calling."[2] If you could hear Paul talk about his farm in person, you would find yourself moved by his unrelenting joy. His tone elevates and his already-wide smile widens even farther when he describes his exuberance at waking up to the rooster's call and trading his professor's tweed for denim and work boots, attire much better suited for the dirty job of preparing his rich, black soil for spring planting.

The fact that on top of this, Paul still has a day job he loves—now a secondary calling, as he puts it—leaves him downright giddy.

Throughout this book we've focused on exploring what having a calling means in the work domain. We've described how people strive to build careers in response to a transcendent summons they perceive that allows them to use their gifts at work in ways that are meaningful and through which they can make a difference. Calling is more than a career-related phenomenon, though. The earliest teachings on the topic have stressed this point, and the research we have conducted on this question is very clear: people perceive callings in many life domains. Of course, pursuing a calling outside of work or striving to satisfy multiple callings can complicate things in a hurry. Our goal in this chapter is to explore what people experience when they perceive a calling within domains of life other than work—parenting, friendships, leisure, or anything else—and what it might mean to experience multiple callings, in and out of work. How can you live out your callings effectively, with Paul's level of vigor and excitement, without being overwhelmed or concerned that one calling may swallow up the next or leave you straining to balance divided loyalties?

Having and Seeking

About seven years ago, as we first started digging into research on calling, we cobbled together some items into a short instrument we thought could efficiently measure two things: the extent to which a person experiences the presence of a calling and the extent to which a person is searching for one. The scale, which has since been dubbed the Brief Calling Scale (BCS), ended up with only four items.[3] We ask research participants to respond to the items using the following five-point scale: (1) not at all true of me, (2) mildly true of me, (3) moderately true of me, (4) mostly true of me, and (5) totally true of me. How would you rate each item?

_____ 1. I have a calling to a particular kind of work.

_____ 2. I have a good understanding of my calling as it applies to my career.

_____ 3. I am trying to figure out my calling in my career.

_____ 4. I am searching for my calling as it applies to my career.

Computing scale scores is easy—just add your ratings for items 1 and 2. That total is your score on the BCS Presence of Calling Scale. Then add your ratings for items 3 and 4. That total is your score on the BCS Search for Calling Scale. The average scores for college students are 6.2 on the Presence of Calling Scale and 5.4 on the Search for Calling Scale.[4] Employed adults representing a wide range of occupations score similarly on the presence dimension (average = 6.1), but lower on the search dimension (average = 3.9).[5] This result makes intuitive sense, considering that many working adults view themselves as currently living out their callings and are less likely than college students to be in an active process of career exploration. Take a moment and compare your scores to the averages from these samples. Statistically speaking, whether you are a student or working adult, if you happen to score 9 or above on the presence scale you are in the upper 16 percent of the population when it comes to experiencing a calling. On the search scale, if you are a student scoring 8 or above, or a working adult scoring 7 or above, you are in the upper 16 percent of the population when it comes to searching for a calling. How do you stack up?

Over the time we have used this little measure, we have distributed it to thousands of people from all walks of life. One of the more intriguing findings we've encountered with these two scales is the nature of the relationship between having a calling to a particular line of work and searching for one. Pause for a moment and ponder how you think these two dimensions might relate to each other. Perhaps, like most people, your guess is that having a calling and searching for a calling are related inversely; when one goes up, the other one goes down. In other words, the stronger the presence of a calling you perceive, the less you are searching for one, and the more you are searching for one, the less likely you are to have one. This expectation is sensible and, in fact, identical to our initial hypothesis. However, the data tell a different story.

Across almost all of our studies using the BCS, the relation between having a calling and searching for a calling is either very small or nonexistent. That's right; these two concepts are only weakly related at best. Put another way, whether a person scores high or low on the Presence of Calling scale tells us almost nothing about how that person will likely score on the Search for Calling scale, and vice versa. How could this be?

Because scores on the two scales are essentially independent, we can segment our respondents into four approximately equal-sized groups:

1. People who find calling irrelevant, who neither have one nor are searching for one
2. People who don't have a calling but want one, and so are searching for one
3. People who have a calling and are content, and therefore are not actively searching for one
4. People who have a calling and yet are simultaneously searching for one

What is this fourth group like? Guided by data from our interviews of employees with a calling, along with data we've collected using a more sophisticated measure of calling than the BCS (which consistently shows a *strong positive relationship* between perceiving a calling and searching for one) the profile of a person who both has a calling and is searching for one is starting to come to light. These folks view a calling to work as an ongoing process rather than a single event; they are constantly on the prowl for ways to maintain, enhance, and expand their calling and are also open to moving into new career paths that can extend their current spheres of influence.

Not only that, but many in this fourth group are eager to venture beyond the role of traditional work and pursue callings within other life domains. Paul fits this profile; he felt that his job as a substance abuse counselor allowed him to live out his calling, but he never stopped looking for ways to enhance that calling, even if it meant moving into other roles. He later decided to pursue his PhD and ultimately became a professor. Even while thoroughly enjoying his job as a professor and viewing it as an avenue for living out his calling, Paul kept searching until he felt called to buy land and start tending it. Now his hobby farm is, in his view, his primary calling; his faculty job is still important, but secondary.

Likely Candidates for Callings Outside of Paid Work

The view of calling as something that can be pursued within various life roles beyond that of paid work is endorsed by a long tradition of philosophers and theologians, but has attracted minuscule attention among researchers in the social sciences. Our research and experiences working with clients in career counseling who do not fit into the typical calling-as-paid-employment box suggest that people who experience a calling outside of work fall into two main categories. The first consists of people who, for any number of reasons, either cannot work in a job that is their calling or do not perceive a calling to paid work, and choose instead to pursue a calling in another area of life. The second group comprises people like Paul who have a strong sense of calling within their careers, but who nevertheless continue searching for callings within other life roles, too.

Compensators and Those Called Elsewhere

Except for people who are independently wealthy and have no economic need for paid employment (wouldn't that be nice?), people have to work, and work takes a lot of time and energy. Part of the appeal of cultivating a calling in one's career is that work is typically a central life role, at least for those who are employed full-time (or wish to be). Yet many people have jobs that they did not choose and do not enjoy, that come with a lot of baggage, and that they do not see as an environment which would reward efforts to improve things through job crafting. For any number of reasons, they'd just rather not go there—yet they do not see changing jobs as a viable option, either. What then?

Some counselors describe the primary goal of career counseling as helping to equip a person with what she or he needs to build a satisfying and meaningful life, of which work is an important part. We've always liked this way of putting it, because it makes explicit the obvious: life is about more than work. Throughout this book, we've reviewed the benefits of a calling for people who experience it in their work: a sense of calling consistently links not only to career-related benefits, but also to an overall sense of well-being. If a calling offers a means of using one's gifts to build or express a sense of meaning for others' benefit, a calling need not be experienced *at work* to reap these benefits. On the contrary, the only requirement is that the calling be lived out somewhere. Sensing a calling within another life role—ideally a highly salient one—could do it just as well, and maybe even better than experiencing a calling in one's work. We might give some of those who take this approach the title of *compensators*, because although they don't view their job as a calling, they have a strategy of making up for it by cultivating a calling within one or more other important life roles. (Ironically for some, their work may still be important in facilitating their calling, in that it may provide the funds they need to invest in living it out. For example, a weekend woodcrafter may use the income from his shipping and receiving job to purchase the supplies needed to make high-quality toys for children.)

Not everyone who forgoes a calling at work to pursue one else-where does so as a compensation strategy, however. Some, such as many stay-at-home parents, opt not to work in a paid role at all, because they may feel called to focus almost exclusive attention on their callings as parents. Having a first child changes everything for parents, from sleep patterns (and amount) to entertainment options to what ultimately matters most in life, and the parent role goes from being an abstract future potentiality to a core life role, central to their identities. In virtually all cultures, especially (but not exclusively[6]) for women, it is not only accepted but assumed that parents will devote immense amounts of time, energy, and emotional investment into raising their children. The desire to make this investment comes easily for most parents, even if the effort itself is anything but easy. Consider this quote from a parent who was interviewed about her calling:

> For me it's a very constant top-of-mind thought process of putting my children first, of putting aside the things that frustrate me and that I want to do often in order to meet the needs that they have. And it's often mundane little things during the day. I'm tired but I need to get up, and I need to get up with a smile on my face so that the kids can have a nice morning, so that they can go to school and have a good day. Days like that are good days for me, because I know that despite the fact that I want to stay in bed and I'm probably cranky, I am choosing consciously to put that aside and show them a happy face.[7]

This parent illustrates the effects of a calling within any life domain, not just parenting. The focus of the calling is constantly on her mind, has an unmistakable motivating effect, and requires a personal sacrifice to live out—and she does so happily.

Of course, descriptions from interview-based studies such as these can only provide so much insight on a topic. At least as important is quantitative research that investigates questions such as this one: Does viewing one's parent role as a calling boost a person's well-being and effectiveness as a parent? Australian researchers Justin Coulson, Lindsay Oades, and Gerard Stoyles have initiated the study of parenthood as a calling, gathering data from over five hundred parents in an attempt to answer this question. Not surprisingly, in line with research on the effects of having a calling in one's work, approaching parenting as a calling is associated with greater happiness and meaning in life. The more that participants viewed their parental role as a calling, the more they gained pleasure from parenting, viewed it as important, and were satisfied in it, and the less they viewed it as a burden. Importantly, all of these relations were considered strong by statistical standards, meaning that viewing parenting as a calling was very closely related to these outcomes. Perhaps equally as intriguing was how approaching parenting as a calling related to the actual parenting styles that participants implemented with their children. Decades of parenting research have consistently shown that having an authoritative parenting style (warm, involved, good-natured, democratic, and high in love but also in setting limits) is more effective than an authoritarian (hostile, punitive, parent as drill-sergeant) or permissive (anything goes, ignoring bad behavior, parent as best buddy) style for all sorts of childhood outcomes, from academic performance to social development to good behavior.[8] Coulson and colleagues found that viewing the parent role as a calling was linked to the healthy, authoritative style. In other words, when parents approach the parent role as a calling, they tend to reap the same types of rewards as do those who think of their work as a calling (e.g., meaningfulness, satisfaction, enjoyment), but they also tend to be more effective parents.

Granted, anyone who has (or wants) children is probably not surprised that many parents approach the task as a calling, in which parenting is every bit as meaningful and valuable as a calling to one's work, and probably more so in most cases. But what about callings to other life roles outside of work or parenting, like organic farming, pottery, music, church involvement, political activism, and so on? What are people who perceive such callings like, and how do they live them out? The only study of which we are aware to explore what it means to have a calling outside of work or parenting was one that we mentioned in the previous chapter. Researchers Justin Berg, Adam Grant, and Victoria Johnson conducted in-depth interviews with thirty-one people about what callings look like when they aren't lived out at the workplace.[9] All thirty-one participants in the study were employed, and of this group, twenty-two were able to distinctly describe "additional callings." The activities targeted by these callings took many forms, including gardening, law, counseling, music, ministry, stand-up comedy, and photography. All twenty-two of these participants were currently employed in jobs that didn't align with their callings. They were compensators, using these callings outside of work to more effectively establish a sense of meaning and purpose in life as a whole.

As an example, Berg and his colleagues discussed Peggy, a lecturer at a university who felt unable to live out her calling to child psychology within her paid employment. As Peggy explained,

> For the last five years, I have been a volunteer at the Ronald McDonald House. It's the house where families stay when their children are sick and in the hospital. I think there is something to be said about consistency of interest and things you find fulfilling. This goes back well beyond the very fact that I was interested in children and illness. [It] goes back to an experience I had in high school working at a children's hospital in Philadelphia, working in their play therapy area, watching kids dealing with illness, and wanting to understand that better and make a difference in things like that. So that's been there for a long time, so it doesn't surprise me that even in my

volunteer work, I seek out something that also feeds that interest.[10]

Andy, another lecturer who sensed a calling that lay elsewhere, shared a similar point of view: "Part of the reason I am working as a lecturer," observed Andy, "is because I am trying to write a novel. So that pays no bills at the moment, but that, in my heart of hearts, is more important to me than the teaching. . . . If somebody said I had to stop writing, I would have no idea who I was, as a person."[11]

For both Peggy and Andy, their respective callings to work with children and to write novels had been long-standing. As compensators, both of them used their relatively flexible jobs as university lecturers to provide the time and financial means to pursue their callings outside of paid employment. Would Peggy and Andy be better off if they were able to live out their calling as paid workers? To the extent that doing so would provide more time to invest in their callings and a stronger sense of coherence and integration, perhaps. But countless people for countless reasons are unable to work in jobs that align with their callings, and find it very difficult to craft their jobs in a sufficiently transformative manner. Especially in such circumstances, pursuing callings within other important life roles provides a very critical pathway for using one's gifts meaningfully to serve the greater good.

Pursuers of Callings in and out of Paid Work

Some people, like Paul, pursue callings in and out of work. These folks are extremely passionate about life. Although they are generally satisfied with how they are using their gifts in service of others through their work, they constantly seek ways to do this more effectively, while striving to identify and live out callings in other spheres of life, too. Some may think of a calling as relevant in *every* life role they inhabit, from worker to spouse to parent to citizen.

How similar are these callings to each other? Do those who pursue multiple callings discern these callings in the same way, and do they approach each calling similarly? How does one find the energy to invest in multiple callings simultaneously without burning out?

Researchers are only beginning to investigate these kinds of questions. One multiple-callings scenario that researchers have studied occurs when women feel called within both their work and parent roles and endeavor to live out the callings simultaneously. For example, in one study, researchers interviewed eleven mothers employed within a religiously affiliated university setting while also raising young children.[12] When these working mothers talked about differences in the nature of their work and motherhood callings, one theme that emerged suggested that a calling to work developed early in life ("I knew probably [by] 7th or 8th grade that I wanted to teach"[13]), whereas the calling to motherhood often arrived after their children were born. Another difference rested in how they described their callings within each role. They used words like "drive," "passion," "longing," and "compelled" to describe work callings, and words like "opportunity" and "responsibility" to describe the calling to parenthood. One woman put it this way: "There was a definite, definite longing to be a doctor, to pursue that. There was not a definite longing to be a mom. It's just something that happened."[14]

How did these women balance their two callings? They were clear that it was often a struggle to stay invested and satisfied in both callings at once, given the magnitude of the demands of each calling. To translate the dynamics of this struggle, imagine that your time and energy must be split approximately fifty-fifty between your work and home duties. Most of the dually called women in this study described feeling most satisfied with how they lived out each calling when they allotted about 75 percent of their time and energy to that calling. Unfortunately we only have 100 percent to work with, and during times when that 75 percent is invested in one calling, the other calling inevitably seems neglected. For the working mothers in this study, nourishing both callings required sacrifices in other areas of life (e.g., less sleep, less exercise) or, for a very fortunate few, a large and extended support network at home and work.

In another, larger study that also focused on Christian mothers called to academia,[15] one participant outlined her experience this way: "For me, I feel like I have two callings [teaching and mothering]. I'm committed to both of those and everything else just falls by the wayside."[16] Themes that emerged from the interviews in this study supported those described above, but also raised a very important additional point: the notion that a calling can be a collective experience. "You're not called to live life alone," said one woman, "[and] you can't work out your calling alone."[17] Callings occur in the context of relationships, and living out a calling inevitably requires understanding and support from others. Another participant explained how this reality played out in her family:

> It's just a sense in the whole family that I have a calling and it's more than just my ambition; it's more than just my thing. And so I think the family, including my daughter, sort of have a sense that it's their responsibility to make it work for me, just as it's my responsibility to make their calling possible for them. So, I think that maybe underlying this whole thing of cooperation among us, in the whole sense of we're in this together, is the idea that this is really God's plan for us.[18]

The interview data from these two studies points to the conclusion that balancing multiple callings can be very enriching, but also is, to say the least, a challenge. More than likely, maintaining multiple callings requires consistent investment that is intermittently distributed across those callings. Think of it as not unlike the plate-spinning act at the circus, in which the performer spins plates and bowls on top of poles quickly, the force generated by their spin preventing them from falling to the floor. The performer shifts constantly from one plate to the next, each time respinning the plate to keep its rotation speed what it needs to be to prevent it from crashing to the ground. Performers who can do this well deserve the applause they earn, because the task looks as exhausting as it is impressive. The same can be said for maintaining multiple callings—doing so well requires a high level of investment, careful planning and prioritizing, and considerable support from others, but when it is done effectively, the benefits to self and others are immense.

Strategies for Living Out Callings beyond Work

People often sense a calling in ways that transcend a particular life role. For example, Paul perceived a calling to leverage his passion for organic gardening into a full-blown farm, a meaningful pursuit which he uses to grow healthy food that provides nourishment for his family and others. This calling could be pursued as a full-time job, and there likely are weeks in which Paul invests close to that level of time and effort into the farm. Yet at the time we interviewed him, Paul had no plans to give up his roles as professor, administrator, and consultant, secondary though they felt at the time. Consciously or subconsciously, he had prioritized his callings based on his values, and although the farm felt primary, there was far less risk in raising crops as a side effort than in giving up his primary income to pursue it. Furthermore, he viewed his day job as still very much a calling, and he was not willing to give that up. Balancing callings in and out of work requires this kind of internal negotiation. Pursuing callings outside of paid work has its own challenges, whether a person also feels called within work or not, because most nonwork domains lack the structure and external supports that work provides. What does this mean for someone trying to effectively pursue callings outside of work or balance multiple callings? If this question applies to you, these three strategies can help you navigate this sometimes rough terrain.

1. Differentiate core and peripheral callings. Some people sense multiple callings, sometimes several, occupying multiple life roles. They are often in a bind, for the reasons we explored above: people simply do not have enough time and energy available to consistently satisfy what each calling requires. To address this issue, revisit the notion of life roles we explored in chapter 6, only replace "roles" with "callings." At any given point in time, a person may have core callings and peripheral callings; the core callings are central, demand considerable time and energy, and occupy the front burners, while peripheral callings are, usually by necessity, relegated to the pantry. A person may still value the peripheral callings, but because the core callings are valued much more, the peripheral callings get short shrift. One thing that can help a person tolerate this scenario is understanding that the relative importance of a particular calling will probably change; callings that are core now will not necessarily remain core, and as things shift over time, peripheral callings may have a chance to come to the fore. You may well experience parenting as a calling for the rest of your life, and early on the parenting role requires inordinate amounts of time and energy. But as children grow up and become more independent, this calling demands less of both and may eventually move to the periphery, as empty nesters discover. As a result, a secondary calling may become primary in the future.

Bryan's constellation of callings is an example of this. He maintains a sense of calling within his roles as parent, spouse, and worker, the three most dominant roles in his life right now. He currently invests very little time in leisure pursuits—not because he has few interests, but because other callings are primary. Lurking on the periphery, however, is a latent passion for art; at one time

Bryan considered choosing art as his major in college, and he craves opportunities to learn new ways to create things, try them out, and give the products of those efforts (the worthwhile ones, anyway) away to people who might enjoy them. Occasionally, opportunities to engage in this calling do arise. For example, twice in the last ten years, Bryan learned that one of his grandmothers was dying of cancer. In each case, the calling to his work suddenly felt much less primary, so he took some time off and invested the thirty to fifty hours needed to create portraits of his grandparents. Doing this helped Bryan cope with his sorrow, giving him time to reflect on their lives and legacies, and the portraits brought an added measure of joy to each of his grandmothers during their final months and weeks. Nevertheless, when the portraits were completed, creating art went back to the periphery, where it remains—but only for now.

If you sense multiple callings, take inventory. Which are your core callings right now, and which are better shelved for the time being, until your roles reorganize in the future? Strive to invest your time and energy in ways that align with your values; clarifying your core and peripheral callings helps you identify, in a systematic way, how you can best accomplish this.

2. Plan and protect time for core nonwork callings. There are some advantages to living out a calling in the work role that many callings outside of work do not enjoy. Work-related callings usually are highly structured. On a workday, most people wear a specific type of clothing, maybe a literal uniform or maybe an attempt to conform to the dress code expected by their profession. Often, simply putting on this clothing has a focusing effect, psychologically preparing the person wearing it for work. On the way to work, people tend to transition their minds from home life to work life. While at work, people map out a set of goals and tasks (or someone else maps them out for them), and spend focused effort striving to meet these goals and carry out these tasks. Informal and formal external rewards are earned for doing work well. There is an expected routine, a rhythm; you know when you need to be engaged in work, and for how long. Living out a calling in this context seems easy; just jump in the stream of your day-to-day work life and know that for some number of hours every week you will be engaged in your calling.

Some nonwork callings have a built-in structure and rhythm of their own; parenting is one. But many do not. On the one hand, this lack of structure can be a blessing; theoretically, it gives you the freedom to pursue your callings on your own terms. On the other, when you aren't getting paid and no employer is tracking whether you complete tasks, or when you don't have a toddler at the side of your bed begging you for breakfast at 6:00 a.m., the onus may be solely on you to fan your calling's flame, which can be a problem. The concern lies not in your motivation to cultivate your calling but in the fact that schedules abhor a vacuum; almost inexplicably, time you think you have to devote to whatever your nonwork calling may be—playing music, perhaps—somehow evaporates. To reap the benefits of living out a calling, however, the opportunities to engage in it must be frequent and regular. The best way to make this happen is to schedule an appropriate block of time and guard it, just like you might do with your job. (See also Q&A 7.) Without imposing this kind of structure, life is likely to get in the way more often than not. Is it better to experience a calling and not be able to live it out, or to have no calling at all? You won't need to think about this question if you plan and protect the time you need to live it out consistently.

3. Invest in what makes your calling a calling. Regardless of whether you experience a calling in work, nonwork, or both, a calling is a transcendent summons to engage a particular life role in a way that helps others and aligns with a sense of personal meaning. Living out a calling means striving to meet the larger goal of using your gifts in ways that promote a sense of purpose and enhance the common good; this is true for callings within any life role, yet accomplishing this goal in some nonwork callings can be challenging.

As we discussed in chapter 5, the workplace provides an obvious setting in which, for most people, opportunities to serve others abound. With a calling to the parent role, the focus of one's efforts to help others is obvious. But consider, say, an accountant who experiences a calling to play music. Without the structured interactions with others that pursuing music as a career provides, it may be easiest for the accountant to spend a few hours a week writing and playing music at home, in solitude. This approach would probably work, but not indefinitely; if his motive to play music is embedded in a sense of calling, as opposed to being a strong leisure interest or simply a fun way to unwind, he will likely sense something missing. A calling in the neoclassical sense requires more than using one's gifts solely for one's own gratification; rather, a calling connects the use of gifts with the benefit of others, an intersection that results in a more deeply rewarding type of gratification.

For this reason, remember to continually return your calling to its roots by using it as a pathway for connecting your gifts with others' needs. Bring your calling into contact with other people and environments. The accountant with a calling to play music can lead others in song, even if those others constitute only his family. He can volunteer to teach guitar to a kid who wants to learn. Meaningfulness arises in such interactions. As you would do with a calling to paid work, engage in ongoing evaluation of your nonwork calling to ensure that it aligns consistently with your broader sense of purpose in life. Paul's exuberance about his organic farm is a product of the meaning he derives from it, because the farm provides a means of using his gifts and satisfying his passion in ways that help families in his community who enjoy his homegrown produce. Centering your calling around strengths and service is an ideal way to foster meaning and purpose within any domain of life.

Along with the crafting strategies we presented in chapter 7, nonwork callings represent another route to experiencing the joy of a calling if doing so in the workplace is, for whatever reason, undesirable or impossible. Many people are in that situation, especially those with few privileges in their work lives. Throughout history and within the body of research on this topic, callings have usually been tied to paid work experiences, yet they certainly have not been relegated only to work. Callings outside of work allow you to express your gifts in service of others meaningfully, without the oversight that comes in a typical job. If you have a calling that cannot be pursued through work, embrace it, invest in it, cultivate it, and enjoy the benefits.

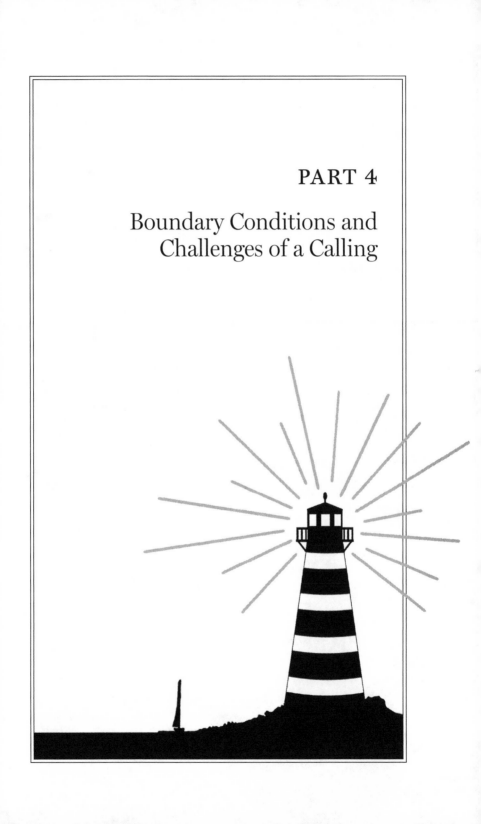

PART 4

Boundary Conditions and Challenges of a Calling

9 Perils and Pitfalls

"FIVE YEARS AGO, Josh gave up being a kid to play the trumpet." Hillary Frank said this about her own brother in a story she filed in 2000 for the radio show *This American Life*.[1] Josh was the most committed, focused, probably obsessed seventeen-year-old trumpet player imaginable. The son of two artists (one a photographer, the other a painter) living in New York, Josh had grown up on music. His mother used to sit Josh at the piano and put a timer on for thirty minutes, but it was torture getting him to sit for that long. Then something happened: he picked up a trumpet and went from a hyperactive, Rollerblading, beachgoing eighth grader to a trumpet-playing automaton, practicing five hours per weekday and fifteen hours (!) in Juilliard's precollege program each Saturday. Most kids need parents to remind them to practice. Josh's parents had to tell him to stop; they wanted to go to bed at midnight and avoid getting calls from neighbors about the noise. Hillary, perplexed at the power this one brass instrument seemed to have over Josh, tried to get him to explain it. He couldn't.

"I can't explain it," Josh said. "It's just, it was right. It was just meant to happen." Malcolm Gladwell somewhat famously reported in *Outliers*[2] that to become truly successful in something, it takes around ten thousand hours of practice. At seventeen, there was little doubt that Josh would surpass this benchmark easily. His passion and enthusiasm for the trumpet were palpable, he became very good at it, and it defined his life.

Josh's obsession with his trumpet, however, had a rather significant downside. "It wasn't until junior year that we just never saw anything of each other," said Eric, one of Josh's old friends from school. "And then this year, I don't know. I meant to call him at the . . . end of summer, and I just never got around to it. And then I think we might have talked once or twice. Oh yeah, we played Frisbee at the beach a couple times. But then school started, Juilliard started, and Josh gets a little consumed. It's a relationship riddled with formalities, and there's really little substance left." Hillary interviewed several of Josh's friends for the story. They spoke in measured tones and noted that the "social Josh" to whom they were once accustomed had transformed into someone distant and removed. It wasn't only the big events that Josh missed, it was the few extra hours each day he spent practicing his trumpet instead of socializing that added up over time. His deteriorating social life was not lost on Josh. "The thing I most dread is lunch, because I have to figure out what I'm going to do with that half hour. . . . And it's really painful. So the way I deal with it is to get into music more. Like maybe I'll practice during lunch. Instead of eating, I'll eat when I get home." The tone of the story became downright sad. It was not as though Josh started assertively pushing his relationships away. Rather, the incredible amount of time it took for Josh to achieve the musical acumen he desired left little space for anyone else in his life. Josh gave up more than being a kid to play the trumpet; he gave up all his friends.

Sometimes, pursuing a calling—with all the passion, excitement, meaning, and pleasure it brings—can have serious consequences. The fuel that feeds a person's passion for work can at the same time be poison to other life roles. This is true when a calling drifts into job idolization and workaholism. We explore these two distortions of a healthy role for work in this chapter, along with two vulnerabilities that can emerge when pursuing a calling: a blindness to useful feedback that might threaten one's aspirations and possible exploitation from opportunistic employers. Finally, we discuss the rare but real possibility of a calling serving as rationale for causing intentional harm. Although a calling can come with perils and pitfalls, there are ways to guard against them. We describe these, too.

Distortions of Calling

Approaching work as a calling differs considerably from other approaches to understanding work. In chapter 2, we described how some people view work as a job, merely a means to make a living. For them, work is worth only the time and energy required to meet that goal. Others view work as a career, providing a path to pursue power, prestige, and wealth. They derive considerable self-worth from what they achieve and accomplish at work. Those with a calling stand in contrast to these two groups, in that they view work in light of a transcendent summons to approach their job in a way that generates positive meaning and expresses purpose, using their gifts to make the world a better place.

Although many people think of these groups as three distinct types, research actually suggests that the job and calling orientations exist on opposite ends of a shared continuum, but that the career orientation occupies a relatively independent dimension.[3] Thus, a person can cross those two dimensions (i.e., the job-calling dimension and high-low career dimension) and create four quadrants, representing four groups of people:

1. Job, low career types
2. Job, high career types
3. Calling, low career types
4. Calling, high career types

The third group represents a "pure" calling orientation, in which a person pursues work as a calling without getting swept up in the trappings of career orientation. The fourth group is more complicated. Some people within this quadrant may pursue their calling while also finding a motivation to achieve, advance, and earn accolades as useful in promoting the broader goals that their calling supports. Others, however, may tie their calling to more self-oriented goals and motives that can typify the career orientation. Taking this approach risks distorting and ultimately undermining what it means to approach work as a calling. If left unfettered, two closely linked syndromes can result, both representing distorted callings: job idolization and workaholism. We explore each of these in turn, then suggest strategies for people with callings to avoid drifting into these distortions.

Job Idolization

In Cameron Crowe's award-winning film *Almost Famous*, set in 1973, a high school student falls into his dream job of traveling with the (fictitious) band Stillwater[4] to write a story for *Rolling Stone*. During one scene, the band attends a raucous teenage house party. After consuming a freakish amount of alcohol and drugs, the lead singer of the band, Russel, climbs onto the roof of the house to jump into a swimming pool below. Both encouraged and hesitant, Russel stands there for a while, shouting to the crowd below, trying to determine his "last words." At some point, pride overcomes reason, and he makes the leap after yelling numerous times, "I am a golden god!"

The film does not provide many insights about Russel's work orientation, but given his obvious drive for success paired with hints of a prosocial idealism, he might occupy the calling, high-career quadrant. At the moment he leaped off the roof and into the pool, the singer indeed felt he had reached "golden god" status. He had worked hard at his craft and had achieved a high and still-rising level of success. People knew who he was and worshiped him for his work. He had groupies! What also came along with this, fortunately and unfortunately, was a great degree of acclaim and prestige. When Russel, who expressed such a hunger for recognition and success, actually began to achieve it, it was difficult for him to avoid developing a god complex along the lines of that hinted by the Renaissance philosophers we noted in chapter 2. Granted, the drugs probably had much to do with his "golden god" proclamation, but nevertheless, when work becomes the pathway to achieving a godlike status, the work itself becomes an idol.

Job idolization simply refers to viewing one's work as being of ultimate importance in the context of life, far greater in importance than any other life role, and far greater than is healthy or than it ought to be. Job idolization occurs when one's work becomes so important that other roles and responsibilities are neglected, or even abandoned. Remember the English stockbroker from *The Moon and Sixpence* we described in chapter 3, who ran away from his family and career to pursue his passion for painting? As we noted, the neoclassical view of calling, with its emphasis on duty and prosocial values, requires that a calling complement, not compete with, one's other roles and responsibilities in life. No empirical research on job idolization per se exists, although a large body of research suggests that a balance of work and nonwork roles predicts greater health and well-being.[5] Job idolization also is reflected in workaholism, a topic of a considerable amount of research, as we review next.

Workaholism

Workaholism is, most simply, an addiction to work. Technically, workaholics are defined as people who enjoy working, who are obsessed with working, and who devote long hours and personal time to work. Workaholism develops much like any addiction. Early on in the process, working makes you feel pretty good; it might give you a sense of mastery and competence, satisfy a need for achievement or power, or provide a sense of excitement or absorption. Over time, you might find yourself needing to work more to experience those same feelings. At some point, work becomes less about feeling good and more about avoiding the bad feelings you get from not doing it—maybe guilt, a fixation on opportunity costs, or a physical feeling of stress. This pattern is similar to that displayed by people who smoke cigarettes not for pleasure but to avoid nicotine withdrawal. As with any addiction, negative consequences—sometimes serious ones, for you and for those around you—are often close at hand.

Workaholism is a bit more complex than many physical addictions, however, because it can seem like a mixed bag, with both positive and negative effects on a person's life. Employers usually love having workaholics on the payroll, for obvious reasons. Workaholics are never afraid to take on big projects. They commit to doing whatever it takes to get the job done well. They create an environment in which other employees often feel like they also have to work hard and make sacrifices, to avoid looking bad in comparison. Workaholics often require big raises to retain, though, and the intensity of some can occasionally create interpersonal strain, but many employers find these trade-offs easy to tolerate. As a result, workaholics are often well respected at work, well compensated, and first in line for promotions. Workaholics usually enjoy the work tasks they are doing a great deal. However, they also think about their work obsessively, from the time they wake up to the moment their heads hit their pillows. They usually work obscenely long hours, which inevitably compromises their relationships, and their foreheads tighten with stress when they are prevented from working not only by frustrating inconveniences but even by family events and vacations.

What types of people are prone to workaholism? Researchers Thomas Ng, Kelly Sorensen, and Daniel Feldman offer six propositions to summarize what research suggests about workaholics and workaholism.[6]

First, *workaholics tend to have lower self-esteem than most people* and deal with this problem by focusing their time and energy in one of the (probably) only areas of life they view as positive: their career. In this straightforward compensation strategy, their inordinate investment in work increases the likelihood of positive feedback and rewards on the job, while simultaneously shifting their attention away from areas of life that may be going poorly. Second, *workaholics are usually extremely achievement oriented.* They intensely crave success and have identified work as one role in life with relatively clear rules for evaluating and achieving success. Of course, success at work doesn't come easily; it requires effort, and the more a person values success, the more effort that person is generally willing to devote to it. If the level of value and commitment to success escalate unabated, without sufficient commitments in other areas of life to serve as a counterbalance, addiction to work is a natural consequence.

Third, Ng and colleagues proposed that like most addictions, *workaholism can be impacted by a dysfunctional family environment* that enables a person to devote excessive amounts of time and energy to work.[7] Think back for a moment to your childhood. How would you describe the atmosphere? The ideal environment is stable and loving, but for those who experience chaos, neglect, and arbitrary punishment growing up, beginning work early in life may provide an easy, socially acceptable way to get out of the house and spend time in an environment that is predictable, supportive, and rewarding. Work could easily be addicting if it provides an adolescent in still-formative stages of development with all of the positives that home does not offer. Even if a person grows up in a context of stability, some families communicate messages in words or deeds that reinforce an unhealthy level of commitment to work. Many parents express a goal of wanting to instill the value of hard work, but some do so to the extreme. We remember classmates in school who grew up in environments that could only be described as stable, but for whom stability meant having at least one parent always absent, working seventy hours a week (and often more). They were very well off, lived in the nicest homes of any of our friends, rode in the best cars, wore the best clothes, and played with the best toys. The relational trade-offs stemming from the parental neglect that accompanies this type of stability are obvious, though, and may lay the groundwork for workaholism later in life.

The remaining three propositions involve particular types of experiences in the workplace itself. Ng and colleagues suggest that people are more likely to drift toward workaholism if they *work in environments in which workaholism is common, or that reward workaholic behaviors.* People also are more likely to become workaholics when they *work in highly competitive environments,* especially where employees must compete for limited resources in a zero-sum game. Consider a car salesperson whose earnings are based off commission, just like the other ten people working alongside him. Putting more time and energy into his work has a direct link to his earnings and his chances for advancement to a managerial role. Such environments also frequently include extra incentives—a free car detailing, a high-definition television, or a cash bonus, for example—dangled by management to even further amp up the motivation to invest in getting results. In such an environment, the pull to work harder and longer can be intoxicating, a term that often shows up in the same sentence as "addiction."

Finally, similar to the issue with self-esteem, *workaholism is more likely to arise among people who have a sizable confidence gap when they are engaged in work activities compared to non-work activities.* Our natural human tendency is to devote time and energy to activities at which we excel. When this tendency is taken to the extreme at work, workaholism can result.

By way of summary, complete the following checklist of workaholism risk factors:

_____ Do you have low self-esteem?

_____ Do you have a high need for achievement?

_____ Did you grow up in a family that was unstable, or that modeled an addiction to work?

_____ Do you work in an environment where workaholism is rewarded?

_____ Do you work in a highly competitive environment?

_____ Are you more confident in your work life than other areas of your life?

These questions are designed to assess the degree of risk you have for developing workaholism, based on the number of risk factors you possess. Answering "no" to all of these questions does not mean you will never be a workaholic, in the same way that answering "yes" to all of them does not mean you certainly are one, or are doomed to become one. Yet the higher the number between 0 and 6, the greater the possible risk. If you replied "yes" to any of these questions, we encourage you to reflect on the role that this factor currently plays in your life and how it may influence the way you approach your work.

Of course, being addicted to work not only has causes, but also consequences, as Ng and his colleagues point out.[8] On the positive side, research suggests that workaholism is related to stronger feelings of satisfaction with work, and also is associated with greater performance and success at work, at least in the short term. The satisfaction probably helps feed the workaholism, and the high degree of performance and success is, understandably, what employers like. On the negative side, workaholism is associated with diminished mental and physical health, as well as relationship problems both in and out of work. When people are obsessed with their jobs, they think about their work constantly, which can leave them feeling stressed most every waking hour of the day. Workaholics also have less time available for leisure or exercise, two activities that are known to provide a boost to mental and physical health. When workaholics chronically neglect such areas of self-care, while also working to the point of exhaustion, it becomes easy to see why their health suffers.

It is no mystery why their relationships are poor, either. On the job, workaholics often find it difficult to trust or respect their co-workers, either because they are competing with them for resources, or because they see their co-workers' level of commitment to work as failing to measure up to their own. This kind of distrust and disrespect is most likely reciprocated by their co-workers, and understandably so. Über-go-getters can be über-annoying at work, and if they appear to think of themselves as better than you, avoiding resentment can be quite difficult. And relationships outside of work? Workaholics are physically absent from their families and friends much of the time, because of the hours they put in at work. In those moments when they are around, they often are mulling over some work-related issue and therefore are often psychologically absent. It is next to impossible for workaholics to avoid experiencing work-family conflict, for reasons of simple arithmetic: there are a finite number of hours in a day, and the more time spent working or obsessing about work, the less that is left for investing in friends and family. Overall, the toll of work addiction on a workaholic's mental and physical health, work relationships, and family life has resulted in a fairly widespread consensus: although workaholism has its upside (in terms of the high levels of satisfaction and performance) in the short term, the negatives far outweigh the positives, especially over the long haul.

Protecting against the Drift into Distortion

People who sense a calling within their work role can be vulnerable to experiencing job idolization and workaholism for a number of reasons. They usually have a strong sense of passion for their work, attribute considerable value and importance to it, and often feel good about themselves when they are carrying it out; all of these are usually very adaptive and desirable characteristics, but all of them can also feed idolization and workaholism. Indeed, for a workaholic, a sense of calling might in some ways be the ultimate drug. It imbues work with meaning and importance. It involves a focus on enhancing the greater good, which carries personal benefits with it. But even more, to the extent that the calling in question is viewed by self or others as admirable and of great moral value, it can serve as a very deep reservoir of rationalization. A workaholic can become convinced, and sometimes convince others, that the outrageous and unhealthy level of investment devoted to work is understandable, even praiseworthy, given the societal value of what they are trying to accomplish. In this way, calling and workaholism can become dangerously linked.

What can a person do to prevent the gradual drift from having a calling to idolizing their work and becoming addicted to it? Arguably the best approach is a positive and proactive one; instead of focusing on a negatively stated mantra like "Just don't let it happen," actively strive for a balance of work with other life roles. In chapter 8 we reviewed research that focused on the experiences of mothers dually called to a demanding career and to motherhood. Some discussed their calling as a family project, with children and spouses actively cooperating to support their callings, with the understanding that they will reciprocate the same level of support in return. To ensure that this system of mutual support works, maintain open channels of communication, keeping your family and friends informed about what is happening in the work to which you are called. Keeping in contact helps them provide much-needed encouragement for you in times of struggle, but also keeps you accountable and in check when your work begins to border on becoming overly consuming and encompassing. Actively striving for balance also means investing in important nonwork activities. This might mean scheduling dedicated time to invest in relationships, such as a biweekly date night with your spouse, one of your children, or a friend; setting aside time for self-care activities, such as exercise or leisure; deepening your spiritual life; and building in time for the equivalent of one full day per week—a Sabbath—to decompress, rest, recharge, and refocus on what ultimately matters. Such an approach encourages and reinforces balance, provides opportunities for cultivating callings in life roles other than work, and keeps you energized and refreshed.

A second recommendation is to strive to keep your work in proper perspective. In his biography on Steve Jobs, author Walter Isaacson paints the portrait of a man who left his fingerprints on an expansive spectrum of the human experience, from computers to music to movies to phones.[9] Consider that the same person who developed Apple computers also spearheaded the studio that brought to the market films like *Toy Story*, *Cars*, and *Brave*. Jobs was a prime candidate for job idolization, and in his early years running Apple, his displays of workaholism, ego, and dictatorial rule were legendary. Over time, however, his nastier interpersonal tendencies mellowed, in part because Jobs developed a more holistic view on life. He married, had children, embraced Buddhist teachings, and focused more on using his wealth and power to serve others.

Despite his enormous level of accomplishment and acclaim, Jobs found a way to avoid the kind of career tunnel vision that is symptomatic of job idolization. Instead of using a self-focused perspective targeting only projects designed to milk the most money from the market, or designing better gadgets principally to further boost his ego, he increasingly viewed his job as about something much greater than just one person. We recommend that you follow Jobs's lead and engage in a continual examination of how your calling is positioned within the constellation of your own life roles, as well as how you are using your calling to help others. Health and well-being are most enhanced when one's work, whether a calling or not, is not an all-consuming endeavor but plays a complementary role in life as a whole, supporting one's relationships and other nonwork roles in life. If your relationships and passions outside of work have suffered because of the time and energy you have funneled into your calling, reevaluate the role that work plays in your life and the extent to which your work is tied to your feelings of self-worth. A calling helps promote a strong sense of identity, but when too much of one's identity is wrapped up in one's calling, job idolization and workaholism may be just around the corner.

Finally—and this point may be obvious—job idolization ultimately undermines a calling's focus on the common good and well-being of others. Idolization necessarily involves a perspective on work in which the work becomes an end in itself (e.g., the belief that nothing is more important than work) rather than the means to improving some aspect of the common good or societal well-being. In contrast, a more other-oriented perspective, integral to the very nature of a calling, is essential for ensuring that one's work retains a healthier role in the context of life. It reinforces the reality that no matter how much a person can accomplish in a job, the needs of others will never be fully met. Ask yourself, *How does the work I do improve other people's lives?* If that answer is not at the tip of your tongue, challenge yourself to think bigger and more broadly about how you can use your gifts in service of others.

Vulnerabilities of Calling

As far as we can tell, no scholar of work behavior understands the world of teenage trumpeter Josh Frank better than Shasa Dobrow, a management professor at Fordham University in New York. She moonlights as a professional bassoonist, currently a member of the Rhode Island Philharmonic who has played with orchestras on Broadway and Carnegie Hall. Some of Dobrow's research has focused on the travails of aspiring musicians, especially those who feel called to their careers. Although Dobrow's definition of calling differs from ours, aligning closer to the "modern" view (i.e., "as a consuming, meaningful passion people experience toward a domain"[10]), it shines light on one potential vulnerability that a sense of calling may evoke: a tendency to ignore good career advice that conflicts with or threatens the calling.

Earning a living can be challenging for even the best classical musicians, given the broader culture's seemingly increasing ambivalence toward classical music. But what about those musicians who are not among the best? New York's three main music conservatories grant degrees to around 500 students per year, a big chunk of the approximately 3,000 graduates in the United States who are added every year to the market of those job seekers hoping to play their instrument in a professional orchestra. Yet only around 150 such jobs become available every year.[11] These odds obviously are not good. In one recent study of 450 elite high school musicians, Dobrow and Jennifer Tosti-Kharas, inspired by the question of whether anyone tells these students not to embark on such a risky career path, examined the extent to which students agreed with the item "If my private music teacher discouraged me from becoming a professional musician, I would follow his/her advice and do something else." They found that students with a very strong sense of calling were more likely than other students to *ignore* the advice of their trusted mentors, not only at the beginning of the study, but even seven years later! The researchers interpreted this finding to suggest that a strong sense of calling, despite all its benefits, may also be associated with inflexible goals and a kind of career tunnel vision.

Although passionate persistence in a particular path can be admirable and inspiring, the pragmatists in us also point out that for many people, just based on sheer arithmetic, such persistence ultimately comes with significant costs. Imagine putting in a Josh Frank–like effort for years, only to come up dry repeatedly when it comes to finding gainful employment. Our response to anyone in this situation is to follow Dobrow and Tosti-Kharas's recommendation of adopting a learning orientation to feedback. Those with a learning orientation hunger for even negative feedback from people whose opinions they trust and value, because they accept such feedback as helpful information they can use to inform the further development and exploration of their gifts and to identify the paths that are particularly promising. This kind of open-minded self-awareness is a very useful attribute to cultivate (see chapter 10), and is at least in theory encouraged by a neoclassical view of calling, with its emphasis on continual, ongoing evaluation of whether one's career path is optimally in alignment with one's gifts and purpose, in service of others. This vulnerability may therefore be especially pronounced among those who look internally rather than externally for the source of their calling, to the extent that a "consuming, meaningful passion" that arises from within may slap blinders on a person, preventing serious attention to evidence that may question the direction of that passion.

To consider another key vulnerability that a sense of calling may create, imagine a zookeeper with a strong sense of calling. Let's call him Rich. Rich, like most zookeepers, has a college degree, but makes very low wages, with a salary below $30,000, in the lowest 25 percent of occupations in the United States. He does get some attention for working so closely with rare animals that usually are found in the African savanna, but much of his job is just plain disgusting—cleaning up elephant feces and scrubbing down cinder block–walled enclosures saturated with very pungent, unpleasant odors, for example. Nevertheless, Rich volunteered at the zoo for nearly eighteen months before finally being offered a paid position and is on record as saying that nothing could possibly make him quit his job there. Why? Because working with animals is simply in his blood. He has wanted to care for animals in one way or another for as long as he can remember, and the zoo always felt like his favorite place in the world. He senses that he was destined to work as a zookeeper, simply drawn to the profession in a way that seems difficult for him to adequately describe. Zookeeping is clearly his calling. Rich identifies very deeply with it, finds it immensely meaningful, and extremely important. Some of the high points of his adult life have been when the animals he cares for have given birth, and few things please him more than hearing children visiting from nearby schools "ooh" and "ahh" at the baby animals.

Although Rich's work brings him immense joy, there are a few downsides, even beyond the low pay and uncomfortable conditions. Sometimes Rich feels burdened by the weight of what he sees as a moral duty to provide the best care possible for his animals. Sometimes, in order to meet his own standards for that level of care, he devotes some of his personal, off-the-clock time to ensuring that things happen as they should. But more than that, Rich hasn't received a raise in four years, despite reading about how the zoo has obtained several new endowments and grants, coupled with record attendance. One of his fellow zookeepers, not the most reliable of employees, complained loudly about pay and saw a raise a month later. Yet when Rich inquired about his salary, he was told that funds were tight but that if all goes well, he would probably see a raise within the next year or so. Rich is aware he is vulnerable. "They know I love this so much I'd do it no matter what, even if they stopped paying me. Why would I be a priority for a raise when that's the case?"

The problem with this, of course, is that the very same calling-driven attitudes that make Rich the absolute model employee also make him a sitting duck for exploitation on the part of his employer.

His managers probably appreciate Rich, but when it comes down to making decisions about where the money goes, they obviously decide they don't appreciate him enough to reward him, especially when he's already working so hard in the absence of such extra rewards. Sometimes only the squeaky wheel gets the grease, and they calculated (correctly) that Rich would work just as hard and be just as likely to stick around without a pay raise than with one. And if a particularly dirty job needed to be done at the zoo, who do you think they ask to do it—the coworker who would complain incessantly (if he didn't refuse outright), or duty-driven Rich?

Stu Bunderson and Jeff Thompson call Rich's predicament the "double-edged sword" of calling.[12] Rich is prototypic of the zookeepers they interviewed in a recent study. Although Bunderson and Thompson didn't set out to investigate work as a calling, participants in their sample of zookeepers mentioned having a calling so much that it became the most frequently coded category found in the interview data. In response, they formulated a more in-depth follow-up study specifically devoted to understanding how zookeepers approach their work as a calling. The results indicated that whereas calling on the one hand led to a strong sense of identification, meaning, and purpose in the work, on the other hand it also came with a burdening sense of moral duty, personal sacrifice, and the kind of vulnerability to exploitation Rich experienced from his employer. Bunderson and Thompson interpreted the double-edged sword as a logical consequence of the sense of duty that comes from a calling: "A neoclassical calling cannot inspire profound meaning without simultaneously requiring profound sacrifice."[13]

Even if vulnerability to exploitation is a logical consequence of pursuing a calling, exploitation is still unacceptable. We strongly urge anyone who resonates with Rich's experience to maintain a firm commitment to boundaries of fairness in such circumstances, which requires wisdom, assertiveness, and perhaps savvy. Some zookeepers in Bunderson and Thompson's study, for example, consciously masked their level of commitment from their employers. "I would not tell them [how committed I am]," one said, "because they can get a strong hold on you that way. If management knows you love your job, they'll try to do things to undercut your pay and stuff like that."[14] Candid discussions about fairness, equity, and legality with a human resources representative, or even an attorney, represent another option that people in such circumstances should not readily dismiss.

Destroying Calling

Workaholism and job idolization are potential outcomes when a person becomes overwhelmingly invested in the work to which she or he senses a calling. Ignoring helpful feedback and attracting exploitative practices from an employer are harmful outcomes that sometimes accompany a calling, too. All of these problems and pitfalls of calling result, on balance, in negative outcomes for the individual worker, for that person's immediate circles of family and friends, and maybe for others. These kinds of negative outcomes, however, pale in comparison to the rare cases in which people may intentionally use what they describe as a sense of calling to advertently hurt others, or far worse. For example, in his book *Vocation: Discerning Our Callings in Life*, Douglas Schuurman describes how the 9/11 hijackers prepared for their acts of terrorism by engaging in a season of prayer; as far as they were concerned, their actions were sanctioned by Allah, and they were obediently carrying out his will. Schuurman also quotes John de Grunchy's account of another tragedy:

> On May 25, 1989, a 23-year-old white Afrikaner, Barend Strydom, was found guilty of murdering eight black people and was sentenced to death by the Supreme Court in Pretoria. Strydom killed all but one of his victims one

morning in downtown Pretoria, shooting them in cold blood . . . . Strydom's father, an elder in the Nederduitse Hervormede Kirk, testified that his son was a devout Christian who had himself told the court that, before he went on his killing spree, he had spent three days and nights meditating and praying to ensure he was doing God's will.[15]

Strydom clearly felt called to do what he apparently perceived to be God's will. When we speak to others about how calling is defined, cynics commonly suggest examples of well-known people who superficially appear to meet the criteria for working with a sense of calling, but who have engaged in egregiously hideous, immoral, unjustifiable, and destructive acts. Hitler is their favorite example. Did Hitler have a calling? The examples need not be so extreme to make the point, of course; some people may hypothetically describe themselves as having a calling to lobby for the tobacco industry or manufacture cigarettes, or to produce pornographic films. John Calvin identified special cases like this centuries ago, when he spoke out against those who claimed a calling to work as pimps, thieves, and adulterers.[16] In all of these cases, one obvious piece to having a calling is missing: contributing to the well-being of others, to the greater good. A calling is not a calling, at least not in the neoclassical sense, if it is disconnected from the common good or well-being of others.

We recognize, of course, that things quickly get complicated when we evaluate callings on the basis of their prosocial contributions. In his diabolical worldview, didn't Hitler think that his policies were designed to advance the common good? A good hard-and-fast rule could be that a calling can in no way advocate for the murder of innocent people. Even this is not always so straightforward; what do we say to the many brave, selfless women and men who feel called to protect U.S. freedom by serving in the military?

If they wind up deployed to a war zone, they may encounter situations in which they are ordered to carry out a mission knowing that some number of innocent civilians will likely die as a result. Is this justifiable, if the mission is undertaken for the purpose of protecting the lives of so many more? If so, how many more lives need to be protected to justify the level of expected civilian loss from the mission? Establishing elaborate ethical decision-making matrices to assist in resolving dilemmas like this lies outside the scope of this chapter, but you can see the challenge.

Obviously we find the examples of the 9/11 terrorists, Barend Strydom, Hitler, pornographers, pimps, thieves, adulterers, and so on to distort a sense of calling to the point of destroying it altogether. To be honest, although we do enjoy engaging in discussion about the boundary conditions of what it means to have a calling, we do not generally encounter too many serious conversations with people arguing personally that their homicidal ideals should be considered a calling. Nevertheless, these examples are real events that did not emerge out of thin air. Could they have been prevented, and if so, how? Not every extreme instance provides sufficient warning signs to ensure its prevention, but we offer three brief suggestions for promoting a climate in which callings stay within the hedges of constructive, not destructive, engagements with society.

One suggestion is to orient to the reality that calling is best discerned and always lived out in the context of a community. We have stressed how valuable it is to identify mentors who can help you think through how your gifts are best suited to meaningfully impact the common good. Research supports the importance and effectiveness of social support and modeling in helping people make good decisions about their careers, but research also indicates that people are most likely to make destructive choices when they occupy a social vacuum, living as a lone wolf without the accountability that emerges naturally in healthy, supportive relationships.[17] Ideally, the journey of discerning and living out a calling becomes a common point of conversation in relationships between people who care about each other, and who are invested in helping positively shape the direction of each other's lives. The protective function in preventing harm from developing is secondary in scope to the additive benefits of such relationships, but perhaps no less important.

The other suggestions center on criteria for evaluating the prosocial benefits of callings. The first is to rely on the moral norm of love. Love can be expressed in myriad ways, from respect shown to customers and competitors, to forgiveness extended to offending coworkers, to discipline enforced for probation violators. "Love may take different forms as its requirements and the needs of the neighbor are refracted through diverse vocational fields," writes Schuurman,[18] but in every instance, love provides sound moral grounding. Any motive that is contrary to love undermines the prosocial dimension of calling, and therefore the concept of calling itself. Second, whereas love is the moral norm for calling, the Hebrew concept of shalom is its "orienting ideal."[19] *Shalom* refers to a sense that everything is the way it is supposed to be, a rich sense of peace intertwined with joy and delight. Shalom refers to a state of wholeness and flourishing, of justice and freedom from oppression—an ideal that will not be reached on this side of heaven. As it applies to calling, however, the point is not so much to reach shalom but rather to strive for it. Does your calling help advance this vision of shalom? Does it move things within your sphere of influence in the direction of "how things are supposed to be"? The sense of drive that can accompany a sense of calling is powerful, and in rare cases it can result in terrible wrongdoing. For every notorious example we reviewed in this section, however, when love and shalom serve as the evaluative criteria, the question of "can such destruction be a calling?" has a clear answer: such destruction obliterates calling.

Complexities of Calling

Throughout this chapter we have highlighted an overarching theme: living out a calling is not without perils and pitfalls. A calling can drift toward the distortion of job idolization and work-aholism. A calling can fall prey to the vulnerabilities of ignoring useful feedback or being exploited by employers with values that do not include your well-being. A calling can destroy itself completely when used as rationale for causing harm. Youssef, another partici-pant from one of our research studies, sensed a calling to psychol-ogy from the time he was an undergraduate student, and a process of questioning, identification of gifts, and exploring opportunities confirmed early on for him that psychology was an ideal fit.[20] He described his calling as a tapestry with one thousand strands; the tapestry as a whole represented the field of psychology, and at the time we interviewed him, his current strand was psychology pro-fessor. His work as a professor gave him tremendous meaning and satisfaction, because he so values mentoring students and contrib-uting to the profession through his scholarship. On the surface, Youssef is a torchbearer for how to discern and live out a calling: he explored it actively, views it as an ongoing process, and recognizes its propensity to change over time.

For Youssef, however, pursuing a calling has come with conse-quences. His passion for work and his eagerness to follow his call-ing has required numerous job changes involving cross-country relocations, which in each case has created considerable turmoil for his family. He seemed burdened by guilt. "I had hoped that I could have provided a better life for my wife," he expressed, with unmistakable sadness, continuing,

> This is just a hang-up that I've had, and a personal one. I've dragged her from one place to another, and it just gets colder each time around, and she hates cold weather. And I make a fraction of what she does. There's a certain amount of guilt sometimes with that, because her career could have flowered. We have had this "target cities"

approach to things where we've applied, and we both have to agree that we both have veto power. There have been times where I had to decide if I'd be willing to give up my career in total.

It was clear in Youssef's voice that he found it difficult to weigh the vigor, excitement, and meaning that comes with his calling against the sense of remorse he feels about the sacrifices his wife has had to make.

And whatever happened to Josh Frank? Perhaps unsurprisingly, Josh went on to earn his Juilliard degree and now plays his trumpet with some of the world's top symphonies. We tracked Josh down to learn if he'd achieved a better sense of balance over the decade since his sister's *This American Life* story. We found major shifts; he developed more friendships with other musicians, in a community for which social connection and musical growth develop in parallel. He married a woman who understood and shared his passion for music. And he learned to practice in a way that required less of his time, a skill he developed both out of experience and necessity. In short, Josh figured out how to retain his calling while also fitting in a life that was supportive and complementary. He mitigated the traps of idolization and workaholism by working not harder, but smarter, and by better integrating his work and nonwork lives.

Living out a calling is not a solitary endeavor; it is inherently relational. Living out a calling affects your life outside of work and the lives of those around you, for better or worse. For Josh and Youssef, living out a calling has brought struggles and sometimes pain. Yet instead of working to avoid the challenges, they learned to manage them; instead of trading their callings for a wider path, they persevered. Calling is indeed not a panacea or a path to problem-free living; perils and pitfalls are part of the territory. But by building in balance, promoting a proper perspective, concentrating on the common good, continually evaluating, building a learning orientation to feedback, maintaining firm boundaries of fairness, orienting to a community of supports, and striving for love and shalom, you can pursue your calling with eyes wide open, anticipating and overcoming the obstacles with assurance that you are up to the task.

10 A Role for Calling in the Changing World of Work

THE CHANGING WORLD of work is a trendy topic today. (We just Googled the phrase and received more than 500 million results— more than what was generated for Lady Gaga, *American Idol*, or Tim Tebow.) The world of work, of course, has never been static; changes in the workplace have always gone hand in hand with societal and economic shifts. Still, it is hard to ignore the countless commentators reporting that a new age has arrived, one in which the incremental, linear progress of the past has been usurped by a climate of unpredictable and jagged change, often abrupt and no longer additive. The wisdom of a carefully evolving, slow-and-steady corporate growth strategy has given way to a climate in which those who are able to adapt quickly and decisively are in the best position to survive and thrive. This is true not only of companies but of individual workers. We live in an increasingly global marketplace in which the Internet renders geography irrelevant, a dramatic shrinkage in the availability of unskilled jobs and the rise of the service sector have taken place, technological advancements unfold at a breathtaking pace, major shifts are occurring in the demographics of the workforce, and career trajectories are marked by unpredictability and constant transition. Media coverage of this "new normal" is incessant and often sensationalized. Nevertheless, most of our grandparents would barely recognize the norms that govern most of today's work environments. It is hard to avoid getting a bit anxious about all this. When one of the very few things we can count on in the new world of work is change, the very fabric of the world (to borrow from Lee Hardy) seems in flux.

What role does the age-old notion of calling play in such a fluid, often oppressive, always changing world of work? This chapter takes on this question. The scope of the topic precludes a comprehensive treatment. Rather, we target how a sense of calling sheds light on three of the most significant issues in the modern work world: the oppressive divide between the haves and the have-nots, the shifting demographics in the workplace, and the increasingly transition-laden norm for individual career development.

Hardship

A recent issue of *Time* magazine featured the image of a ladder with broken rungs, along with the question "Can you still move up in America?" The lead photo accompanying the cover story captured Lesley Perez, seated on her bed in her parents' apartment in New York City. At age twenty-four, Lesley still lives with her parents— or rather, lives with them again. She can't afford to do otherwise; her salary as a kindergarten teacher is just $23,000 a year, and she carries $35,000 in debt from college loans. For the increasing number of people in the United States like Lesley, the cover's question strikes a heart-sinking chord. Rana Foroohar's lead article in that issue makes a compelling case that the U.S. meritocracy—the shared vision that in the land of opportunity, citizens can do anything to which they aspire if they simply put their minds to it and work hard—is now more than ever a myth for many.[1] Foroohar cites research from the Pew Charitable Trusts' Economic Mobility Project suggesting that those born in 1970 in the bottom fifth of the U.S. socioeconomic stratum had just a 17 percent chance of making it into the upper two-fifths as adults.

Of course, some people have better odds than others. As vocational psychologists Nadya Fouad and John Bynner note, "People are constrained from the time they are born by such structural factors as gender, socioeconomic status, ethnicity, and geographic location. . . . Along with curtailing the young person's aspirations and dreams, economic hardship, in particular, can lead to lack of opportunity and restriction of progress in the education system and throughout adult life."[2] Tangible resources are just one piece of the puzzle; the cultural environment that accompanies the social class into which a child is born pervades the full range of emotional, educational, and social resources that parents can provide. Think about a child growing up in a single-parent household, with that parent struggling to hold down two jobs just to provide the basic needs for survival. School budgets are often tied to taxes on income or property within a district, which makes it likely that this child attends an underfunded school that cannot attract top teachers and is surrounded by peers who have low expectations for the kind of work opportunities that will eventually be open to them. What kind of life will this child envision as she anticipates the future, and how will that vision of the future translate into the goals she sets for herself? Even with high aspirations, this child will not enjoy the benefits that come from having well-connected parents who can help arrange opportunities for summer internships, or who can model what is required for success as, say, a high-achieving white-collar professional. To be clear, all legitimate areas of work have dignity and meaning; we do not wish to imply that some job types are inherently "better" than others, only that the "if you dream it, you can do it" ideal is overly simplistic, overlooking the reality that people are starting at very different points.

The economic disparities that help explain the rich getting richer while the poor get poorer are real, but they only tell part of the story. Economist Alec R. Levenson points out that recent decades also have seen a dramatic increase in the disparity of wages for people *within the same segments of the labor market.* In other words, it is now more likely than ever that people even within the same occupation are "ending up with what could be viewed as arbitrarily different compensation." Levenson offers this example: "Two white male lawyers in their early 30s a generation ago might have received compensation that was relatively equal, yet by the 1990s they were much more likely to have dramatically different compensation because of organizations' increasing willingness to differentiate rewards and pay both across organizations and within the same organization."[3] Levenson describes these differences as apparently arbitrary, but systematic differences in compensation have long occurred across gender and for people of color as well. Even while women's participation in the workplace has increased more than 70 percent over the last thirty years—around 75 percent of women between the ages of twenty-five and fifty-five are currently employed—gender-based salary discrepancies have barely budged; women currently earn about 75 percent of men's wages in the same jobs. Among full-time employees, people of color also are paid considerably less on average than white workers, even when education, occupation, geographic region, and work-related experiences are equivalent, and even larger gaps exist for sexual minorities and those with disabilities.[4] As Boston College professor David Blustein has argued, the workplace can often be a hub of social oppression by virtue of its role as, for most people, their primary source of interactions with society.[5]

And this is just in the United States. In many places in the world, the picture is devastatingly grim. A full one-third of the 7 billion people on earth today have to somehow scrape by on incomes of two dollars a day or less, many toiling under conditions that can only be described as modern-day slavery. This degree of poverty is universally accompanied by severe constraints on freedom, including substandard housing, poor health, malnutrition, illiteracy, and all manner of exploitation and human rights abuses.[6] Fred Borgen, professor emeritus at Iowa State University, used such facts to raise some critical questions for those interested in understanding what career development means for most people:

> How many of the world's teenagers can say with realism, "I have a dream in my career"? How many of those teenagers have the prospect of freely picking a career about which they are passionate, pursuing it without major societal obstacles, and finding satisfaction and meaning in that career? Sadly, that number is less than 10% of the world's teenage population. For all age groups currently on the globe, the number of people who will find or have found self-actualization in their careers (as typically defined by Westerners) is no more than 500 million, and the case could be made that the number is much lower. . . . Vocational psychology as we know it today does not apply well to most of the world. If our purview is the United States, we must address the "forgotten half." . . . If our purview is global, we must, alas, address a "forgotten nine-tenths."[7]

Who Is Calling For?

The Francis Ford Coppola film *Powaqqatsi* opens with images from a gold mine in Brazil. Hundreds of workers wearing tattered, sweat-drenched, and dirt-caked tank tops and shorts are shown carrying burlap bags of earth up treacherously steep pathways in an open-pit mine. The workers toil mercilessly in the heat, most dragging on cigarettes, all appearing gaunt, dehydrated, and ready to collapse from exhaustion. At one point, the camera focuses on two workers hoisting up a fellow miner on their shoulders. The man squirms in pain; he had been drilled in the head with a falling rock. Setting their bags aside, the man's coworkers carry him to the top of the pit, where they presumably left him, turned, and headed back down for another burdened trip to the top. None of the other workers seemed even to notice, much less slow down. When Bryan teaches his career development course to his PhD students in counseling psychology, he spends the first few weeks marching through all the major psychological theories of career choice and development. Nearly all of these theories build on the assumption that people have the opportunity to make relatively unconstrained choices about what type of work they will pursue. Once students are familiar with the theories, Bryan shows this scene from *Powaqqatsi* and asks, "Who are these theories really for?"

The "who is this for?" question is even more poignant when applied to the notion of work as a calling. Is having a calling merely a luxury for the shrinking segment of the world—certainly fewer than 10 percent, according to Borgen—privileged enough to make unconstrained choices about their careers? Can people pursue their callings when they are just trying to survive, barely scraping together enough income to pay for the necessities of living, and saving anything that remains in the hopes that they can provide a better life for their children? Myriad constraints can serve as barriers to approaching work as a calling, and they are not equally distributed; some people clearly face more obstacles than others. Yet paradoxically, some evidence suggests that at least in some circumstances, a calling may be most needed and more readily attainable for those faced with unemployment and oppression.

Unemployment. Immediately following the first semester of his sophomore year of college, Ryan flew home to Dallas, Texas, for the winter break. He was feeling good. He had just become swept away by a new love interest, totally nailed his final exams, and was ready to spend the next three weeks at home doing not much of anything. As the designated airport chauffeur, Ryan's dad picked him up that morning and drove him to a local Denny's for breakfast. Some weak coffee was served, a couple of Grand Slams were ordered, and Ryan's dad proceeded to lead off with the prototypical parent question: "How's school?" Probably because he was in a good mood, Ryan decided against the expected response for nineteen-year-olds—"Fine"—and detailed the positive developments in his love life and grade point average. After about fifteen minutes, Ryan had run out of steam and lobbed a question back to his dad: "So what's new around here?"

The response caught Ryan off guard: "Well, today is my last day at Blockbuster." For the previous seven years, Ryan's father, Mike, had worked in the marketing department for Blockbuster Video, developing and sending out mailings to customers offering coupons, discounts, and descriptions of new releases about to hit the shelves. The son of a bricklayer and homemaker, Mike immigrated to the United States from England at age six. Armed only with a high school education, he worked his way up the corporate ladder over a thirty-year career to achieve what many might consider the American dream—married, three kids, a four-bedroom house in a desirable suburban neighborhood, a well-paying middle management job, an Acura SUV, and even a Golden Labrador. With that dream, of course, came expenses: a sizable mortgage, $80,000 a year in loans so Ryan and his sister could attend elite private colleges, and medical costs associated with Ryan's younger sister's hearing disability. Mike detailed the circumstances of why and how he was "let go" from Blockbuster, but Ryan could barely hear any of that; he was in a state of shock. His dad, pink-slipped? The possibility had just never occurred to him; he simply took his dad's job for granted, and the consequences of his own father being out of work for any lengthy period of time were too far-reaching to fully grasp just then.

Ryan stepped back into the moment and asked: "How are you doing with this?" His dad's response was simple and quick. "Well, this is the first time I have been unemployed since I was fifteen years old." Like many Americans, work was not only embedded in Mike's identity, but it allowed him the satisfaction of providing certain opportunities for his family, opportunities that he never enjoyed himself. The loss of work and the massive changes that came with it—from identity to lifestyle—were scary, almost paralyzing.

This very position is one that millions of people in the United States face right now. Many who don't face it now will confront it soon, and some people will endure several bouts of unemployment over the course of their careers. The effects of unemployment on mental health are well documented by researchers, consistently showing problems with self-esteem, conflicts in relationships, substance abuse, and a number of other, more substantial mental health problems.[8] One study conducted in Germany even found that unemployment altered (downward) people's well-being set point—that is, participants experienced a marked decline in their sense of satisfaction with life after losing their job and failed to return to their previous levels of life satisfaction even after finding new employment.[9]

One might expect that people who lose work they had experienced as a calling may suffer the most, given the extent to which calling enhances the connection of one's work to one's identity and sense of purpose. Research has not yet shed light on this question directly, but we suspect among those for whom their specific job is very closely tied to their sense of calling, the negative effects of unemployment may indeed be exacerbated. Ample evidence shows that when people think of their work as central to their sense of self, they experience significantly worse mental health and lower life satisfaction when they become unemployed, compared with those who view their work as less tied to their identity.[10] However, a calling is not the same as work centrality; as we addressed in chapter 3, a sense of calling usually transcends a particular job. For example, a veterinary assistant may feel called to promote health and relieve suffering for animals and view her job at a local animal hospital as very important in facilitating her pursuit of that calling. If her position was terminated, her concern would likely not be with losing her sense of calling, but rather with losing her primary vehicle for living out that calling. Another job could support her calling just as well, but until that job comes along, she can do other things to live out that calling aside from paid employment. Given that possibility, a sense of calling could even buffer the negative effects of job loss, serving to help people cope with the hardships they face in unemployment. In short, if one's job is a means to living out a calling rather than *being* the calling, losing the job does not mean losing the calling.

In some situations, unemployment can actually spark a sense of calling where one didn't previously exist. Many of the miserable middle-career employees we have encountered in career counseling describe feeling stuck, because although they hate their jobs, they cannot easily quit because the pay and benefits (the "golden handcuffs") are so good. Job losses and layoffs are rarely a net positive, but they do cut the golden handcuffs, which then opens up new possibilities in which a sense of calling may emerge. Douglas T. Hall, in a *Journal of Organizational Behavior* article with Dawn Chandler, describes how this unfolds for some among the ranks of the unemployed:

> [I am] currently conducting research on unemployment and [am] hearing unemployed people from diverse backgrounds talk about their sense of calling. In fact, several of these people have reported that it was not until their resources ran out, when they "reached bottom," that they were able to discern what they described as their true calling. In a discussion with a group of unemployed professionals there was consensus that having resources can in some cases be a barrier to discovering a calling, as that removes a source of motivation to self-explore and try out

different kinds of work. To maintain one's unemployment benefits, people reported that they were required to apply for many different full-time and part-time jobs, for work that they would not otherwise have even considered, and this forced exploration and trial work helped them discover work for which they had great passion.[11]

Perhaps economic resources are a mixed bag when it comes to pursuing a calling. With a dependable source of good income, people have more latitude to freely explore ways to use their gifts meaningfully, in service of the greater good, without worrying about having to meet their basic needs. Yet as Hall and Chandler note, "A position of privilege can insulate a person from having to take work seriously, so that [she or] he never does the self-exploration and trial work activities necessary to discern [her or] his calling."[12] (For more on living out a calling in unemployment, see Q&A 12.)

Oppression. Unemployment is often demoralizing, but for some, maintaining employment comes with its own set of costs. Above, we noted that compensation for employment is not distributed proportionally across groups. Here are some of the details: According to the U.S. Census Bureau, average 2010 earnings among full-time workers with bachelor's degrees were $45,223 for white women and $71,958 for white men.[13] In contrast, African American women and men earned $41,653 and $48,068, respectively, while Hispanic/Latino American women and men earned $39,321 and $56,774, respectively. Vocational psychologist Ruth Fassinger noted that the advancement pipeline also "leaks" for people of color; nearly a third (29.2 percent) of white men are managers or professionals, but only 18.5 percent of African American men and 11.4 percent of Hispanic/Latino men are. For women representing these groups, the percentages of managers and professionals are 33.4 percent, 24.8 percent, and 17.8 percent, respectively, and for both sexes, African

Americans and Hispanic/Latino Americans represent only 3 percent and 3.8 percent of CEOs.

Part of what accounts for these wage and advancement disparities is that women and people of color tend to funnel into a comparatively narrow range of occupations and work roles, particularly those on the low end of the compensation spectrum. In the high-growth and often very lucrative STEM (science, technology, engineering, and math) fields, which have been identified as extremely important to the economic strength and global leadership of the United States, whites (77.1 percent) and Asian Americans (11.2 percent) hold nine-tenths of the jobs. Despite earning half of the college degrees in the U.S. workforce, women constitute just one-fourth of the STEM workforce, and women of color only 4 percent. These numbers, of course, are at least in part the result of other barriers that exist in a much broader context. Well-documented inequalities embedded in social structures like education, health care, training opportunities, and access to work perpetuate these differences between groups. Fassinger points out, for example, that high percentages of African American (27 percent) and Hispanic/Latino (13 percent) youth live in "severely distressed" neighborhoods, and that children educated in such concentrated areas of poverty receive not only less schooling but schooling of a much lower quality than is found in more economically advantaged areas.[14] Few children from such areas are adequately equipped to thrive in college.

Inequalities in the distribution of resources that perpetuate down-the-road inequalities elsewhere are macro-level issues that, without a doubt, require complex and multifaceted solutions. How do they translate into an individual's actual experience in the world of work? People of color often experience discrimination in job selection and hiring. Economists Marianne Bertrand and Sendhil Mullainathan demonstrated this very creatively in a study in which they sent fictitious resumes in response to "help wanted" ads in Boston and Chicago newspapers. The resumes were identical except for the names; some were given African American–sounding names like Tamika, Lakisha, Jamal, or Tyrone, and others were given white-sounding names like Geoffrey, Todd, Meredith, and Carrie. What did they find? The white-named resumes received approximately 50 percent more callbacks for interviews than did the African American–named resumes. Remember, the resumes were in all other respects *exactly the same*. The researchers followed this up by sending out a batch of higher-quality resumes in which the applicants had more experience, training, and skills; these also were identical except for the names. Astoundingly, they found a statistically significant increase in the number of callbacks for the higher-quality resumes with white names, but the callback rate did not differ for the lower- and higher-quality resumes with African American names.[15] Unfortunately, barriers persist even after finding a job; a large volume of research indicates that people of color are disproportionately excluded from information and support networks, have relatively few mentors and role models, and often feel pressure and isolation from being a "token" minority. Negative racial stereotypes also abound, and research in social psychology shows that fear of being judged according to such stereotypes actually impedes performance and achievement.[16]

These concerns are magnified for women of color. Indeed, women in general also experience considerable career-related barriers.[17] For example, research has described many educational and workplace contexts as "chilly" and unwelcoming to women, an outrageously high percentage report having experienced sexual harassment (two-thirds in one study of college students[18]), double standards are frequently expressed in response to women's behavior and accomplishments (e.g., disapproval of expressions of strength and assertiveness among women, but not among men), and the intersection of work and family life is arguably more complex for most women than for most men.

The larger point is that the world of work simply does not treat all people the same. Some people, by virtue of characteristics out-side of their control, have much steeper hills to climb. Here again, this discussion has focused on the U.S. context; work-related oppression takes on a whole new meaning elsewhere in the world, where laborers toil in sugar cane fields for the equivalent of fifteen dollars a month[19] and where children quit school to work for three dollars a day in unmonitored, extremely dangerous, abandoned coal mines.[20] What role for a calling can there possibly be in such circumstances?

Profoundly oppressive conditions around the globe, such as forced labor and extreme poverty, are patently antithetical to seek-ing and experiencing a sense of calling. The best evidence on the relationship between wealth and well-being suggests that hap-piness is lower among the very poor, who struggle with very real concerns over matters basic to survival, such as finding adequate nourishment and a safe, secure place to sleep at night. But once these survival needs are met, the link between income and well-being evaporates.[21] Maslow's needs hierarchy, which suggests that basic needs for survival and safety must be met before higher-order needs such as belongingness and esteem even become relevant, serves as a useful rule of thumb: calling matters once more basic needs are covered. When we've worked with clients in career coun-seling who are one step away from eviction—or whose children have been living off ramen noodles, peanut butter, and saltines for weeks—the topic of calling usually never comes up. In such cases we focus instead on finding ways to ensure, as quickly as possible, that the household stays safe, warm, and well fed.

Similar to economic hardship, when exploitative or prejudicial practices set the norms that govern one's livelihood and restrict one's freedom, an emphasis on living out a sense of calling seems misplaced. The utterly disturbing inequalities that pervade the world of work run counter to, certainly not in support of, a sense of calling. Yet consider the story of the *arpilleristas* of Chile, intro-duced by vocational psychologist Ellen McWhirter and colleagues as impoverished women living under the brutality of General Augusto Pinochet's dictatorship that began in 1973. These wives, mothers, and daughters of those who were murdered or tortured or who had disappeared survived an atmosphere of terror about which the outside world knew little because of extreme censorship. . . . The women banded together in small groups for economic survival and sewed bits of cloth onto rough fabric backings to sell as handicrafts. Their work of survival was also a powerful protest: their brightly colored work depicted the brutality of the regime in their neighborhoods and in their daily lives. The simple artwork of poor women was beneath the notice of the dictatorship, and their efforts, which were exported to the outside world, provided powerful testimony of what was happening in Chile. They who were powerless opened the eyes of the international community.[22]

The available research evidence tells us very little about how those working under severe oppression and poverty experience a sense of calling, including how many find it relevant at all. Nevertheless, the *arpilleristas* are an example of how infusing work with purpose in ways akin to a calling can serve as a powerful source of resilience and imbue the work with an unmistakable sense of dignity and meaning. Is calling really irrelevant in such circumstances? Perhaps such circumstances are when a sense of calling is most needed.

Shifting Demographics

Within the United States and most other developed nations, the mix of people in the workforce is changing fast.[23] The baby boomers—children of the Greatest Generation, born roughly from

1946 to 1964—recently began reaching the official retirement age of sixty-five. Yet many are choosing to remain in the workforce; whether their investment portfolios fell victim to economic slowdowns or whether they just enjoy working (or both), the number of American workers age sixty-five and older increased by nearly one-third in the last decade. The number of workers ages fifty-five to sixty-four increased by more than 50 percent during that time, and although the average age of retirement is sixty-four, 75 percent of retirees plan to launch new careers after retiring.[24] By 2016 more than 35 percent of the workforce will be over fifty-five.[25] All this makes the boomers, for now anyway, still a dominant age cohort in the workplace. Their influence is approximated by that of Generation Y, born roughly between 1979 and 1994, the younger portion of which also goes by "the Millennial Generation." The baby boom generation and Gen Y are both roughly double the size of Generation X (born between 1965 and 1978), the age cohort sandwiched between them.

Boomers and Gen Y, Unite!

The sheer numbers of boomers and Gen Y employees in the workforce means that, whether they are deliberate about it or not, they are collaborative shapers of the norms in most workplaces. Hearing about vast differences between generations is common, but especially with these two generations. (Gen Y members are more likely to Google "Lady Gaga" or "*American Idol*" than are the boomers, for example. We're not sure who likes Tim Tebow more.) The topic of generational differences is especially hot in the workplace, and more than a few consultants are making a handsome living providing training to help companies bridge the perceived generation gap. The members of Gen Y, says conventional wisdom, love multitasking, are obsessed with technology, are used to getting what they want whenever they want it, and are very tolerant. Boomers are prone to workaholism, like to have meetings and communicate in person, adapt eventually to new technology that is constantly thrust upon them, and like to know what to expect.

These are just a few examples, but despite all their differences—many of them real, some of them overblown[26]—Gen Y and the boomers have some important things in common, too. According to a provocative *Harvard Business Review* article, their vision and values for the workplace bear considerable similarity.[27] The authors of the article cite evidence from a survey suggesting that Gen Y and the boomers share the view that financial gain is not the best driver for deciding where to work or to keep working, and that no less than 85 percent of both Gen Y and boomers value the chance to give back to society as a critical feature of a good place to work. (More than 75 percent of Gen X employees also expressed this value.) The survey also revealed that Gen Y workers value mentoring from boomers more so than from Gen X employees, and seem oriented to a "trust those over fifty" dictum. For their part, even while sometimes referring to their Gen Y counterparts as Kippers (an acronym decoded as Kids in Parents' Pockets Eroding Retirement Savings), boomers appear to delight in sharing their wisdom with their younger colleagues.

To summarize, the two largest generational cohorts in today's workforce (1) see financial gain as a secondary consideration in evaluating their place of employment, (2) place a premium on making a positive contribution to society, and (3) seem to enjoy working with each other. We can't help but look at this evidence in light of the research we reported earlier that a sense of calling is far more prevalent than is often assumed. At a time when discussions related to purpose and meaning in the workplace are increasingly common in organizations,[28] it seems as good a time as ever to encourage workers to invest in discerning and living out their callings in work and in life. As we noted briefly in chapter 4, a transformational leadership style that expands the goals and aspirations of employees, while effectively communicating a shared vision that employees value, is one key pathway that leaders can use to promote a sense of calling, and in turn, psychological health. Another strategy, given the benefits of mentoring and its value to employees of all age cohorts, is to establish formal or encourage informal mentoring relationships in the workplace that specifically include discussion of, and support for, discerning and living out a calling at work. We provide more information about these and other strategies for promoting a sense of calling in the workplace at the book's companion website, www.makeyourjobacalling.com.

Calling and Retirement

As dominant a force as the baby boomers remain in today's workforce, and as many of them are delaying retirement, massive numbers are nevertheless poised to retire, and soon. The decision to retire or continue working is often very complex, involving all kinds of factors, such as finances, health, interests in leisure and volunteering, relationships, and attitudes about work, among other things. The actual transition to retirement can go smoothly or not so well, depending on another complex interaction of factors. One consistent research finding is that the more deeply a worker identifies with one's work, the more difficult the transition to retirement can be.[29] As was the case with unemployment, does this mean that people who approach work as a calling are likely to struggle when they retire?

Research that could provide a window into this question has not yet been undertaken, so we can only speculate. We suspect, much like we did for those with callings who suffer unemployment, that workers who tie a calling narrowly to their specific jobs are most at risk for a tough retirement transition—particularly if that retirement is involuntary. But here again, there is likely a flip side in which a sense of calling serves as a resource, paving a smooth path for the postcareer journey. If a calling transcends a particular job, retirement becomes an opportunity to seek new ways to live out that calling. Some may opt to do this with new employment, an option that will become common in the next decade when shortages of skilled labor are expected and "bridge employment"—a transition phase between full-time employment and full-time retirement—will likely be encouraged and incentivized by many employers desperate for talent. Others may embark on entirely new pathways for living out a calling that would never have been possible under the constraints of having to earn a full-time living. Either way, committing to using retirement as a new opportunity for living out a calling may prove freeing, enriching, and meaningful.

Looking back on his career, now at age sixty-five and (at the time we interviewed him) in his last month as a partner in a successful obstetrics and gynecology group in Fort Collins, Colorado, Larry Kieft explains that living out his calling has always been an ongoing process of seeking and discovering new ways to use his gifts to serve others. Born to working-class parents of deep faith in Grand Haven, Michigan, Larry first aspired to a teaching career. Eventually, a teacher—one whom Larry profoundly admired—recognized how Larry's affinity for science could support his values for building relationships and suggested that Larry consider living out his faith through medical missions. That encouragement stuck with Larry, and a series of formative experiences (e.g., a summer workshop in missions, attending a Christian college that stressed how faith applies to all of life, a coming-of-age hitchhiking trip across Europe) reinforced for him that he could use his skills in service of others through medicine. The thought of sharing in some of the most sacred times in patients' lives led him to pursue obstetrics. That was more than thirty-five years and approximately forty-five hundred delivered babies ago.

Larry clearly viewed his work as a calling, and his faith was more than an add-on; it was embedded in every aspect of his job, even though the medical missions trajectory didn't materialize in the way he expected. "I had no qualms about that," he explains. "For my family, especially when our children were young, it seemed right to stay in Fort Collins. I felt a sense that wherever I was, I could serve." And he did, in ways that extended beyond the walls of his practice. He helped establish a prenatal program for women who couldn't afford obstetrics care. He became politically active within his profession, trying to engage other physicians in expanding care to the uninsured and working with the hospital foundation to do so. He helped raise money to endow a children's clinic. He serves on the board of the Colorado Coalition for the Medically Underserved, trying to get everyone in the state covered with health insurance. "All of these are parts of what I think of as my calling—and not in a sweet, sentimental way. These were just the right things for me to do with where I am in my faith and with the opportunities that God has given to me."

Larry's profession matters to him and has provided him with opportunities for using his gifts in service of others, but his sense of calling was never wrapped up in being a physician. "That is not to say I ever had doubts about becoming a doctor, I just thought there were other ways I could have served. I love being a doctor, but it doesn't define me. My calling has made me constantly think about what is next, where I am going—not because I am discontent, but because there is something out there still for me to do." As he began to anticipate his retirement, Larry turned the possibilities around in his head, exploring some options for leveraging his gifts. He read news about the challenge of meeting medical needs in some parts of the world and looked into ways he could help. Soon Larry found himself in Bangladesh, Mali, and Nigeria, confronting the soul-stirring realities of medicine in the developing world: children dying of diarrhea and respiratory infections, women dying in childbirth because necessary medications are unavailable, a medical school with twelve hundred students but not a single working cardiac monitor in its intensive care unit.

Larry saw the needs and mapped out a dream for his "retirement": linking medical schools and residencies in the United States with those in the developing world, so that training for doctors in Africa could be enhanced in ways that are appropriate to the local culture and resources; not overwhelming them with technologies they are not able to achieve, but building on what they already have. As an initial step in realizing this dream, Larry enrolled in a master's program in international public health. Wherever his calling leads, he's committed to following it. "I'm healthy. I'm wired to be around people and to work. I have skills. The needs in the developing world are real, and they matter. I could live another thirty years. How am I going to use that time?"

Larry's experience reinforces a few things about the nature of calling. First, a calling is an ongoing process that unfolds over time, not a singular event. As Larry put it, "Calling is not a onetime deal; you get more opportunities to listen again and do new things." Second, very closely related to this, a calling is usually broad, transcending any particular job. Larry's dream for his retirement continues a pattern that has marked his entire career, in which he continually sought new ways to use his gifts meaningfully to better serve the underserved. The advantage of retirement is that Larry's options are about to expand, now that he will soon be free from having to work his share of his medical group's service hours. Third, although research has not yet examined how a sense of calling relates to well-being in retirement, we can vouch for the fact that Larry shows as much energy and excitement about his next steps as we've ever seen from someone charting a new career path. The lesson here for those who sense a calling, but who are anticipating retirement: Approach your retirement as a new beginning, one that creates new opportunities for living out your calling, without the tethers of your day job.

Calling in the Age of Free Agency

With boomers soon to retire en masse, the number of workers leaving the workforce will outpace the number of workers entering it. Economists suggest that these changes will not necessarily lead to labor shortages, but will probably create shorter employment relationships, more contingent work, more independent contractors, and other such arrangements.[30] The transition from careers that progress in a linear manner following advancement templates put in place by organizations to more of a "free agent"–oriented environment involving highly individualized career trajectories has been unfolding over the last half century. Many economists, psychologists, and management scholars suggest that the rate of this type of change is increasing rapidly, and will continue to do so.

An adaptive approach to navigating this type of change is to develop what Douglas T. Hall and colleagues describe as a protean career orientation.[31] Hall defines the *protean career* as "one in which the person, not the organization, is in charge, the core values are freedom and growth, and the main success criteria are subjective."[32] A protean career orientation has been found not to vary across various career stages (for example, between undergraduates, graduate students, and middle managers), and is not linked to mobility, but is more common among people who are open to new experiences and driven to master their goals.[33] When people have a protean career orientation, they are self-directed and driven by their own values, motivated to pursue a path that expresses their gifts and facilitates personal growth. A protean career orientation is not the same as a calling, but when protean attitudes combine with a sense of purpose, and an awareness of how one's gifts can promote the greater good, the concepts converge.

How does a sense of calling support a protean strategy for managing a career in a turbulent work world? Hall and Chandler answer this question by pointing to two critical *metacompetencies* (i.e., overarching skills that encourage the development of other, more specific skills): self-awareness and adaptability. People with a high degree of self-awareness are good at gathering feedback from others about what they are like at work; using that feedback to develop an accurate sense of their strengths and weaknesses; and changing their self-perception when necessary, as they come across new information. Adaptability in this context refers to the capacity to adjust to the needs of whichever situation a person confronts. People with a high degree of adaptability not only have the ability to change, they are motivated to do so. Those who are blessed with both of these metacompetencies are proactive people who are down to earth and humble; they don't think of themselves as any better or worse than they ought. They can sense when they need to update skills, and because they love learning, they are generally adept at doing so. A sense of calling brings with it a clarity of goals and motivation for one's work, and part of having a calling also means continually seeking ways to better align one's gifts with needs in the world. Hall and Chandler suggest that having a protean career is a necessary but not sufficient condition for having a calling.[34] We agree and point out an important implication: By cultivating a calling, you are automatically developing a protean approach to work marked by metacompetencies that will prove critical in helping you adapt to the free agent–oriented work environment that continues to evolve. For this reason, a sense of calling helps you thrive in the changing world of work.

The Future of Calling

At the beginning of this chapter, we summarized the trends that commentators describe when they suggest we are at the dawn of a new era of change. Forecasting the future of the world of work with accuracy is inordinately difficult, dependent as it is on multiple factors that are themselves unpredictable, but that change will happen is certain. Some change, like the shift to a less organization-oriented and more individual-oriented world of work, may play to the strengths of what a sense of calling provides, for reasons we summarized in the preceding section. Other change, such as increasing economic disparity and inequality, may threaten a sense of calling. Regardless, the notion remains that work can be approached as a calling. What people mean when they use the term "calling" may continue to diversify, but if history is any guide, the neoclassical approach to calling is very robust, having already survived half a millennium of constant cultural and economic change.

Think back to the diverse group of people we've introduced who are discerning and living out callings in their work and lives. The road construction flagger who keeps people safe. Roger, the cop called into the ministry. Rohit, the warehouse-manager-turned-disaster-relief-worker. Maria, called to landscape architecture. Emily, called to support her psychotherapy clients in their life journeys. Sheryl, the engineer now working on new treatments for heart disease. Maggie, the janitor who helps sick children heal. Paul, the professor and organic farmer. Larry, called to use his retirement to improve health care in the developing world. And many others. These folks, along with a recent flurry of social science research and centuries of other scholarship, have taught us much about what it means to have a calling. A calling can transcend a particular job or paid employment in general. A calling can change over time, and can be discerned within the context of any life role. A calling can have a dark side and introduce perils and pitfalls but also can serve as a support in times of hardship, help manage transitions in life, and provide coherence and stability in an increasingly unstable world of work. A calling can provide a deep sense of well-being, in work and in life.

What steps are you taking to discern your callings? How will you respond to the callings you sense in those places where your gifts align with opportunities and needs in the world around you? Another certainty about the future of calling is this: however the future of the world of work unfolds, the role of calling in *your* future depends on you.

Questions and Answers

*Q&A 1. It seems surprising that people use "calling" to mean
such different things. On the one hand a calling is a prompting
from an external caller to approach work in a way that helps
others; on the other, a calling is an inner drive toward
self-fulfillment. Why such a difference?*

We approach this question in a couple of ways. The first approach
looks at it through a psychological lens, reframing it this way: What
personal characteristics differentiate people who adopt a neoclassical understanding of calling (e.g., transcendent summons, purpose and meaningfulness, prosocial values) from those who adopt
a modern approach (e.g., inner drive toward self-fulfillment)? No
study of which we are aware has examined this particular question directly, although a few have investigated similar questions
that shed light on this one. One study, conducted in Germany by
psychologist Andreas Hirschi, found that people who thought of
their careers as a calling could be divided into three groups: one
focused on their own self-enhancement, one was highly religious
with strong prosocial values, and one felt their work was important in their lives but otherwise had fairly diverse values in which
no obvious pattern emerged.[1] The self-enhancement group placed
a much higher level of importance on the role of work in their
lives than the other two groups but also tended to have somewhat
negative views of themselves. (Hirschi explains, "Apparently, this

calling group consists of self-centered and insecure students whose primary goals in work are gaining personal benefits. This indeed constitutes a very peculiar type of calling."[2] We suspect that their negative views of themselves may have driven their quest for self-enhancement, and that they viewed discerning a calling as a path leading to such self-enhancement, but this interpretation is only speculative until more research is undertaken.) Despite these differences, all three groups appeared rather advanced in terms of their career development, with a high degree of identity achievement, confidence, and engagement in their work.

Hirschi's research converges somewhat with evidence from our own studies, which usually suggest that the neoclassical view seems to resonate with people who have stronger religious commitments and prosocial values, who are less materialistic, and who are somewhat more agreeable, conscientious, and open to experience than others. However, despite the fact that people tend to define "calling" in overlapping yet clearly distinct ways, researchers have not found consistent differences across these various ways of understanding calling in terms of their relationships with career development and well-being. This point bears repeating because it is a rather striking and important result: When it comes to predicting people's career development progress and general well-being, it doesn't seem to matter which particular definition of calling people use.

The other approach looks at the word itself rather than characteristics of the people who use the word in different ways. A linguist would take this approach, especially one who specializes in semantics. We are not linguists and we don't specialize in semantics, but it doesn't take an expert to see that the term "calling" is in a state of flux; as should be obvious by now, the word has taken on different meanings when applied to work. In his book *The Mother Tongue*, Bill Bryson includes a chapter that explores where words come from and why they mean what they do.[3] Point number four in that chapter is that words change by doing nothing. Almost inexplicably, their meanings shift over time. Often, words even take their opposite meaning; he noted that "counterfeit" once meant a legitimate copy, and "brave" once suggested cowardice. The technical term for this kind of drift in meaning is *catachresis*, a phenomenon Bryson notes is "as widespread as it is curious." Perhaps "calling" has entered a state of catachresis. Why? The growing secularization of the culture? Maybe a societal shift in values from the well-being of the common good to the best interests of the individual? It is hard to say; here again, in the absence of good data one can only speculate.

Of course, the fact that the term "calling" means somewhat different things to different people does not mean one has to believe that all definitions are equally accurate. We define "calling" the way we do—as a transcendent summons to approach a particular life role in a way that demonstrates or derives a sense of purpose or meaning, motivated by other-oriented values and goals—because we find it both useful and faithful in spirit to the historic usage and literal meaning of calling, factors that we find important. With other people who value these particular criteria, we sometimes argue that our definition is, if not the "right" one, at least a very good one. But as psychological scientists we are mostly interested in understanding how people think about calling and the difference it makes in their lives. Therefore, in many (although not all) of our studies, we do not impose our definition of the term on people, but rather use a more open-ended approach in which people can appeal to whichever definition of the term they usually use.

Q&A 2. In defining "calling" the way you do, you seem to be making some assumptions. Can you be explicit about what those are?

Absolutely. As a quick refresher before we dive in, assumptions are beliefs that people hold without necessarily having evidence to support them; they are things that people simply take for granted, serving as a foundation on which they build other beliefs. In our scholarly work, we have tried to make our assumptions very clear from the outset—a much more helpful approach, we think, than keeping people guessing. In a recent article in the *Counseling Psychologist*, one of the flagship journals in our field, we laid out five assumptions that form a backdrop for our approach to understanding calling. We paraphrase them as follows:

1. *We assume that people are active agents.* In other words, we assume that people have the free will required to be genuinely intentional in making choices. We also assume that people are capable of thinking through possible outcomes ahead of time and using that ability to their advantage. Furthermore, it means we assume people are able to regulate their own behavior and to engage in self-reflection, evaluating their own actions and considering changes they feel might be needed. In short, people are not robots; they have the ability, freedom, and responsibility to think and make choices for themselves. Having said all this, however, we also assume that the freedom that people have in their behavior is limited in important ways by biological, environmental, and spiritual influences. As one obvious example of such influences, both of us, at one time or another in childhood, aspired to a career as a professional athlete. Unfortunately, our biologically rooted athletic ability placed too low a ceiling on the level at which we could ultimately perform (although we sure enjoyed trying). As another example, maybe you can think of a friend who was raised by unloving, neglectful parents and now tends to make really awful choices in his relationships. Those choices are his and he is responsible for them, but you don't have to be a psychoanalyst to conclude that his earlier experiences probably influenced his later decisions. People make willful choices for which they are ultimately responsible, but those choices are never made in a vacuum—or so we assume.

2. *We assume that people are meaning-makers.* Consciously and subconsciously, as people think through their experiences, they construct general and specific meanings that help them make sense of those experiences. Typically, this meaning-making happens when people look back on things. We can't always see in the moment how one event in the present leads to the next, but in reviewing our past experiences, we are usually pretty good at finding a thread that weaves things together and makes the big picture sensible and coherent.

3. *We assume that people have all kinds of different roles and responsibilities in life and that these roles usually interact in complicated ways.* Work is just one of these life roles, and we define "work" broadly to include any activity or effort, paid or unpaid, that is directed toward accomplishing or producing something that fills a societal or organizational need. There is a lot more to life than work, and the distinctions between work and nonwork are often very fuzzy. Sometimes the same activity can be viewed through the lens of more than one life role—like caregiving for a disabled family member, for example.

4. *We assume that humans, by necessity, live in societies bound by common needs and mutual service*—and because of this, work role activities generally make some kind of difference for other people. The influence may be large or small, direct or indirect, but generally speaking, every legitimate job has some kind of social impact.

5. *We assume that people have to deal with all kinds of obstacles to meaning and purpose at work*—on an individual level, an organizational level, and on a societal level. But we also assume that these obstacles are amenable to change. Change isn't necessarily easy, but it is possible.

These assumptions are not intended to be comprehensive, but in terms of beliefs that we hold as we define "calling" and think through these kinds of issues in general, these are probably the big ones. Different combinations of these assumptions have appeared at different points throughout the book.

Q&A 3. Calling seems to be a very Western, Christian concept. Are you taking a teaching from one religious tradition and trying to apply it to everyone?

In short, yes. But let's unpack this a bit. Two issues seem relevant when this question arises. The first is whether a single cultural or religious tradition can have an exclusive claim on a concept like calling. The second is whether we can take a concept from one tradition or worldview and apply it broadly, including to people who don't come from or approach things from that perspective.

In response to the first issue, we have always been very clear that the concept of calling—at least the neoclassical understanding of the term—emerged from a Western, Christian context. As we explained in chapter 2, the roots of the neoclassical understanding of calling took hold during the Protestant Reformation in Europe, although official Catholic teaching related to work and career now takes essentially the same approach. Many people identify with this tradition, especially in the United States, in which close to 80 percent of the population say they are Christians.[4] However, scholars and spiritual leaders from other traditions have generally embraced this approach, too. For example, Marcia Hermansen, director of the Islamic World Studies program at Loyola University Chicago, suggests that although calling per se has not been a focus within Islamic theology, "It is clear that questions of human purposiveness and labors of this world . . . have been addressed in numerous [Islamic] contexts,"[5] including the Qur'an; Islamic philosophy, theology, and mysticism; and the work of contemporary Muslim writers. These sources teach that

- ▶ Diverse gifts and talents are part of Allah's plan.
- ▶ People are bound by mutual needs that a cooperative division of labor addresses.
- ▶ All aspects of life are sacred.
- ▶ Ethics and virtues should govern on-the-job conduct.
- ▶ Work should be undertaken with care for important social needs.
- ▶ Spiritual meaning is not limited to clerics and contemplative orders.
- ▶ Each person has a purpose to discover and foster.

See any overlap here?

As another example, authors such as Marsha Sinetar have applied the Buddhist concept of "right livelihood," which refers to the natural path, guided by people's own abilities and passions, to work and career.[6] This concept may not seem to align directly with a sense of calling, but when the Dalai Lama was presented with a summary of calling research, he responded by discussing how Buddhist teaching supports a calling orientation and offered his own hypothesis that approaching work as a calling would likely prompt a range of key benefits to self and others.[7]

Our point here is not that our approach to calling is universal, applying equally well to everyone, across all world religions. We have never made such a claim. We do, however, think that the concept of calling could be sufficiently broad so as to find relevance across a wide range of religious and nonreligious perspectives.

Then there is the second issue—whether it is okay to take a concept that emerged within one tradition and apply it broadly, including to people who do not adhere to that perspective. Ideas don't come out of thin air; they are always rooted in a particular context. Should ideas that originate within one tradition be reserved only for those who lay claim to that tradition? We find this alternative immensely unappealing. It is useful, for clarity's sake, to make the cultural or religious context of an idea—to the extent that it is known—clear rather than hidden. But ultimately—well, ideally anyway—ideas live or die on the basis of their own merit. Is it useful? Can it help me get more out of life? Can it somehow make me a more effective person? We happen to think that, with respect to the notion of approaching work as a calling, the answer to these questions is yes for most people. Research supports this conclusion, at least indirectly. In the end, though, you have to answer these questions and judge for yourself the merits of the ideas we advance in this book.

Q&A 4. By doing empirical research on calling, aren't you taking an inherently spiritual concept and stripping away its spiritual meaning by reducing it to scientific explanations and principles?

We aren't anywhere near a level of scientific understanding of calling that could explain it all in scientific terms, even if this was our goal. But this isn't our goal. There are multiple ways of knowing things; philosophers often point to authority, reason, experience, and intuition or inspiration as some of the main ways that people know what they know. Psychological science, which draws from experience as a way of knowing through its use of the scientific method, is an important strategy for understanding human behavior, one that we obviously like to use. In our research, we do strive to build an increasingly clear understanding of how people approach their work as a calling, and the difference it makes for their career development and workplace behavior. However, even the most thorough explanation of a phenomenon on a scientific level does not mean that a spiritual explanation of that phenomenon is therefore false or superfluous.

This issue is even more pronounced in other fields within psychology, such as the psychology of religion and spirituality. Some of the most interesting research within this field, for example, looks at brain function during a spiritual experience. Researchers have investigated, among others, Franciscan nuns deep in prayer and Buddhist monks in the midst of meditation using functional magnetic resonance imaging (fMRI) technology, which measures the rate of blood flow to various regions of the brain. During intense prayer or meditation, blood flow increases to the parts of the brain involved in intense concentration and emotional experience, and reduces to the areas involved in perceiving sensory information and one's location in physical space.[8] Some analysts have interpreted such results as evidence that there is no such thing as a real religious or spiritual experience, because it can all be explained in physiological terms. This conclusion, however, commits what scholars have dubbed "the fallacy of nothing-but-ery"—that is, the flawed assumption that explaining a spiritual experience using natural processes explains it away as "nothing but" a natural phenomenon. Science is good at explaining things in naturalistic terms, and in general, we find great value in such explanations. But science, by definition, cannot possibly investigate influences that exist outside of nature. Thus, a good scientific explanation of a particular phenomenon can be useful in understanding the natural processes that might be involved in that phenomenon, but that doesn't mean that there are not also spiritual factors at work.

In short, we do not believe that a scientific understanding of calling strips its meaningfulness or explains away any spiritual understanding of the concept. Although in this book we generally approach the topic through the lens of psychological science and theory, we do not intend to imply that this approach offers a comprehensive understanding of the topic. There are very rich religious and spiritual perspectives on calling, and the most thorough understanding of the concept would incorporate them—as well as historical, philosophical, sociological, and economic treatments of the topic. We urge readers who desire comprehensiveness to investigate the topic and its personal applications at every level.

Q&A 5. I think my employer may find it inappropriate if I took steps to integrate such deeply held personal values with my job. How should I approach this?

We recognize a valid fear some people might have: that because a calling is so highly tied to what one values, it may not be appropriate for the workplace, which some people still, somewhat incredibly, describe as a value-free zone. An important distinction focuses on the questions of the source of a calling and how it is expressed. The sources from which people perceive a calling may differ considerably, but regardless of the source, the manner in which a calling is expressed is usually fairly uniform: an approach to work that allows a person to demonstrate or derive a sense of meaning and purpose, which is motivated by a desire to be helpful to others. We suspect that the source of a calling is most likely where a fear of integrating values explicitly may arise, especially when the source is external to the self (e.g., a higher power or one's country). How would you tell your boss or coworkers that you chose your current career, or approach your work the way you do, as a response to a calling from God? What would happen if you did?

If it seems likely that an external calling source might rub some people at work the wrong way, then use a healthy dose of caution when discussing it. A work environment that encourages all employees to openly discuss the values underlying their career paths without judgment is the ideal, but this kind of environment, unfortunately, is likely far from the norm. Our advice is to be shrewd.

Pick and choose your spots. Bring people into your circle whom you are confident would be supportive, or at least tolerant and respectful, of where your calling originated. However, don't stray from integrating the values your calling promotes into your work. Apart from the fact that doing so would leave you feeling fragmented and compartmentalized, employees who actively focus on making work meaningful, and who strive to serve the greater good, are considered model workers to most employers. Decades of research by scholars who study the best kinds of employees in the workplace support this assumption. These employees are more likely than others to engage in "organizational citizenship" behaviors, which consist of five personal dimensions: altruism, civic virtue, conscientiousness at work, courtesy, and sportsmanship. By aggregating data from many similar studies into one omnibus quantitative summary, a technique known as meta-analysis, researchers have found that employees who engage in citizenship behaviors are happier at work, more committed to the organization, and more supportive of leadership than those who seldom express citizenship behaviors.[9] If you have values that are focused on helping others and finding meaning at work, express those values loudly. Employers will be thrilled that you did.

Q&A 6. I had what I thought was a "transcendent summons" experience, but now I have doubts about whether it was real or just my imagination. How can I tell?

Formulating a general response to this question is hard, because these experiences vary tremendously from situation to situation. Many people long for a burning bush–type event in which they experience a calling, but most never get one, at least not in the way they hope for or expect. As we said in chapter 3, experiencing some kind of life-altering revelation about your calling is not typical, and seeking such an event is not a strategy we would recommend. Nevertheless, it does happen. Earlier we shared the stories of Roger Visker, the cop who was dramatically called into the ministry, and Rohit, the warehouse manager, who quit his job to operate a forklift at the makeshift Salvation Army center in North Dakota. Both men felt a strong sense of having been called. Roger took a measured response, in part because so much was riding on making the change, given his other commitments. He entered a period of exploration and soul-searching and ultimately concluded that pursuing the ministry was, in fact, something he had to do. Rohit, on the other hand, responded to his summons by making a major change almost immediately.

We have heard of transcendent summons experiences that are as convincing as they are dramatic, leaving people with little question about the legitimacy of the experience. However, sometimes people have seemingly earth-shattering experiences that are traceable to dubious sources, such as their own exhaustion; a heavy intake of caffeine, alcohol, or something stronger; a response to an emotionally intense or unfamiliar situation; or even simply very strongly desiring such an experience. In situations where a person has what feels like a summons but is left with doubts about its legitimacy, we strongly recommend taking Roger's approach. Our assumption is that, in general, a calling aligns a person's gifts with an opportunity to work meaningfully, in a way that fits within that person's broader sense of purpose in life and enhances the greater good. If this assumption seems reasonable to you, start by asking yourself these questions:

- ▸ Is the path to which I sense a calling consistent with my strongest areas of interest? Does it fit well with what I value most? Does it capitalize on my areas of ability or skill? Would it allow me to be myself in my work?
- ▸ When I discuss this kind of career change with people whom I

deeply respect, who know me well, who can be objective, and who have my best interests in mind, what do they say?

▸ How would this kind of change impact my ability to carry out my other responsibilities in life?

▸ What needs in my community or in the world around me would I positively influence through my work if I made a change like this?

Take time for self-reflection and thoroughly (and if you are a person of faith, prayerfully) investigate these questions. If this process leaves you with a strong sense that the pathway to which you sense a calling is a good fit with your gifts, draws support from the people around you whom you trust, fits well within your other roles and responsibilities, provides a means through which you can make a positive difference in the world, and is accessible to you, these characteristics seem supportive of the legitimacy of the experience. If any of the above questions give you reasons to reconsider, don't ignore them.

Q&A 7. I work for a wholesale distributor right now, but I have a passion for art, and I sense a calling to a career as an artist. However, I am very concerned that pursuing art full-time will make it difficult for me to earn a living. How can I pursue my calling if I'm not sure I'll be able to pay the bills?

This question is common, especially for those interested in the arts or in other fields for which adequately paying jobs are scarce. In chapter 9 we profiled Josh Frank, a Juilliard-trained, internationally renowned trumpeter who still struggles with the financial ups and downs of the professional music world. Josh makes it work, in part by getting a little entrepreneurial (e.g., offering trumpet lessons from his apartment via Skype to supplement his pay as a performer) and in part because he has fewer financial responsibilities given that he has no children and a spouse who also earns an income.

One option, of course, is to step out in faith and give it a shot as a full-time artist. Before taking that step, weigh the costs and the benefits. Do you sense that if you don't do this now, you'll look back in the future and wish you had at least tried? If you do this and it doesn't work out, what are the consequences? One thing is certain: you will never succeed as a full-time artist if you don't ever give it a try. With apologies to Alfred Lord Tennyson, perhaps the key question is this: Is it better to have tried and failed, then never to have tried at all? If your answer to this is yes, you know what you have to do.

We are tempted to promise that if you do what you love, the money will follow, but we are also pragmatic. Furthermore, we know very talented artists who have gone in the opposite direction of what you describe, making the tough choice of giving up full-time art to look for a "regular" job that could better help them meet their financial obligations. For artists unlike Josh who may not have the financial backing of a spouse or who may have additional mouths to feed, pursuing that calling as a primary income source may simply feel not worth the risk. If you are confronted with this scenario, don't lose hope. We suggest taking a multipronged approach to the problem.

First, make it a point to invest in your art as a side job, paid or unpaid. Without the structure and obligations that come with a full-time job, and all the other demands that compete for your attention, your studio time may be vulnerable to getting swallowed up by your other commitments. So treat it like a job: Set up a consistent schedule clearly indicating the time you will devote to your art and protect that time. For example, set aside Tuesday and Thursday nights from 7:00 to 10:00 as your studio time, let your family and friends know about these times, and guard them as you would guard the time you are required to spend at your day job. Plan out the projects you want to complete and establish timelines for them. Let people know about these timelines, and ask them to keep you accountable for meeting them. Building in this degree of structure helps ensure that you will maintain the boundaries you establish for pursuing your calling to art.

Second, part of what probably makes art your calling is that it provides you with a way to use your gifts meaningfully to serve the greater good. Have you tried to approach your day job this way, too? Doing so may not turn your wholesaling distribution gig into a calling, but it may move things in that direction. Read again through the various job-crafting strategies we discussed in chapter 7, and try to create opportunities to use your creativity and artistic ability in your current job. Perhaps you can adapt some of your existing tasks, or add to them, in ways that can showcase your creativity. You might try by simply approaching your direct supervisor, clue her or him into your (possibly) hidden passion for art, and ask if there are opportunities for you to use your talents to improve your current projects or help the organization better meet its goals.

Although it doesn't involve art, here is an example: During Ryan's last year of graduate school, he worked full-time as a psychotherapist at a college counseling center. He mostly enjoyed the job, but the requirements of his day-to-day activities did not allow him to pursue his calling, which centers around conducting research. Acutely aware of this conflict, about midway through the year Ryan made it a point to let his bosses know that he had a very strong interest in research and would be thrilled for any opportunity to use his research skills in his job. Surrounded by therapists whose passions mainly involved working with people, his supervisor was pleasantly surprised that someone on staff was willing to work with numbers. This simple conversation ultimately resulted in Ryan becoming involved in two research projects that helped advance the goals of the counseling center—one that involved analyzing data from people applying for jobs within the center, and another that involved building an electronic database that therapists could use to better refer clients to counselors in their community. It was a win-win for the organization and for Ryan, but it would never have happened if he hadn't taken the initiative of talking with his boss about his situation.

Q&A 8. In a big-picture sense, I feel like my job is a calling, but sometimes the daily grind really does feel like a grind. How can I experience more meaning when things get really tough in my job?

We suspect almost everyone encounters the grind from time to time. To better understand the dimensions involved in this question, let's look at a quick research example. Ryan and his students recently conducted a study with a group of eminent research psychologists, each of whom had been in the field for over twenty-five years, had achieved the highest rank of full professor, and whose scholarly work was regarded by their peers as top notch. All of these people were extremely passionate about their jobs and viewed helping others in some way as an important part of their work. However, equally pervasive were complaints about seemingly unending administrative work—from student evaluations to putting together hundred-page documents to help their graduate programs remain nationally accredited. Talk about a grind! How do these scholars tolerate the tedious and time-consuming parts of their job descriptions? They engaged in resigned indignation. That's right; over time, they learned to simply plow through these painstaking tasks and complete them, even though they could hardly stand them. Such deplorable tasks were viewed simply as "the costs of doing business."

We mention this group of extremely successful scholars to make our first point. Virtually every job is going to have certain tasks or periods of time that are especially grinding. Indeed, if a job exists out there with people who feel like they are living out their callings in 100 percent of their duties, we have yet to hear of it. Therefore, make sure your expectations about your job and your calling are realistic. Even the most poignant and profound callings will occasionally require tasks that are just plain unpleasant.

However, suppose you don't expect perfection, and the grind is not sporadic but is more like an everyday onslaught. Maybe you have waited it out for a few months to see if things might improve, and they haven't. If this describes your experience, start by assessing how well your big-picture calling fits with what you are currently doing. Throughout this book we've highlighted how callings are usually at least somewhat fluid; they change over time, as do the demands of any particular job. Perhaps your sense of calling, your job demands, or both have changed so that they are no longer in alignment, and the friction you are feeling may be an indication that a larger change is needed.

If this situation resembles yours, consider the realistic prospect of crafting your current job in ways that match your calling. Perhaps a good starting point is to assess what the grind is really about for you. Is it something to do with the work tasks, the work hours, your boss, your coworkers, or some combination of all of the above? Whatever the source of the problem, assess your level of ability to craft your job in ways that allow you to navigate these obstacles. To spark some ideas for changing your work tasks and environment, read through chapter 7 and implement the job-crafting exercise we describe.

If the grind doesn't come to a halt through job crafting, start to appraise your options for a job that would fit better with your sense of calling. Although difficult, job changes are extremely common. Most changes are best thought of not as indications of failure, but as new beginnings. For some, transitioning from the grind to a more calling-appropriate job match means keeping the same job title, but finding a new environment that offers a better fit. For others, it might require leaving an occupation entirely and taking on a brand-new trade. For more to think through as you anticipate this process, read through chapter 6. Although the thought of completely shifting career trajectories might seem scary and intimidating, across all the people we've interviewed who have used their calling as a guide for a major job change, each and every one of them has expressed great joy in taking that step.

Q&A 9. I'm a mother of two young children. What kinds of things can I do to help my kids foster a sense of calling in their work as they grow up?

We wish all parents would ask this question. We are not the kind of psychologists who are accustomed to doling out parenting advice, but we can offer a few recommendations based on Bryan's personal experience as well as the observations of developmental and vocational psychologists. To keep it simple, here are four guidelines:

1. *Help your children develop their inherited gifts.* With apologies to John Locke, children are not blank slates when they are born. They have inherited, among other things, a budding set of gifts—interests, abilities, personalities, and needs—that are incubating within them. You have undoubtedly seen evidence of such inheritance. Depending on their ages, one of your children might seem naturally drawn, for example, to expressing herself or himself through finger painting, sculpting Play-Doh, making crafts, and enjoying other creative activities, whereas the other might be a rough-and-tumble kid who loves running around, wrestling, and getting dirty outside. Maybe one is fascinated by animals, while the other can't get enough of number puzzles like Sudoku.

Whatever the particulars, all children have certain signature tendencies that they express consistently and that probably seem to have emerged all on their own. You may have noticed how these kinds of tendencies have shaped the way you parent each of them. Do you find yourself getting animal-themed toys for your child who is obsessed with animals and puzzle books for your child who loves numbers? Such personalized presents serve to strengthen these particular interests. This kind of environmental shaping happens very naturally; you want to satisfy your children's interests, so you create opportunities in which they can do more of the things to which they are naturally attracted or for which they show an aptitude. In parenting in this manner, you help them further develop those gifts that make them unique. This process of identifying children's preferences, abilities, personalities, and needs, and creating opportunities for them to further develop these gifts, is both adaptive and important. If your child loves sports, register her in the local rec league and play catch with her in the park. If your child loves music, sign him up for piano lessons and sing songs around the dinner table. Keep doing things like this, because such reinforcement helps them develop their potential, an important step in their increasing awareness of what makes them unique. Such awareness will eventually help them discern their callings in life.

2. *Help your children expand their gifts and explore the world around them.* As important as it is to recognize your children's gifts and create environments in which they can develop them, parents can go overboard with this principle. We have encountered parents who put their finger on a particular skill or ability a child seems to have and proceed to overwhelm the child with a rigidly constrained environment that seems designed to squeeze every bit of that particular ability out of the child. Even with the best parental intentions, sending an eleven-year-old to a special school where she can train year-round for six or more hours a day to perfect her tennis game, at the expense of other activities, for example, probably has far more potential for harm than good.

Decades of research evidence suggest that important individual differences like interests and personality are not fixed during childhood and adolescence, but rather fluctuate considerably before stabilizing during early adulthood. Due to this finding, we usually urge middle and high school students to avoid committing too early to a particular career path. Doing so has the potential to close the child off from learning about other opportunities that may ultimately lead to a better fit with her or his developing gifts. Our advice to parents is to encourage your children to explore the activities in which they are particularly interested, but also to try new activities and experiences, strive for well-roundedness, and keep options open. Take your children not only to the zoo but also to the art gallery and the museum of nature and science. Get tickets not only to a baseball game but also to the local community theater. Connect them with role models representing a wide array of occupational spheres. By exposing them to such diverse experiences, your children will undoubtedly find some things more enticing and enjoyable than others, but they will learn more along the way and may surprise you and themselves with interests or abilities that could otherwise have gone untapped.

3. *Help your children develop a concern for others in their community and world.* As children develop, expand their gifts, and explore the world around them, they start to develop a curiosity and concern about their future. They project themselves into various roles and imagine what serving in those roles might be like. As they do so, they begin to develop a sense of motivation. In what is that motivation rooted? For children who are insulated from the world around them, the source of motivation may center around themselves. For those who visit unfamiliar places, build new relationships with peers outside their comfort zone, and experience the plight of those much less fortunate, their motivation will likely better account for the experiences of others. Travel with your children to new places, especially as part of a short-term service trip,

and interact with the locals. Volunteer with your children at a soup kitchen, homeless shelter, local hospital, or assisted living facility. Get to know the people you are serving and listen to their stories. Talk about them with your children. Such experiences help your children develop a sensitivity to the very real needs of people in their community and world. As they continue to grow, this other-oriented focus helps them identify how their gifts may be uniquely useful in contributing to the common good and well-being of others.

4. *Model what it means to live a calling.* Your children naturally look to you as their primary role model. If you approach your job or other life roles as a calling, they pick up on it. At the same time, we are often surprised by how little people know about their own parents' values in life and experiences at work. Therefore, we recommend not only modeling what it means to live out a calling, but also taking an active approach to helping your children understand your experiences and motivations. Talk with your children often about what you value in life, what you see as the big-picture goals, and what you are striving for through the work or other activities in which you are engaged. If you can't stand your job and think of it as the farthest thing from a calling, share this with your children, too; help them understand what you like and what you wish was different about your experience. Bryan recently worked with a middle school counselor to design a parent interview assignment for students. Students were instructed to spend an hour asking their parents questions about what they think of their work. In a follow-up focus group, the students who followed through with this interview described it as enlightening and as something that encouraged them to think more about what they aspire to do one day.[10]

Your influence on your children's career development and emerging sense of calling can best be accomplished through conversations with your children about your work life, goals, and motivations, combined with your long-term effort to establish a supportive environment in which your children can freely develop their gifts, explore the world around them, and establish a concern for others. Create these opportunities, encourage your children as they engage in them, and model these behaviors yourself.

Q&A 10. When I Google "career counseling," I get information about counselors, psychologists, and career coaches. This is confusing. What are the differences? How should I choose a career counselor?

We feel your pain! According to Rich Feller, president of the National Career Development Association, there are actually thirty-five unique titles that people offering career counseling services use![11] The differences between the three types of providers you mention are as follows:

Counselors usually have master's degrees and typically carry a certification, such as Nationally Certified Career Counselor (NCCC), Nationally Certified Counselor (NCC), or Licensed Professional Counselor (LPC). A master's degree in counseling usually takes two to three years to complete. NCCC certification recognizes specialized training and experience related to career counseling, but this credential is no longer being offered; NCCC counselors are a dying breed. NCC and LPC certifications recognize general counseling training and expertise; they do not necessarily require career counseling training.

Psychologists who provide career counseling usually have a doctoral degree—either a PhD (doctor of philosophy) or a PsyD (doctor of psychology)—and have a state license to practice psychology. A doctoral degree usually requires between five and seven years of graduate training (including, not in addition to, a master's degree). Psychologists who provide psychotherapy services can be either *counseling psychologists* or *clinical psychologists*, but usually counseling psychologists are the ones who provide career counseling. (A lot of overlap exists between these two areas of psychology, but clinical psychology has historically focused on helping sick people get well, and counseling psychology has focused on helping well people flourish. Most counseling psychology programs provide career assessment and counseling training to its students, and most clinical programs do not. Counseling psychologists who have specialized in career counseling may use the title "vocational psychologist"; this term describes one's area of focus, not a degree or a credential.)

Career coaches or *life coaches* are often harder to gauge. Some have master's-level training as a counselor or even doctoral-level training as a psychologist and simply prefer to use the "coach" title, but others have as little as a weekend seminar's worth of training.[12] The latter category of coaches are, in theory if not always in practice, para-career counselors equipped to successfully work with relatively straightforward problems (e.g., setting goals or redoing a résumé), referring more complex cases to career counselors or psychologists. Many coaches with whom we have interacted are bright, warm, and supportive, and they seem quite skilled. However, there are undoubtedly some who may have entered the profession for the wrong (usually financial) reasons, enticed by Internet banner ads promising high salaries. In most states, the credentialing process for career and life coaches, if there is one at all, bears little resemblance to the regulatory rigor that governs professional counselors and psychologists, a much-discussed issue in the coaching profession.

The best advice we can give is that if you opt to work with a counselor, do your homework. Unless your concerns are fairly simple, find one who is well trained. In theory, such training is not hard to evaluate; simply ask a provider to give you a summary of her or his training and experience in career counseling. Some make this information available on a website or have a summary available on a brochure; others can summarize it in person or over the phone. Whether the counselor has a doctoral degree or a master's degree may not matter—research has not found a difference in effectiveness between services delivered by doctoral- and master's-level counselors. However, you should evaluate two things: whether the counselor has at least a master's degree, and whether the counselor has specialized training or experience related specifically to career counseling.

Once you have identified a well-trained counselor (or two or three), arrange a meeting and evaluate whether you think you would work well together. Come prepared with questions (e.g., What is your approach to working with clients? What kinds of things would I be doing? How do you use assessments? What outcomes do people usually experience, over what number of sessions? What are the costs? What is your success rate?). Many career counselors provide initial consultation sessions for free or at a reduced cost. Use this session to experience what working with this counselor would be like; if you feel that establishing a good working relationship together would be difficult, you are probably right; move on to another option. If you hit it off, give it a try, and evaluate how well things are going as you work through the process. We provide more detailed suggestions for choosing a counselor at the book's companion website, www.MakeYourJobaCalling.com.

Q&A 11. I have worked in my current job for the last twenty years, and I always thought of it as a calling. Lately, though, I feel very stagnant in it. I think it still makes a difference for people, but it's become too much of a routine, is no longer very challenging, and

is almost getting boring. However, I really can't afford to change careers right now. What suggestions do you have to help me reinject some excitement into my calling?

It sounds like you are in a funk, which is normal. Remind yourself that a calling is never static; in all the interviews we've conducted with people we consider to be exemplars of calling, we can count on one hand the number who describe having discovered a calling in a single event, then riding off into the figurative sunset without experiencing a change in their callings after that. Instead, think of your calling as dynamic and evolving, and start by adapting it using *scaffolding.* Scaffolding usually brings to mind those temporary lattice structures that construction workers use for support when they are working on a building's exterior. During the 1950s, psychologist Jerome Bruner applied the term within the field of education, using it metaphorically to refer to a particular method of teaching.[13] According to this approach, to help students learn, teachers provide a series of supports, then gradually remove them as students learn the material. As students move on to more complex material, new supports are put in place to help them learn, and the same cycle commences in which these supports are gradually removed as the material is learned. Throughout the learning process, the teachers instruct students to build on past knowledge to uncover new knowledge. For example, division is usually taught after students begin to grasp multiplication, which is introduced after students first learn addition and subtraction, and so on. Students are encouraged to scaffold their knowledge over time, building on what they previously knew to learn more and more.

Expanding beyond education, scaffolding has started to become widely used in the broader culture, usually referring to the notion that people build off previous knowledge or skills to learn higher-order knowledge and skills. This may be a little abstract, but think for a moment about the most famous rock bands over the last half century—not the one-hit wonders, but those that thrived for long periods of time, like the Beatles, the Rolling Stones, or U2. All of these groups started out playing a particular style of music, with particular types of songs. Along the way, though, they evolved, taking on new challenges and performing new types of music. If any of them experienced a calling to perform as musicians, that probably didn't change, but the ways they approached their trade changed considerably over time. Take the Beatles, for example. When they introduced an Eastern flair into their later albums, it was seen as a pretty big shift—but it's not like they went from making music to writing computer programs. They simply went from making music one way to making it another way. The Beatles built from their foundation of music and added new twists that required them to expand their comfort zone and learn new ways to do things. You can take this same approach in your job. Think of things you do very well at your work. How can you build off of that foundation? How can you tweak your work a bit and build new skills or knowledge? Taking on new or more complex tasks might just provide the level of challenge needed to pump some excitement into your calling again.

Another option is to challenge yourself to come up with new ways for using your job to help others. We offered some ideas for this in chapter 5, but for a good example of someone who is doing this well, turn back to chapter 10 and read Larry Kieft's story. Here is a guy who for decades worked closely with women and mothers as an obstetrician and gynecologist. For many people, providing medical care and delivering babies would go pretty far in satisfying a desire to help others. But Larry has gone much farther than this, establishing a prenatal program for mothers in need, working to secure health care for the uninsured, and raising money for a children's clinic, all efforts to live out his calling more effectively. As he enters retirement, Larry has an even bigger dream of linking medical schools and residencies in the United States and Africa to

help physicians in developing countries obtain high-quality, cultur-
ally appropriate training. Larry has held essentially the same job for
thirty-five years, but his calling has always been about finding new
ways to use his gifts to better serve those in need. If you're feeling
stagnant, think like Larry. What are some new ways you can use
your gifts in your work to make a difference?

*Q&A 12. I was just laid off from a job that I felt was my calling.
I would like to maintain my calling but am not sure what to do.
Any advice?*

You have just suffered a significant loss. We want to acknowledge
that for starters and recognize that like other types of loss, job loss
can be emotionally devastating. Some people who experience job
loss have depressive feelings; they might feel really down in the
dumps, and can experience thoughts related to worthlessness,
helplessness, fatigue, insomnia, or restlessness. Others feel anxious; they worry a great deal, or feel afraid, panicky, or impatient.
Some people feel physical symptoms, too, like headaches or back
pain or a racing heart. If any of these feelings or symptoms are
part of your experience, please seek some help immediately from a
psychologist or from your doctor. As with any other significant loss,
you also may need to permit yourself the chance to grieve, and you
will probably benefit by seeking support from people who mean a
lot to you. Seek that support, because it will help you cope and give
you a boost as you begin to anticipate your next steps.

Your question suggests that you view your calling as bigger than
the job you lost, which is an important belief on which to build.
A calling transcends any single job, but at the same time, a job
is an important vehicle for living out a calling. You have at least

two options for proceeding. The first, of course, is to set out for new employment that fits at least as well as the job you lost. Some fortunate percentage of people who seek a replacement job similar to the one they lost find one quickly, and if you sense that your job was a calling and you excelled at it, this could be you. Update that résumé, prepare some new cover letters, brush up on your interviewing skills, and work with your network of colleagues to identify new, potentially satisfying options as quickly as possible. (For some useful resources to help you navigate each of these steps in the process, go to www.makeyourjobacalling.com.) We recognize, of course, that this kind of quick advice is easy to give. Actually carrying it out is much harder because each of these tasks requires considerable effort, and there is no guarantee that a new job is right around the corner.

If your search for a job similar to the one you lost takes an extended period of time, your other option is to take whatever job you can find that brings in some income and strive to live out your calling outside of work, at least for now. With this approach, you could get some of the same psychological benefits your job provided and also help buffer the feelings of loss you are experiencing. In chapter 8 we provided recommendations for how you might accomplish this, but for people suffering with unemployment, living out a calling outside of work may have some additional rewards:

1. *Sense of identity and self-worth.* Filling the "identity void" left by losing your job is not easy, and experiencing that void may reduce your overall sense of self-worth, especially if your identity was closely tied to your job. Performing activities that align with your calling may provide you with a similar sense of purpose, mission, and accomplishment compared to what you experienced while you were employed.

2. *Connecting with others.* What image comes to mind when you think of someone who is unemployed and looking for a new job? It might be someone with a naturally occurring "bed head" hairdo

wearing pajama pants, holding a cup of coffee, and staring glassy-eyed at the computer screen with a résumé open on one tab and Monster.com on the other. Indeed, unemployment can result in a very solitary existence. Attempting to live out your calling while unemployed can help circumvent that pattern, because a calling necessarily involves other people and can help you remain connected. Chapter 5 discussed the basic need that people have for a human connection. Engaging in activities related to your calling even while unemployed can be a great way to connect with like-minded folks while helping others in the process.

3. *A gateway to employment.* When working with unemployed clients, career counselors frequently recommend volunteering during the job hunt. Working for free exposes people to new career options they hadn't previously considered. Ask yourself: If you could do anything for your job without having to worry about money, what would it be? Whatever comes to mind is probably a good fit with your calling, and offering to perform your services for free to an organization at a minimum can help you feel better (see point 1 above) and could ultimately lead to a paid position. Performing your calling is something you naturally do with passion, energy, and commitment—all traits that stand out to any employer.

Q&A 13. I'm running a business that emerged from my sense of calling, and I'd like for my employees to experience the same sense of purpose and mission that I do. What kinds of things can I do to help facilitate this?

Throughout this book we have focused on discerning and living a calling at the level of the individual employee or job seeker. However, people in a position to influence organizations on a broader scale have a unique opportunity to positively impact larger groups of employees. When employees view their work as a calling, they experience a greater degree of career-related and general well-being, and are likely to perform well as a result. Helping employees cultivate their callings is therefore beneficial not only to the individual employee but to the organization; it is both the right thing to do and also good for the bottom line. We offer three brief suggestions to facilitate this process; more information is available at www.makeyourjobacalling.com.

1. *Assess and match their gifts.* In order for employees to approach their work as a calling, they need a good understanding of their unique gifts. What makes each individual employee special? In chapter 6 we discussed the importance of forging a path by discovering gifts through informal self-assessment (e.g., writing down the strengths you display when you are at your best), psychological inventories (e.g., using tests that measure a person's vocational interests), or with the help of a trained career counselor. We suggest that employers offer career development interventions such as workshops that can help employees assess their gifts in large- or small-group settings. An efficient way to do this is to have employees complete a set of psychological inventories and then hire a psychologist or counselor to facilitate a group interpretation of these results.

Helping employees understand their gifts is useful by itself, particularly so if job opportunities are provided that match their gifts. An employer can allow employees to alter their job tasks in ways that make the tasks better matched to their unique gifts. One recommended approach would be for an employer to meet individually with each employee and discuss how their gifts can better fit the available opportunities within the workplace. These opportunities may range from redesigning a subset of an employee's job tasks to moving that employee into a new position altogether. This commitment to smart fluidity helps employees experience greater satisfaction over time, especially in cases where their strengths shift.

2. *Get buy-in for your organizational mission.* Like many employers, you probably have a clearly articulated mission statement to which you may turn for help with big-picture decisions. How well do your employees know this mission? How well do they buy into it? Employees who understand the larger purposes and goals of the organization for which they work derive a greater sense of meaning from their work tasks. Many of the most successful companies in the United States (e.g., Google, Microsoft, Whole Foods) host regular group sessions in which employees are reminded of the company's overall mission and encouraged to find new ways to implement that mission in their respective jobs. We recommend this same strategy in your business: implement training activities that highlight the company's mission and that make clear and unambiguous how each employee helps advance that mission.

3. *Create opportunities for employees to serve others.* Helping employees sustain a calling over time requires a combination of using their gifts, experiencing meaningfulness and purpose, and serving others. As an employer, you can nourish this final piece in a variety of ways. One simple strategy for creating these opportunities is to ensure that the mission of your business itself is linked to the greater good. If this value is explicit, you can use this as a selection criterion and hire people who buy into that mission. To the extent that you are able to do so effectively, you add employees who are not only aware of their desire to help others but also more likely to naturally engage in service within their work tasks. If helping others is a secondary part of your organization's mission, consider other ways your employees can meet the needs of others. Many businesses incorporate regular outside work service activities, such as building Habitat for Humanity houses or serving food at a soup kitchen. These types of activities certainly have value, but the effect is likely maximized when the available activities align

with the unique strengths of the employees. For instance, while a group of lawyers might have fun pulling out their hammers and trying to build a house, it may be more meaningful (and useful) if they used this time to provide pro bono legal services to disadvantaged clients. We recommend that you assess your employees' strengths and use this information to create regular opportunities to actualize these strengths in the service of others.

Notes

Chapter 1

1. Isaac Hunter, Bryan J. Dik, and James H. Banning, "College Students' Perceptions of Calling in Work and Life," *Journal of Vocational Behavior* 76.2 (2010): 178–86.
2. Isaac Hunter, Bryan J. Dik, and James H. Banning, "Perceptions of Calling in Work and Life," American Psychological Association, San Diego, CA, August 2011.
3. Roy Baumeister, *Meanings of Life* (New York: Guilford, 1991).
4. Amy Wrzesniewski, "Callings," in *The Oxford Handbook of Positive Organizational Scholarship*, ed. Kim Cameron and Gretchen Spreitzer (New York: Oxford University Press, forthcoming).
5. Stephen W. Hawking, *A Brief History of Time: From the Big Bang to Black Holes* (New York: Bantam, 1988).
6. Nancy E. Abrams and Joel R. Primack, "Einstein's View of God," in *God for the Twenty-first Century*, ed. Russell Stannard (Radnor, PA: Templeton Foundation Press, 2000), 153–57.
7. Steven Weinberg, interview from the PBS film *Faith and Reason* (1998), New River Media and Five Continents Music (Ronald Bailey and Andrew Walworth, executive producers; Ronald Ailey and Cameron Allan, producers; Margaret Wertheim, writer and host), www.pbs.org/faithandreason/.
8. Stuart Bunderson and Jeffery A. Thompson, "The Call of the Wild: Zookeepers, Callings and the Double-Edged Sword of Deeply Meaningful Work," *Administrative Science Quarterly* 54.1 (2009): 32–57, 50.
9. Bryan J. Dik and Ryan D. Duffy, "Calling and Vocation at Work: Definitions and Prospects for Research and Practice," *Counseling Psychologist* 37.3 (2009): 424–450, 427.
10. William C. Placher, *Callings: Twenty Centuries of Christian Wisdom on Vocation* (Grand Rapids: Eerdmans, 2005).
11. Drawn from the 2007 Pew Forum Religious Landscape Survey, http://religions.pewforum.org.
12. Because we were unable to track this person down to request permission to use his real name, Rohit is a pseudonym.

13. With a goal of being as clear as possible, we define "purpose" as "a stable and generalized intention to accomplish something that is at once meaningful to the self and of consequence beyond the self" (William Damon, Jenni Menon, and Kendall C. Bronk, "The Development of Purpose during Adolescence," *Applied Developmental Science* 7.3 [2003]: 119–28, 121). We define "meaning" or "meaningfulness" as "the sense made of, and significance felt regarding, the nature of one's being and existence" (M. F. Steger, Patricia Frazier, Shigehiro Oishi, and Matthew Kaler, "The Meaning in Life Questionnaire: Assessing the Presence of and Search for Meaning in Life," *Journal of Counseling Psychology* 53.1 [2006]: 80–93, 81). One further point of clarification: A recent review by Rosso, Dekas, and Wrzesniewski encouraged scholars to differentiate between the terms "meaning" and "meaningfulness" at work, because "meaning at work" usually refers to the type of meaning that employees derive from work, whereas "meaningfulness at work" refers to the amount of significance they attach to it. We have opted to use "meaning" rather than "meaningfulness" because it is the more frequently used term in common vernacular and is two fewer syllables in length; also, our hope is that, in its context, it is clear that our use of "meaning" refers to the positive significance that people experience (Brent D. Rosso, Kathryn H. Dekas, and Amy Wrzesniewski, "On the Meaning of Work: A Theoretical Integration and Review," *Research in Organizational Behavior* 30 [2010]: 91–127).

14. Roy F. Baumeister and Kathleen D. Vohs, "The Pursuit of Meaningfulness in Life," in *The Handbook of Positive Psychology*, ed. C. R. Synder and Shane Lopez (New York: Oxford University Press, 2002), 608–18.

15. Douglas T. Hall and Dawn E. Chandler, "Psychological Success: When the Career Is a Calling," *Journal of Organizational Behavior* 26.2 (2005): 155–76.

16. Amy Wrzesniewski and Jane E. Dutton, "Crafting a Job: Revisioning Employees as Active Crafters of Their Work," *Academy of Management Review* 26.2 (2001): 179–201.

17. Jesper Isaksen, "Constructing Meaning Despite the Drudgery of Repetitive Work," *Journal of Humanistic Psychology* 40.3 (2000): 84–107.

18. Blake E. Ashforth and Glen E. Kreiner, "'How Can You Do It?': Dirty Work and the Challenge of Constructing a Positive Identity," *Academy of Management Review* 24.3 (1999): 413–34.

19. James C. Davidson and David P. Caddell, "Religion and the Meaning of Work," *Journal for the Scientific Study of Religion* 33.2 (1994): 135–47.

20. Dik and Duffy, "Calling and Vocation at Work."

21. Ryan D. Duffy, Bryan J. Dik, and Michael F. Steger, "Calling and Work-Related Outcomes: Career Commitment as a Mediator," *Journal of Vocational Behavior* 78.2 (2011): 210–18.

22. Michael F. Steger, N. Pickering, J. Y. Shin, and Bryan J. Dik, "Calling in Work: Secular or Sacred?" *Journal of Career Assessment* 18.1 (2010): 82–96.

23. Ryan D. Duffy, Elizabeth M. Bott, Blake A. Allan, Carrie L. Torrey, and Bryan J. Dik, "Perceiving a Calling, Living a Calling, and Job Satisfaction: Testing a Moderated, Multiple Mediator Model," *Journal of Counseling Psychology* 59.1 (2012): 50–59.

24. Lee Hardy, *The Fabric of This World: Inquiries into Calling, Career Choice, and the Design of Human Work* (Grand Rapids: Eerdmans, 1990).

25. Amy Wrzesniewski, Clark McCauley, Paul Rozin, and Barry Schwartz, "Jobs, Careers, and Callings: People's Relations to Their Work," *Journal of Research in Personality* 31.1 (1997): 21–33.

Chapter 2

1. Robert N. Bellah, Richard Madsen, William M. Sullivan, Ann Swidler, and Steven M. Tipton, *Habits of the Heart: Individualism and Commitment in American Life* (New York: Harper & Row, 1985).

2. Studs Terkel, *Working* (New York: New Press, 1997), xi.

3. Ibid., xviii.

4. Bellah et al., *Habits of the Heart*, 68.

5. Ibid., 66.

6. Michael G. Pratt, Camille Pradies, and Douglas A. Lepisto, "Doing Well, Doing Good, and Doing With: Organizational Practices for Effectively Cultivating Meaningful Work," in *Meaning and Purpose in the Workplace*, ed. Bryan Dik, Zinta Byrne, and Mike Steger (Washington, DC: APA Books, forthcoming).

7. A factor analysis of Wrzesniewski et al.'s measure of work orientations in 1997 suggests that job and calling anchor the ends of a bipolar continuum, while the career orientation is a separate dimension (Amy Wrzesniewski, Clark McCauley, Paul Rozin, and Barry Schwartz, "Jobs, Careers, and Callings: People's Relations to Their Work," *Journal of Research in Personality* 31.1 [1997]: 21–33).

8. Faulkner's famous quote is uttered by the character Gavin Stevens near the end of act 1, scene 3, of *Requiem for a Nun*. It's taken a bit out of context here—Stevens's point is that an individual's past actions are never truly in the past because they continue to shape the present—but nevertheless we believe the general principle applies broadly, extending beyond individuals to Western civilization.

9. Lee Hardy, *The Fabric of This World: Inquiries into Calling, Career Choice, and the Design of Human Work* (Grand Rapids: Eerdmans, 1990).

10. *Plutarch: The Lives of the Noble Grecians and Romans*, translated by John Dryden and revised by Arthur Hugh Clough (New York: Modern Library, n.d.), 182–83. Quoted in *Working: Its Meanings and Its Limits*, ed. Gilbert Meilaender (Notre Dame, IN: University of Notre Dame Press, 2000).

11. Eusebius (c. 260–c. 339), *Demonstration of the Gospel*; discussed in Darrow L. Miller, *LifeWork: A Biblical Theology for What You Do Every Day* (Seattle: YWAM Publishing, 2009).

12. They aren't as famous as Plato and Plutarch, but include guys like Gordiano Bruno, Giovanni Pico Della Mirandola, and Marsilio Ficino.

13. Hardy, *Fabric of This World*, 27.

14. Ibid., 28.

15. Patricia A. Emison, *Creating the "Divine" Artist: From Dante to Michelangelo* (Leiden: Brill, 2004).

16. Hardy, *Fabric of This World*, 28.
17. Agnes Heller, *Renaissance Man* (London: Routledge, Kegan and Paul, 1978), cited in Hardy, *Fabric of This World*.
18. We're being facetious.
19. Some scholars question whether the nailing on the church door actually occurred, or whether they were instead presented to church authorities in a letter. Either way, the theses were written and presented to church authorities, which is usually considered the starting point of the Reformation.
20. Miller, *LifeWork*, 22.
21. Alister McGrath, *Reformation Thought: An Introduction* (Malden, MA: Blackwell, 2001).
22. Hardy, *Fabric of This World*, 76.
23. Gordon T. Smith, *Courage and Calling: Embracing Your God-Given Potential* (Downers Grove, IL: InterVarsity Press, 1999).
24. Roy Baumeister, *Meanings of Life* (New York: Guilford, 1991), 125.
25. Amy Wrzesniewski, Clark McCauley, Paul Rozin, and Barry Schwartz, "Jobs, Careers, and Callings: People's Relations to Their Work," *Journal of Research in Personality* 31.1 (1997): 21–33.
26. Remember our discussion about differences in definitions of calling from chapter 1? Our way of conceptualizing calling differs a bit from Wrzesniewski et al.'s. For example, pursuing a calling in a neoclassical sense involves placing one's work into proper perspective, a point we discuss briefly in chapter 3 and in somewhat more depth in chapter 9. Taking work home and on vacations, as C does in this paragraph, doesn't seem consistent with this; such behavior may in fact make C a candidate for workaholism, which we describe in chapter 9 as a distortion of calling. Nevertheless, there is clearly overlap between C's approach to work and our way of conceptualizing calling.
27. Christopher Peterson, Nansook Park, Nicholas Hall, and Martin E. P. Seligman, "Zest and Work," *Journal of Organizational Behavior* 30.2 (2009): 161–72.
28. Ibid., 162.

Chapter 3

1. A popular theory in psychology, Maslow proposed that in order for higher-order needs (such as self-esteem or self-actualization) to be met, lower-order needs (such as hunger and thirst, safety and security) have to be met first (Abraham H. Maslow, *Motivation and Personality* [New York: Harper & Row, 1970]).
2. Michael J. Breslin and Christopher A. Lewis, "Theoretical Models of the Nature of Prayer and Health: A Review," *Mental Health, Religion and Culture* 11.1 (2008): 9–21.
3. http://religions.pewforum.org/pdf/report2religious-landscape-study-key-findings.pdf.
4. Brandy M. Eldridge and Bryan J. Dik, "Calling vs. Vocation: The Role of a Transcendent Summons," American Psychological Association, Boston, August 2008.
5. Jose F. Domene, "Calling and Career Outcome Expectations: The Mediating Role of Self-Efficacy," *Journal of Career Assessment* (forthcoming).

6. Cristina Jenaro, Noelia Flores, and Benito Arias, "Burnout and Coping in Human Service Practitioners," *Professional Psychology: Research and Practice* 38.1 (2007): 80–87; Alan M. Saks, "Multiple Predictors and Criteria of Job Search Success," *Journal of Vocational Behavior* 68.3 (2006): 400–415.

7. Douglas J. Schuurman, *Vocation: Discerning Our Callings in Life* (Grand Rapids: Eerdmans, 2004), 37.

8. Schuurman describes these elements of the process in the context of the community of Christian believers. They align so closely with directives stemming from theory in vocational psychology that we take the liberty of applying them more broadly. As Schuurman explores elsewhere in his book (ibid., 32–36), generalizing these principles in this manner has precedent and is theologically legitimate.

9. Steven D. Brown and Nancy E. Ryan-Krane, "Four (or Five) Sessions and a Cloud of Dust: Old Assumptions and New Observations about Career Counseling," in *Handbook of Counseling Psychology* (3rd ed.), ed. Steven Brown and Robert Lent (New York: Wiley, 2000), 740–66.

10. Ibid.

11. The concept of "life space," with its core and peripheral roles, was articulated by vocational psychologist Donald Super; see Donald E. Super, Mark L. Savickas, and C. Super, "The Life-Span, Life-Space Approach to Careers," in *Career Choice and Development* (3rd ed.), ed. Duane Brown and Linda Brooks (San Francisco: Jossey-Bass, 1996), 121–78.

12. Roy Baumeister, *Meanings of Life* (New York: Guilford, 1991).

13. We explore this further in chapter 8.

14. Jeffrey H. Greenhaus and Gary N. Powell, "When Work and Family Are Allies: A Theory of Work-Family Enrichment," *Academy of Management Review* 31.1 (2006): 72–92.

15. We explore this point more fully in chapter 5.

16. In chapter 8.

17. http://www.goodreads.com/author/quotes/19982.Frederick_Buechner.

18. We take our duty to protect the identity of our clients very seriously. Maria is not her real name, and her story is in fact a composite of more than one client with whom Bryan has worked.

Chapter 4

1. M. F. Steger, Patricia Frazier, Shigehiro Oishi, and Matthew Kaler, "The Meaning in Life Questionnaire: Assessing the Presence of and Search for Meaning in Life," *Journal of Counseling Psychology* 53.1 [2006]: 80–93, 81.

2. See Michael F. Steger and Bryan J. Dik, "Work as Meaning: Individual and Organizational Benefits of Engaging in Meaningful Work," in *Oxford Handbook of Positive Psychology at Work*, ed. Alex Linley, Susan Harrington, and Nicola Garcia (Oxford: Oxford University Press, 2010), 131–42.

3. William Damon, Jenni Menon, and Kendall C. Bronk, "The Development of Purpose during Adolescence," *Applied Developmental Science* 7.3 (2003): 119–28, 121.

4. Peggy Lowe, "Work and God? Not Mutually Exclusive, Exec Says," *Orange*

County Register, March 10, 2011, http://www.ocregister.com/articles/mutually
-291713-county-orange.html.

5. Brent D. Rosso, Kathryn H. Dekas, and Amy Wrzesniewski, "On the Meaning of Work: A Theoretical Integration and Review," *Research in Organizational Behavior* 30 (2010): 91–127.

6. This research comes from Hackman and Oldman's Job Characteristics Model. They wrote, "An individual experiences positive affect to the extent that he learns (knowledge of results) that he personally (experienced responsibility) has performed well on a task that he cares about (experienced meaningfulness)." A meta-analytic study (that is, a study that quantitatively aggregates results from multiple studies of a particular research question) by Fried and Ferris supports the relationships we describe here (J. R. Hackman and Greg R. Oldham, "Motivation through the Design of Work: Test of a Theory," *Organizational Behavior and Human Performance* 16.2 (1976): 250–79, 255–56; Yitzhak Fried and Gerald R. Ferris, "The Validity of the Job Characteristics Model: A Review and Meta-Analysis," *Personnel Psychology* 40.2 (1987): 287–322.

7. Matthew B. Crawford, *Shop Class as Soulcraft: An Inquiry into the Value of Work* (New York: Penguin Press, 2009), 4.

8. http://www.newbelgium.com/culture/our-story.aspx.

9. Two examples: Michael G. Pratt, "The Good, the Bad, and the Ambivalent: Managing Identification among Amway Distributors," *Administrative Science Quarterly* 45.3 (2000): 456–93; Jeffery A. Thompson and J. S. Bunderson, "Violations of Principle: Ideological Currency in the Psychological Contract," *Academy of Management Review* 28.4 (2003): 17–39.

10. Gerald R. Salancik and Jeffery Pfeffer, "A Social Information Processing Approach to Job Attitudes and Task Design," *Administrative Science Quarterly* 23.2 (1978): 224–52.

11. Amy Wrzesniewski, Jane E. Dutton, and Gelaye Debebe, "Interpersonal Sense-Making and the Meaning of Work," *Research in Organizational Behavior* 25 (2003): 93–135.

12. Indeed, relationships with coworkers are one of the scales on several available assessments of work values, which are designed to measure individual differences.

13. Fred O. Malumbwa, Amanda L. Christensen, and Michael K. Muchiri, "Transformational Leadership and Meaningful Work," in *Purpose and Meaning in the Workplace*, ed. Bryan Dik, Zinta Byrne, and Michael Steger (Washington, DC: American Psychological Association, forthcoming).

14. Kara A. Arnold, Nick Turner, Julian Barling, Kevin E. Kelloway, and Margaret C. McKee, "Transformational Leadership and Psychological Well-Being: The Mediating Role of Meaningful Work," *Journal of Occupational Health Psychology* 12.3 (2007): 193–203.

15. Amy Wrzesniewski and Jane E. Dutton, "Crafting a Job: Revisioning Employees as Active Crafters of Their Work," *Academy of Management Review* 26.2 (2001): 179–201.

16. Richard J. Leider and David A. Shapiro, *Whistle While You Work: Heeding Your Life's Calling* (San Francisco: Barrett-Koehler, 2001), xiv.

17. Robert A. Giacalone, Carol L. Jurkiewica, and Louis W. Fry, "From Advocacy to Science: The Next Steps in Workplace Spirituality Research," in *Handbook of the Psychology of Religion and Spirituality*, ed. Raymond F. Paloutzian and Crystal L. Park (New York: Guilford, 2005), 515–28, 515.

18. Marjolein Lips-Wiersma, "The Influence of Spiritual 'Meaning Making' on Career Behavior," *Journal of Management Development* 21.7 (2002): 497–520; Susan C. Sullivan, "The Work-Faith Connection for Low-Income Mothers: A Research Note," *Sociology of Religion* 67.1 (2006): 99–108.

19. Sullivan, "Work-Faith Connection for Low-Income Mothers," 105.

20. Crystal L. Park, "Making Sense of the Meaning Literature: An Integrative Review of Meaning Making and Its Effects on Adjustment to Stressful Life Events," *Psychological Bulletin* 136.2 (2010): 257–301.

21. Bryan J. Dik, Ryan D. Duffy, and Andrew P. Tix, "Religion, Spirituality, and a Sense of Calling in the Workplace," in *The Psychology of Religion and Workplace Spirituality*, ed. Peter Hill and Bryan Dik (Charlotte, NC: Information Age Publishing, forthcoming).

22. Peter C. Hill and Bryan J. Dik, "Toward a Science of Workplace Spirituality: Contributions from the Psychology of Religion and Spirituality," in *The Psychology of Religion and Workplace Spirituality*, ed. Peter Hill and Bryan Dik (Charlotte, NC: Information Age Publishing, forthcoming); Lowe, "Work and God?"

23. Pete Hammond, R. Paul Stevens, and Todd Svanoe, *The Marketplace Annotated Bibliography: A Christian Guide to Books on Work, Business, and Vocation* (Downers Grove, IL: InterVarsity Press, 2002).

24. www.cardus.ca.

25. http://www.faithandwork.org/.

26. http://www.princeton.edu/csr/current-research/faith-and-work/.

27. Christopher Peterson and Martin E. P. Seligman, *Character Strengths and Virtues: A Handbook and Classification* (Oxford: Oxford University Press, 2004).

28. Martin E. P. Seligman, Tracy A. Steen, Nansook Park, and Christopher Peterson, "Positive Psychology Progress: Empirical Validation of Interventions," *American Psychologist* 60.5 (2005): 410–21.

29. Hadassa Littman-Ovadia and Michael F. Steger, "Character Strengths and Well-Being among Volunteers and Employees: Towards an Integrative Model," *Journal of Positive Psychology* 5.6 (2010): 419–30.

30. Martin E. P. Seligman, "Positive Psychology: Fundamental Assumptions," *Psychologist* 16.3 (2003): 126–27.

31. Côté and Moskowitz actually describe the benefits of acting in ways that are consistent with their strongest personality traits in their behavioral concordance model, but other research—for example, Steger, Hicks, Kashdan, Krueger, and Bouchard—shows consistent links between strengths and other personality dimensions, so this explanation seems likely to fit (Stephane Côté and D. S. Moskowitz, "On the Dynamic Covariation between Interpersonal

Behavior and Affect: Prediction from Neuroticism, Extraversion, and Agreeableness," *Journal of Personality and Social Psychology* 75.4 (1998): 1032–46; Michael F. Steger, Brian M. Hicks, Todd B. Kashdan, Robert F. Krueger, and Thomas J. Bouchard Jr., "Genetic and Environmental Influences on the Positive Traits of the Values in Action Classification, and Biometric Covariance with Normal Personality," *Journal of Research in Personality* 41.3 (2007): 524–39.

32. This point, along with additional context for this discussion, comes from this chapter: Bryan J. Dik, Michael F. Steger, Arissa R. Fitch-Martin, and Casey C. Onder, "Cultivating Meaningfulness at Work," in *The Experience of Meaning in Life: Classical Perspectives, Emerging Themes, and Controversies,* ed. Clay Routledge and Joshua Hicks (New York: Springer, forthcoming).

33. Rebecca J. Schlegel, Joshua A. Hicks, Laura A. King, and Jamie Arndt, "Feeling Like You Know Who You Are: Perceived True Self-Knowledge and Meaning in Life," *Personality and Social Psychology Bulletin* 37.6 (2011): 745–56.

34. Apparently this story has a long history, but we first read it in this essay: John J. Ryan, "Humanistic Work: Its Philosophical and Cultural Implications," in *A Matter of Dignity: Inquiries into the Humanization of Work,* ed. William J. Heisler and John W. Houck (Notre Dame, IN: University of Notre Dame Press, 1977), 11–22.

35. Social psychologists point to data showing that people thrive when they are "self-concordant"—that is, when they pursue goals that align closely with their interests and values. Similarly, construal level theory suggests that overarching purposes may be difficult to link to activity in the here and now, but that connecting work activities to purpose in life should make such self-concordant pathways to purpose more concrete and tangible.

36. Michael F. Steger, Bryan J. Dik, and Ryan D. Duffy, "Measuring Meaningful Work: The Work and Meaning Inventory (WAMI)," *Journal of Career Assessment* (forthcoming).

37. Elliot Sober and David S. Wilson, *Unto Others: The Evolution and Psychology of Unselfish Behavior* (Cambridge, MA: Harvard University Press, 1998).

38. Daniel C. Batson, *The Altruism Question: Toward a Social-Psychological Answer* (Hillsdale, NJ: Lawrence Erlbaum, 1991).

39. Robert B. Cialdini, Stephanie L. Brown, Brian P. Lewis, Carol Luce, and Steven L. Neuberg, "Reinterpreting the Empathy–Altruism Relationship: When One into One Equals Oneness," *Journal of Personality and Social Psychology* 73.3 (1997): 481–94.

40. M. E. McCullough, Marcia B. Kimeldorf, and Adam D. Cohen, "An Adaptation for Altruism? The Social Causes, Social Effects, and Social Evolution of Gratitude," *Current Directions in Psychological Science* 17.4 (2008): 281–85.

41. By "we" here, we mean Bryan along with our colleague Michael Steger. Here's the reference: Michael F. Steger and Bryan J. Dik, "If One Is Looking for Meaning in Life, Does Finding Meaning in Work Help?" *Applied Psychology: Health and Well-Being* 1.3 (2009): 303–20.

42. We don't want to overstate these results: This experiment was limited by having a smaller number of participants than we had hoped for, and because of this,

the pattern of results we describe here is better characterized as suggestive than definitive. Nevertheless, the results fit with the survey data, with other research on related questions, and with what we would expect based on theory.

43. All of what follows is summarized in Brent D. Rosso, Katherine H. Dekas, and Amy Wrzesniewski, "On the Meaning of Work: A Theoretical Review," *Research in Organizational Behavior* 30 (2010): 91–127.

Chapter 5

1. Jared M. Diamond, *Collapse: How Societies Choose to Fail or Succeed* (New York: Viking Press, 2005).
2. David M. Buss, *Evolutionary Psychology: The New Science of the Mind* (New York: Allyn & Bacon, 2007).
3. http://www.bls.gov/news.release/archives/atus_06222010.htm.
4. http://www.cnn.com/SPECIALS/cnn.heroes/.
5. Michael F. Steger, Todd B. Kashdan, and Shigehiro Oishi, "Being Good by Doing Good: Eudaimonic Activity and Daily Well-Being Correlates, Mediators, and Temporal Relations," *Journal of Research in Personality* 42.1 (2008): 22–42.
6. Netta Weinstein and Richard M. Ryan, "When Helping Helps: Autonomous Motivation for Prosocial Behavior and Its Influence on Well-Being for the Helper and Recipient," *Journal of Personality and Social Psychology* 98.2 (2010): 222–44.
7. Trust us, we do enjoy such debates, and there is no shortage of opportunity in which to engage in them.
8. Not her real name.
9. Adam M. Grant and Justin M. Berg, "Prosocial Motivation at Work: When, Why, and How Making a Difference Makes a Difference," in *Handbook of Positive Organizational Scholarship*, ed. Kim Cameron and Gretchen Spreitzer (Oxford: Oxford University Press, 2011), 28–44.
10. Adam M. Grant, Elizabeth M. Campbell, Grace Chen, Keenan Cottone, David Lapedis, and Karen Lee, "Impact and the Art of Motivation Maintenance: The Effects of Contact with Beneficiaries on Persistence Behavior," *Organizational Behavior and Human Decision Processes* 103.1 (2007): 53–67.
11. Adam M. Grant, "Relational Job Design and the Motivation to Make a Prosocial Difference," *Academy of Management Review* 32.2 (2007): 393–417.
12. Grant and Berg, "Prosocial Motivation at Work."
13. Adam M. Grant and James W. Berry, "The Necessity of Others Is the Mother of Invention: Intrinsic and Prosocial Motivations, Perspective-Taking, and Creativity," *Academy of Management Journal* 54.1 (2011): 73–96.
14. Ryan D. Duffy and William E. Sedlacek, "What's Most Important to Students' Long-Term Career Choices: Analyzing 10-Year Trends and Group Differences," *Journal of Career Development* 34.2 (2007): 149–63.
15. Peter Marshall, *Mr. Jones, Meet the Master: Sermons and Prayers of Peter Marshall*, ed. Catherine Marshall (New York: Revell, 1951), 147–48.
16. Amy Wrzesniewski and Jane E. Dutton, "Crafting a Job: Revisioning Employees

as Active Crafters of Their Work," *Academy of Management Review* 26.2 (2001): 179–201.

17. John Rosecrance, "The Invisible Horseman: The Social World of the Backstretch," *Qualitative Sociology* 8.3 (1985): 248–65.

18. Arthur P. Brief and Stephan J. Motowidlo, "Prosocial Organizational Behaviors," *Academy of Management Review* 11.4 (1986): 710–25.

19. Grant, "Relational Job Design and the Motivation to Make a Prosocial Difference."

Chapter 6

1. Donald H. Blocher, *The Evolution of Counseling Psychology* (New York: Springer, 2000), 14.

2. M. Pope and M. Sveinsdottir, "Frank, We Hardly Knew Ye: The Very Personal Side of Frank Parsons," *Journal of Counseling and Development* 83 (2005), 105–15.

3. This phrase is borrowed from Mark Savickas.

4. Frank Parsons, *Choosing a Vocation* (Boston: Houghton Mifflin, 1909), 5.

5. Mark L. Savickas, "Constructing Careers: Actor, Agent, and Author," *Journal of Employment Counseling* 48.4 (2011): 179–81.

6. Henry A. Murray and Clyde Kluckhohn, *Personality in Nature, Society, and Culture* (New York: Knopf, 1953).

7. Susan C. Whiston, Thomas L. Sexton, and David L. Lasoff, "Career-Intervention Outcome: A Replication and Extension of Oliver and Spokane (1988)," *Journal of Counseling Psychology* 45.2 (1998): 150–65; Susan C. Whiston, Briana K. Brecheisen, and Joy Stephens, "Does Treatment Modality Affect Career Counseling Effectiveness?" *Journal of Vocational Behavior* 62.3 (2003): 390–410.

8. Steven D. Brown and Nancy E. Ryan-Krane, "Four (or Five) Sessions and a Cloud of Dust: Old Assumptions and New Observations about Career Counseling," in *Handbook of Counseling Psychology* (3rd ed.), ed. Steven Brown and Robert Lent (New York: Wiley, 2000), 740–66.

9. We say this is better because the limited research comparing these approaches finds the incumbent approach to be slightly more effective (Bryan J. Dik, Ryan S. C. Hu, and Jo-Ida C. Hansen, "An Empirical Test of the Modified C Index and SII, O*NET, and DHOC Occupational Code Classifications," *Journal of Career Assessment* 15.3 [2007]: 279–300).

10. We take our duty to protect the identity of our clients very seriously. Sheryl is not her real name, and her story is in fact a composite of more than one client with whom Bryan has worked.

11. Donald E. Super, "A Theory of Vocational Development," *American Psychologist* 8.5 (1953): 185–90.

12. www.bls.gov/news.release/pdf/nlsoy.pdf.

13. http://www.bls.gov/news.release/tenure.nr0.htm.

14. Anya Kamanetz, "The Four-Year Career: Lessons from the New World of Quicksilver Work Where 'Career Planning' Is an Oxymoron," *Fast Company*, February 2012.

15. Douglas T. Hall, *The Career Is Dead: Long Live the Career* (San Francisco: Jossey-Bass, 1996).
16. Donald E. Super, Mark L. Savickas, and C. Super, "The Life-Span, Life-Space Approach to Careers," in *Career Choice and Development* (3rd ed.), ed. Duane Brown and Linda Brooks (San Francisco: Jossey-Bass, 1996), 121–78.
17. Mark L. Savickas, *Career Counseling* (Washington, DC: American Psychological Association Books, 2011).
18. Frederick Buechner, *Wishful Thinking: A Theological ABC* (New York: Harper and Row, 1973), 95.
19. 2009 Global Women in Engineering survey by the U.K. Resource Centre for Women in Science, Engineering, and Technology, http://www.ieee.org /portal/site/tionline/menuitem.130a3558587d56e8fb2275875bac26c8 /index.jsp?&pName=institute_level1_article&TheCat=2201&article=tionline /legacy/inst2010/mar10/featureWIE.xml&.

Chapter 7

1. Amy Wrzesniewski and Jane E. Dutton, "Crafting a Job: Revisioning Employees as Active Crafters of Their Work," *Academy of Management Review* 26.2 (2001): 179–201, 179.
2. Justin M. Berg, Jane E. Dutton, and Amy Wrzesniewski, "Job Crafting and Meaningful Work," in *Purpose and Meaning in the Workplace*, ed. Bryan Dik, Zeeta Byrne, and Michael Steger (Washington, DC: American Psychological Association, forthcoming).
3. Justin M. Berg, Adam M. Grant, and Victoria Johnson, "When Callings Are Calling: Crafting Work and Leisure in Pursuit of Unanswered Occupational Callings," *Organization Science* 21.5 (2010): 1–22.
4. Ibid.
5. Justin M. Berg, Amy Wrzesniewski, and Jane E. Dutton, "Perceiving and Responding to Challenges in Job Crafting at Different Ranks: When Proactivity Requires Adaptivity," *Journal of Organizational Behavior* 31.2 (2010): 158–86.
6. Ibid., 166.
7. Ibid.
8. Roy Baumeister and Mark R. Leary, "The Need to Belong: Desire for Interpersonal Attachments as a Fundamental Human Motivation," *Psychological Bulletin* 117.3 (1995): 497–529.
9. Berg, Wrzesniewski, and Dutton, "Perceiving and Responding to Challenges in Job Crafting at Different Ranks," 166.
10. Ibid., 167.
11. Ibid.
12. This comes from a description by Amy Wrzesniewski and Jane E. Dutton, "Crafting a Job: Revisioning Employees as Active Crafters of Their Work," *Academy of Management Review* 26.2 (2001): 179–201 of a working paper by Jane E. Dutton, Gelaye Debebe, and Amy Wrzesniewski, "A Social Valuing Perspective on Relationship Sensemaking," working paper: University of Michigan, Ann Arbor.

13. Berg, Dutton, and Wrzesniewski, "Job Crafting and Meaningful Work."
14. Thomas N. Bradbury, Frank D. Fincham, and Steven R. H. Beach, "Research on the Nature and Determinants of Marital Satisfaction: A Decade in Review," *Journal of Marriage and the Family* 62.4 (2000): 964–80.
15. Robert Epstein, "How Science Can Help You Fall in Love," *Scientific American Mind*, January/February 2010, 26–33.

Chapter 8

1. Research has found that because of the high levels of stress and easy access to legal and illegal substances, those in the food service industry are especially prone to such vices (Amy Zuber, "Restaurant Workers Worst Drug Abusers," *Nation's Restaurant News* 17 [February 1997]: 31.7, 1).
2. Ryan D. Duffy, Pamela F. Foley, Trisha L. Raque-Bogdan, Laura Reid, Bryan J. Dik, Megan C. Castano, and Christopher Adams, "Counseling Psychologists Who View Their Careers as a Calling: A Qualitative Study," *Journal of Career Assessment* (forthcoming).
3. Bryan J. Dik, Brandy M. Eldridge, Michael F. Steger, and Ryan D. Duffy, "Development and Validation of the Calling and Vocation Questionnaire (CVQ) and Brief Calling Scale (BCS)," *Journal of Career Assessment* (forthcoming).
4. Ryan D. Duffy and William E. Sedlacek, "The Salience of a Career Calling among College Students: Exploring Group Differences and Links to Religiousness, Life Meaning, and Life Satisfaction," *Career Development Quarterly* 59.1 (2010): 27–41.
5. Ryan D. Duffy, Bryan J. Dik, and Michael S. Steger, "Calling and Work-Related Outcomes: Career Commitment as a Mediator," *Journal of Vocational Behavior* 78.2 (2011): 210–18.
6. Fortunately, new research indicates that societal attitudes toward stay-at-home dads have become much more favorable over the last decade (Aaron B. Rochlen, Ryan A. McKelley, and Tiffany W. Whittaker, "Stay-at-Home Fathers' Reasons for Entering the Role and Stigma Experiences: A Preliminary Report," *Psychology of Men and Masculinity* 11, no. 4 (2010): 7–14.
7. Justin Coulson, Lindsay Oades, and Gerard Stoyles, "Parent's Conception and Experience of Calling in Child Rearing: A Qualitative Analysis," *Journal of Humanistic Psychology* (forthcoming), 233.
8. Nancy Darling and Laurence Steinberg, "Parenting Style as Context: An Integrative Model," *Psychological Bulletin* 11, no. 3 (1993): 487–96.
9. Justin M. Berg, Adam M. Grant, and Victoria Johnson, "When Callings Are Calling: Crafting Work and Leisure in Pursuit of Unanswered Occupational Callings," *Organization Science* 21.5 (2010): 1–22.
10. Ibid., 12.
11. Ibid.
12. Tina S. Sellers, Kris Thomas, Jennifer Batts, and Cami Ostman, "Women Called: A Qualitative Study of Christian Women Dually Called to Motherhood and Career," *Journal of Psychology and Theology* 33.3 (2005): 198–209.
13. Ibid., 201.
14. Ibid.

15. Kerris L. M. Oates, M. E. L. Hall, and Tamera L. Anderson, "Calling and Conflict: A Qualitative Exploration of Interrole Conflict and the Sanctification of Work in Christian Mother in Academia," *Journal of Psychology and Theology* 33.3 (2005): 210–33.
16. Ibid., 217.
17. Ibid., 215.
18. Ibid.

Chapter 9

1. Hillary Frank, "The Miseducation of Josh Frank" in "Kids as Adults," *This American Life*, Episode 150, NPR, January 21, 2000.
2. Malcolm Gladwell, *Outliers: The Story of Success* (New York: Little, Brown, 2008).
3. Amy Wrzesniewski, Clark McCauley, Paul Rozin, and Barry Schwartz, "Jobs, Careers, and Callings: People's Relations to Their Work," *Journal of Research in Personality* 31.1 (1997): 21–33.
4. Not to be confused with the real band Stillwater from Warner Robins, Georgia, which existed from 1973 to 1982.
5. Jeffrey H. Greenhaus and Gary N. Powell, "When Work and Family Are Allies: A Theory of Work-Family Enrichment," *Academy of Management Review* 31.1 (2006): 72–92.
6. Thomas W. H. Ng, Kelly L. Sorensen, and Daniel C. Feldman, "Dimensions, Antecedents, and Consequences of Workaholism: A Conceptual Integration and Extension," *Journal of Organizational Behavior* 28.1 (2007): 111–36.
7. Ibid.
8. Ibid.
9. Walter Isaacson, *Steve Jobs* (New York: Simon & Schuster, 2011).
10. Shoshana R. Dobrow and Jennifer Tosti-Kharas, "Calling: The Development of a Scale Measure," *Personnel Psychology* 64.4 (2011): 1001–49, 1005.
11. Daniel J. Wakin, "The Juilliard Effect: Ten Years Later," *New York Times*, December 12, 2004; Andrew Druckenbrod, "Many Small Orchestras Whistle a Happier Tune," *Pittsburgh Post-Gazette*, November 27, 2005, http://www.post-gazette.com/pg/05331/613157.stm.
12. Stuart Bunderson and Jeffery A. Thompson, "The Call of the Wild: Zookeepers, Callings and the Double-Edged Sword of Deeply Meaningful Work," *Administrative Science Quarterly* 54.1 (2009): 32–57.
13. Ibid., 52.
14. Ibid., 43.
15. Douglass J. Schuurman, *Vocation: Discerning Our Callings in Life* (Grand Rapids: Eerdmans, 2004).
16. John Calvin, "Treatises against the Anabaptists and against the Libertinese," ed. and trans. Benjamin Farley (Grand Rapids, MI: Baker Academic, 2001), cited in Schuurman, *Vocation*.
17. Ervin Staub, *The Psychology of Good and Evil: Why Children, Adults, and Groups Help and Harm Others* (New York: Cambridge University Press, 2003).
18. Schuurman, *Vocation*, 79.

19. Ibid.
20. Not his real name.

Chapter 10

1. Rana Foroohar, "What Ever Happened to Upward Mobility?" *Time*, November 14, 2011.
2. Nadya A. Fouad and John Bynner, "Work Transitions." *American Psychologist* 63.4 (2008): 241–51, 245.
3. Alec R. Levenson, "Millennials and the World of Work: An Economist's Perspective," *Journal of Business Psychology* 25.2 (2010): 257–64, 262.
4. Ruth E. Fassinger, "Workplace Diversity and Public Policy: Challenges and Opportunities for Psychology," *American Psychologist* 63.4 (2008): 252–68.
5. David L. Blustein, *The Psychology of Working: A New Perspective for Career Development, Counseling, and Public Policy* (Mahwah, NJ: Erlbaum, 2008); Blustein, "The Role of Work in Psychological Health and Well-Being: A Conceptual, Historical, and Public Policy Perspective," *American Psychologist* 63.4 (2008): 228–40.
6. Tod Sloan, "Global Work-Related Suffering: A Priority for Vocational Psychology," *Counseling Psychologist* 33.2 (2005): 207–14.
7. Fred H. Borgen, "Advancing Social Justice in Vocational Theory, Research and Practice," *Counseling Psychologist* 33.2 (2005): 197–206, 201.
8. This research is summarized in Blustein, *Psychology of Working*.
9. Richard E. Lucas, Andrew E. Clark, Yannis Georgellis, and Ed Diener, "Unemployment Alters the Set-Point for Life Satisfaction," *Psychological Science* 15.1 (2004): 8–13.
10. Frances M. McKee-Ryan, Zhaoli Song, Connie R. Wanberg, and Angelo J. Kiniki, "Psychological and Physical Well-Being during Unemployment: A Meta-Analytic Study," *Journal of Applied Psychology* 90.1 (2005): 53–76.
11. Douglas T. Hall and Dawn E. Chandler, "Psychological Success," *Journal of Organizational Behavior* 26.2 (2005): 155–76, 167.
12. Ibid.
13. http://www.census.gov/hhes/www/cpstables/032011/perinc/toc.htm.
14. American Psychological Association, *Report of the APA Task Force on Socioeconomic Status* (Washington, DC: American Psychological Association, 2007), http://www2.apa.org/pi/SES_task_force_report.pdf.
15. Marianne Bertrand and Sendhil Mullainathan, "Are Emily and Greg More Employable than Lakisha and Jamal? A Field Experiment on Labor Market Discrimination," *American Economic Review* 94.4 (2003): 991–1013.
16. Claude M. Steele, "A Threat in the Air: How Stereotypes Shape the Intellectual Identities and Performance of Women and African Americans," *American Psychologist* 52.6 (1997): 613–29.
17. All of this is reviewed in Ruth E. Fassinger, "Workplace Diversity and Public Policy: Challenges and Opportunities for Psychology," *American Psychologist* 63.4 (2008): 252–68.
18. There were some men in the sample used in this study, too, but not many (American Association of University Women, *Drawing the Line: Sexual*

Harassment on Campus [Washington, DC: American Association of University Women Educational Foundation, 2006]).

19. Barbara L. Bernier, "Sugar Cane Slavery: Bateyes in the Dominican Republic," *New England Journal of International and Comparative Law* 9.1 (2003): 17–45.

20. http://news.bbc.co.uk/2/hi/asia-pacific/6955202.stm

21. David G. Myers, "The Funds, Friends, and Faith of Happy People," *American Psychologist* 55.1 (2000): 56–67; Daniel Kahneman and Angus Deaton, "High Income Improves Evaluation of Life but Not Emotional Well-Being," *Proceedings of the National Academy of Sciences of the United States of America* 107.38 (2010): 16489–93.

22. Ellen H. McWhirter, David L. Blustein, and Justin C. Perry, "Annunciation: Implementing an Emancipatory Communitarian Approach to Vocational Psychology," *Counseling Psychologist* 33.2 (2005): 215–24, 222.

23. Ken Dychtwald, Tamara J. Ericson, and Robert Morison, *Workforce Crisis* (Boston: Harvard Business School Press, 2006).

24. Kelly Greene, "When We're All 64," *Wall Street Journal*, September 26, 2005; cited in Wayne F. Cascio, "The Changing World of Work," in *Oxford Handbook of Positive Psychology and Work*, ed. P. Alex Linley, Susan Harrington, and Nicola Garcea (New York: Oxford University Press, 2010), 13–23.

25. United States Department of Labor, Aging Workforce Initiative, 2011, http://www.doleta.gov/brg/indprof/AWI/.

26. Alec R. Levenson, "Millennials and the World of Work: An Economist's Perspective," *Journal of Business Psychology* 25.2 (2010): 257–64.

27. Sylvia A. Hewlett, Laura Sherbin, and Karen Sumberg, "How Gen Y and Boomers Will Reshape Your Agenda," *Harvard Business Review* 87.7-8 (2009): 1–6.

28. Bryan J. Dik, Zinta S. Byrne, and Michael F. Steger, eds., *Purpose and Meaning in the Workplace* (Washington, DC: American Psychological Association, forthcoming).

29. Heather E. Quick and Phyllis Moen, "Gender, Employment, and Retirement Quality: A Life Course Approach to the Differential Experiences of Men and Women," *Journal of Occupational Health Psychology* 3.1 (1998): 44–64.

30. Cascio, "Changing World of Work."

31. E.g., Douglas T. Hall, *Careers in and out of Organizations*, 1st ed. (Thousand Oaks, CA: Sage Publications, 2002); Jon P. Briscoe and Douglas T. Hall, "The Interplay of Boundaryless and Protean Careers: Combinations and Implications," *Journal of Vocational Behavior* 69.1 (2006): 4–18.

32. Douglas T. Hall, "The Protean Career: A Quarter-Century Journey," *Journal of Vocational Behavior* 65.1 (2004): 1–13, 4.

33. Briscoe and Hall, "Interplay of Boundaryless and Protean Careers."

34. Hall and Chandler, "Psychological Success."

Questions and Answers

1. Andreas Hirschi, "Callings in Career: A Typological Approach to Essential and Optional Components," *Journal of Vocational Behavior* 79.1 (2011): 60–73.

2. Ibid., 70.

3. Bill Bryson, *The Mother Tongue: English and How It Got That Way* (New York: William Morrow, 1991).
4. http://religions.pewforum.org/reports.
5. M. Hermansen, "Islamic Concepts of Vocation," in *Revisiting the Idea of Vocation: Theological Explorations*, ed. John Haughey (Washington, DC: Catholic University of America Press, 2004), 77–96, 77–78.
6. Marsha Sinetar, *Do What You Love, the Money Will Follow: Discovering Your Right Livelihood* (New York: Paulist Press, 1987).
7. Dalai Lama and Harold C. Cutler, *The Art of Happiness at Work* (New York: Riverhead Books, 2004).
8. Andrew Newberg, Michael Pourdehnad, Abass Alavi, and Eugene O'Aquili, "Cerebral Blood Flow during Meditative Prayer: Preliminary Findings and Methodological Issues," *Perceptual and Motor Skills* 97.2 (2003): 525–30.
9. Jeffrey A. LePine, Amir Erez, and Diane E. Johnson, "The Nature and Dimensionality of Organizational Citizenship Behavior: A Critical Review and Meta-Analysis," *Journal of Applied Psychology* 87.1 (2002): 52–65.
10. Bryan J. Dik, Michael F. Steger, Amanda Gibson, and William Peisner, "Make Your Work Matter: Development and Pilot Evaluation of a Purpose-Centered Career Education Intervention," *New Directions in Youth Development* 132, Winter (2011): 59–75.
11. Rich Feller, personal communication with the authors, January 31, 2012.
12. Try Googling "career coach certification." When we tried this, the first hit trumpeted: "Become a Certified Career Coach—High 6-figure Income Possible." Another pitched. "How You Too Can Be a Career Coach—and Enter the Fastest Growing Profession Today—and Helping Hundreds of People Find Work While Making $200/Hour or More, Working from Home or Anywhere!" Don't get us wrong, most coaches are *not* get-rich-quick hacks who charge thousands for services they are poorly equipped to deliver. But some are.
13. David Woods, Jerome S. Bruner, and Gail Ross, "The Role of Tutoring in Problem Solving," *Journal of Child Psychology and Psychiatry* 17.2 (1976): 89–100.

Index